The Voice

THE VOICE
Life at
The Village Voice

by Ellen Frankfort

WILLIAM MORROW AND COMPANY, INC.
NEW YORK   1976

Printed in the United States of America

1 2 3 4 5 80 79 78 77 76

Library of Congress Cataloging in Publication Data

Frankfort, Ellen.
    The Voice: life at the Village voice.

    1. The Village voice. I. Title.
PN4900.V5F7   071'.47'1   75-42321
ISBN 0-688-03044-0

BOOK DESIGN: HELEN ROBERTS

For my father,
who always encouraged me
to have a voice of my own.

Preface

A word or two about how this book came to be. In May, 1974, I attended the A. J. Liebling Counter Convention, sponsored by *(MORE)*, a paper devoted to scrutinizing the media. It was an exciting time; Nixon was about to fall and we didn't know when. The atmosphere combined the excitement of a horse race and the seriousness of an illness. I was proud to be a member of the media.

Ironically, I think it was this pride that made me more sensitive to the failings of *The Village Voice*—the publication with which I had been professionally identified for several years. How, I wondered, could a paper that was so astute at sensing the dishonesty of everyone, including the President (long before the Dan Rathers, the Walter Cronkites, even the Tom Wickers did), be so unjust, so unfair, so damned hypocritical about working conditions at home. I proposed writing an article on the subject to Richard Pollak, Editor of *(MORE)*.

I thought I'd record—in just a few pages—exactly what had happened when in 1971 a group of *Voice* writers tried to discuss money matters with Dan Wolf, who was then the Editor of the *Voice*. But the piece, which I called "Confrontation with the Father," ran on for sixty pages. It was hardly suitable for *(MORE)*. Perhaps a magazine would be interested.

As I was finishing it, I read that Clay Felker of the New York Magazine Company had purchased the *Voice*. It was as if I had been handed an ending. The sale had an aesthetic rightness about it. The *Voice*, the Village, and Dan had all been shifting away from bohemian rags to bourgeois riches, and the sale to *New York* magazine seemed merely the last and most visible sign of that shift.

As I tried to incorporate the sale into my story, I realized that I was no longer dealing with only an abortive attempt at organizing for more money. It seemed I was writing an allegory of middle-aging as well as a chronicle of a certain time—the late sixties and early seventies—and a certain place—bohemian America (whether it be Greenwich Village, Berkeley, or the only head shop in Peoria, Illinois).

But above all, the *Voice* story turned out to be that of a family—"just one big unhappy family," as Dan was fond of saying—and not even a magazine seemed large enough to contain such a saga. And so I settled down to write a book.

As I began to interview people, I felt I was in possession of the densest collection of ambivalences on record. Almost everyone with whom I spoke described a strong love–hate bond with the *Voice*. Discovering the source of this ambivalence was key to understanding why we couldn't get more money, or, for that matter, understanding much else about the *Voice*.

What was clear from almost the beginning of the writing was that the book was *not* a history of the *Voice*. Otherwise there would be no excuse for the absence—other than an occasional mention—of Jill Johnston, Nat Hentoff, Andrew Sarris, and other pioneers who helped establish the paper's distinctive "voice" after it was started in 1955.

At times, writing about the people involved with the politics of the *Voice* between the two changes of ownership—the sale by Dan Wolf and Ed Fancher to Carter Burden and Bartle Bull in January, 1970, and the sale by Bull and Burden to Clay Felker of *New York* in July, 1974—felt like more than I could handle. Although the changes of ownership provide convenient time markers, the primary reason I focus on that period is that it coincides with the time I was writing for the *Voice* on a weekly basis and knew, in a firsthand way, what was happening.

Even within the confines of the early seventies, the possibilities of people to interview were numerous. When, in the fall of 1974, I started to call people, the *Voice* had just changed hands. Many individuals were not certain how they felt about the change; some were reluctant to speak, unsure whether they wished to damn the whole thing in print or adopt a more prudent attitude.

Others, who no longer felt at home at the *Voice*, either because they no longer had a job there or felt they would not wish to work there in the future, were anxious to open up. A few, who were convinced that the change could only be for the better, were also eager to have their thoughts on record.

I spoke (or more accurately, listened) to anyone who wished to talk. The one person who would not speak at all was Dan Wolf. I telephoned him, wrote to him, even sent a registered letter to his door. Short of camping out in his building, I could not make contact with him. With the exception of Don McNeil, who died in 1968, only one other person profiled—Alexander Cockburn—refused to go on record officially (although we did have an informal sidewalk chat).

Otherwise, those who sat down with me seemed delighted to say, at last, how they *really* felt about life at *The Village Voice*. Through their tales and mine, I hope the reader will experience some of the richness of feeling that comes from being a member of "just one big unhappy family."

ELLEN FRANKFORT
October, 1975

Acknowledgments

Hal Davis, who sent me seemingly obscure clippings that he sensed before anyone would be key to my story; for his sharp editorial guidance; and above all, for his generous spirit.

Daniel Kaiser and Edythe Greissman, for giving a critical reading of the manuscript when it was only scribblings and notes.

Betty Anne Clarke, my agent, who helped make the scribblings and notes into a book.

Media Women, for making me more sensitive to the position of women journalists, and Dr. Donna Allen, in particular, for providing a role model for all women in the profession.

Claudia Dreifus, who helped me develop a worker's consciousness and encouraged me to stick with the project, even at its most difficult moments.

Julie Coopersmith, for discouraging two dozen coy titles and being a friend throughout.

Gayle Benderoff, for keeping track of the details and always being there when I called.

All the people who shared their experiences with me. I regret that I could not include them all in the book.

Jim Landis, for being a superlative editor. Although I never felt a voice other than my own intruding, working with him on the manuscript helped me become a better writer.

Contents

14

It is not necessary to slay your father, time will slay him, that is a virtual certainty.

—from "Manual for Sons,"
by Donald Barthelme

The Death of a Favorite Son

Fred W. McDarrah

". . . If you wade in too deep, you may learn that
the East Village undertow is no myth."

Don McNeil

Don McNeil seemed like the perfect son. Having grown up in Alaska, he had a touch both of the exotic and the exile—a loner among the polar bears. And then, too, he was a dropout (he never finished college), giving Dan Wolf a sense that there was something for him to complete. For it was clear that Don McNeil was, by temperament, a quester.

Yet Don's biography would make his explorations less metaphysical; the ice, the sparse physical surroundings in which he grew up were inconsequential details. The most important fact transcended geography: Don McNeil, like Ross Wetzsteon from Montana, like Bartle Bull from Britain, like Jack Newfield from Brooklyn, like Joe Flaherty from New York, like Dan himself, had lost his father when he was young. And it had been no ordinary death—his father had died in a submarine bombing, leaving the son of a legendary war hero for Dan to adopt.

Don came to New York just as the flower children were in full bloom, holding their first Be-In, a glorious event, genuine enough in spirit to overcome the cynicism of the city, the sense of put-on pervasive among media people. So when someone in a fanciful outfit looked down from a limb of a tree in Central Park that sunny Sunday afternoon and offered the nearest passerby half a sandwich, it seemed wrong not to accept. The message was be open, and with it came a spirit of not wanting to hurt others, of wanting to accept others. For a moment, the city was the prisoner of a beautiful captor—a vision, a rainbow, a collage of childish dreams in the middle of a concrete forest. The tall dense skyscrapers formed a ring of protection around those gathered in the park, and Don McNeil, the young writer from Alaska, saw it as the start of something new.

"The Be-In Was the Beginning," he called the spring 1967 *Village Voice* story in which he wrote:

> As the sun gleamed off a backdrop of molded metal sky-scrapers on Easter Sunday, a medieval pageant began in the middle of Manhattan. Laden with daffodils, ecstatic in vibrant costumes and painted faces, troupes of hippies gathered on a hill overlooking Central Park's sheep meadow to Be-In. By sunset, ten thousand celebrants swarmed in great rushes across the meadow, and thousands more were dispersed throughout the rest of the park. Bonfires burned on the hills, their smoke mixing with bright balloons among the barren trees and high, high above, kites wafted in the air. Rhythms and music and mantras from all corners of the meadow echoed in exquisite harmony, and thousands of lovers vibrated into the night. It was miraculous.

That was Don's voice. It was not a sneering one; he was a sympathetic observer. However, one senses Dan's presence: Dan listening to Don with a skeptical look that modulated the lyricism and made Don wonder whether this Be-In was anything more than a onetime novelty; Dan, the cynic, unconvinced that a new age was dawning, communicating to the young writer his own sense of doubt, and Don listening, adding an amendment to his own enthusiasm in the form of a final paragraph:

> Another Be-In has been scheduled in conjunction with the Spring Mobilization to End the War in Vietnam, but some people are skeptical about mixing Be-Ins with politics. The Be-In seems almost a sacred event, harking back to medieval pageants, gypsy gatherings, or the great pow-wows of the American Indians. At the same time it is a new and futuristic experience which, once refined, offers great promise. But it should be refined carefully. It is a lot of energy to deal with.

Dan's sense of caution becomes the final coda, a questioning acceptance, for who could not appreciate the icons of ceremony? But a gentle note of warning: don't be taken in entirely. And it was this seesaw of the emotions, this dialectic of the psyche, that characterized Don's work throughout the year. One could turn to any piece and it would be there: "the glamour and the gloom," "the famous and the friendless"—phrases attempting to articulate the divided self, the alien who yearns above all to feel part of a community but who is always aware of the barriers, the person who feels at home only with others who are uprooted and even then retains an observer's sense of the outsider.

As Don, the ambassador to the kingdom of the hippies, moved between it and the Village, there was always Dan to rock him back and forth. But with time Don started to make his own roots, and the balance between distance and involvement became more difficult to maintain. Dan, perceiving, perhaps, that Don was slipping, guided him back, and it is Dan's voice one recognizes when Don writes:

> When the psychiatrist gives up, when they take another acid trip or go back to their East Village lovers amid the final fury of a father's threats . . . life becomes difficult. For the kick is no longer experience per se. The theme has changed to the melange of escaping, soul-searching, and discovering thyself: a difficult agonizing process whether on an acid trip or an analyst's couch.

For a while Don seemed to heed Dan's unspoken advice—don't get too deep; observe, report, but always keep your distance—which Don echoed in his writing:

> The transient rut is not a creative one . . . For more, it is a long road down, laced with drugs, especially amphetamine. Many dig the descent; oblivion can be seductive . . .

But simultaneously Don was beginning to drop hints that Dan's hold was no longer the same, that oblivion was becoming more seductive. For while the *Voice* was supposed to be a home, it was, as Dan himself said, "just one big unhappy family." And Don felt the sibling rivalries and fierce competitiveness had little to do with his reach for the oneness he had initially experienced in the Be-In. Again he turned to his writing to work out the conflict.

> What brings people together in a tribe . . . There's a feeling of "oneness" [were the quotation marks those of Dan or Don?] in the Group Image. They came together by accident or intuition. They are artists, dancers, musicians, high school dropouts, college graduates, a few kids, a few dogs, and a cab driver.

At the end of the piece called "Tribes and Tribulations," the caution is less noticeable, as if the scales are now tipping on the other side, that of abandonment—of the group, of the community, of the tribe, of all the things the *Voice* seemed to offer but did not deliver.

> Going to a Group Image hearing can be an engulfing experience. Like the Easter Be-In, you may be in for a surprise. The tribal spirit is contagious and it can catch you off guard. Be prepared to plunge in and feel what's happening.

Had Dan read Don's writing as a key to Don's psyche, he might have been worried by the constant imagery of drowning. But Dan was confident that Don would not plunge in. And perhaps Don might not have, had the times been the same as the beginning of his days at the *Voice,* where he could write about a glorious Be-In, where cosmic love was in the air. But times reversed themselves, as Don came to understand. Not without significance is his March 1968 piece on the Yip-In at Grand Central Station entitled "Leather Is In; Love, Flowers Are Out."

> The crowd simply made a U-turn in a connecting corridor and flowed back into the terminal, and the cops went wild. Now another formation of cops charged toward the stairs where I was standing, and I made for the street again, rounded the corner, and returned to the 42nd Street entrance, which was now entirely filled with police. . . . They looked at my credentials, cursed the Voice, grabbed my arms behind my back, and joined by two others, rushed me back towards the street, deliberately ramming my head into the closed glass doors, which cracked with the impact.

And now it was the hard side of the city granite, buildings no longer lit by sun and the people in them no longer behaving gently. Brutality was in the air as clearly as cosmic love had been in the beginning. Who had betrayed whom? The constellations still whirl. Had Don betrayed Dan by getting too involved? Had the police betrayed the flower children who had written a communiqué to the community which Don had quoted only a few months earlier: "Let us accept the police as people in a gentle manner. They are civil servants and in that capacity let us love them." Was Dan right after all not to have been taken in by the first Be-In, to view it as nothing more than a bit of spring fever, a hippie version of the Easter Parade, scented with "grass" instead of artificial flowers? But if Dan was right that the gentle rebellions could not overcome the harshness of authority, he could be right also that the whole counterculture was merely an adolescent striving to untie

24

umbilical cords, a phase in development before a settling down to the real world, the adult world, the world of family and children and property.

Yet Don had experienced other things, things that a man like Dan might not approve of. There were the acid trips, which Don himself knew the dangers of. But there was something else, something that a father, a family man, a conventional Jewish boy, might not forgive, and that was love between two men.

Don was having a writer's block. Perhaps it was the need to make sense of his own course, during the year he had charted the change from love to leather. What did it all mean? Dan wanted to get Don back to the days when he was writing like a detached observer, sympathetic but apart, coming only to Dan to work out the confusions. For a while, he gave someone else Don's "beat"— Steve Lerner was to cover the counterculture or whatever was left of it before it became openly combative and campuses all over the country started to erupt one after another.

Don withdrew from the competition of family combat and with a male friend went away to the country, to a place where things still seemed sweet, where there were no forests of concrete, only of trees, and Bob Dylan echoed in the air. Trying to separate the paranoia from the reality, Don took refuge in a homosexual affair, which he intuitively knew Dan could not accept as easily as he had accepted all his other quests for love, community, meaning. Only in his head had Dan ever quested. Dan, the original philosopher, the great cerebral pilgrim, walking through the lives of others while never leaving his office at *The Village Voice*.

When Don, walking out into a pond, stoned, ignored his own warning, written earlier in the year, ". . . if you wade in too deep, you may learn that the East Village undertow is no myth," and did not come out alive, something in Dan seemed to die too.

Don had been the favorite son, the one who happened along during the honeymoon days of the *Voice* and the decade, the two— the paper and sixties politics—as symbiotically connected as the editor and writer, the father and son. Don was different from all the others who had come (and were still to come) to Dan in search of the father they had lost. Don appeared to lack the ambition of Jack Newfield, a son self-made in the tradition of the father; he seemed to have none of the hunger for power that festered in Ross Wetzsteon nor the fake bravado of Joe Flaherty, who approached something of a folk hero in the dark publike interior of the Lion's Head Bar, where everyone knew that Joe's father had been killed by mobsters and found floating in the cold waters of the Hudson River. And later on there would be Bartle Bull, whose father, like Don's, had been killed in combat. But Dan could not be moved by Bartle in the same way. He understood that Bartle, a wealthy young Wall Street lawyer, would continually carry on about how liberal he was, not because he wasn't, but because he felt uncomfortable in Bohemian quarters with people who were not always correct, who liked sloppiness, and who liked to display their mistakes right there in print for everyone to witness.

Don had come along at the right moment, and now there was a real loss. Only one other person had the potential to take Don's place—Sally Kempton—but Dan was a bit in awe of her. She was, after all, the daughter of Murray, a father all too real. (Could Dan really replace Murray?) And besides, she was a woman and could always turn to another man, which would strike Dan as not only natural but even inevitable. None of the strangeness of Don's turning away.

How much Dan had orchestrated Don's downward course became a haunting question. Dan was not responsible for the changing times, the shifting moods. And there was that period—if only a year or so—that Don found love in Dan. As the dedication of Don's book puts it, "I always knew in my heart that I'd find a newspaper to love, and I've found one. To Dan Wolf, Editor of *The Village Voice.*" Those are words that not even Clay Felker can take away. The notion that only in death is permanence won is far too simple for the counterculture children of the sixties. There were to be no echoes of Tristan and Isolde when they go; no, the Aquarian Age had its own texts, and it is in the Epilogue to Don's book, written by his intimate friend, Paul Williams, that the flavor of the times is captured.

> I will neither affirm nor deny our immortality . . . It is September 9th, 1969, more than a year after your death, I do not know where you are Don McNeil. Are you a part of me, writing these words? . . . Don is now neither mortal nor immortal, and . . . you too, reader, are alive. This I affirm.

Only on the eve of the seventies, as a decade was dying out, along with its drug victims and other innocent adventurers, could these words escape the sneering that would attend such mush today. Then there were still a few moments left to believe that the world was pure, free of boundaries, clear-cut divisions, rivalries, sides, and that Don had joined a cosmic something—a vague, uncertain, there-and-not-there force, his spirit still seesawing somewhere in the cosmos, no one quite sure exactly where but everyone remembering with great innocence (and not a morsel of guilt) the epiphanies they shared high on acid and were still sharing a year after Don was dead at twenty-three.

Dan was no more sympathetic to sentimentality than to acid trips. The seventies had been upon him before they arrived. And slightly more than a year after Don died, Dan sold *The Village Voice*.

Confrontation with
the Father:
Dan Wolf and His Writers

It was barely visible but it was there. Not in the fingers or hands but around the mouth, which tightened as mouths do when rage is muzzled. For a moment, it looked as if the words might break through. *How dare they, these children of mine who came to me when they were nobodies and whom I made into somebodies. How dare they gang up and attack. Where would they be without me?*

But Dan Wolf knew not to say it aloud. Better a tightening of the mouth than a torrent of abuse. For at the very moment when the sons and daughters are up in arms is exactly when a father must not reveal the slightest sign of insecurity. And so Dan issued himself imperatives: *Appear calm, collect yourself. After all,* New York, Rolling Stone, Psychology Today *might continue to chip away, but my children, the writers . . . NEVER.*

That week in December, 1971, had been tense for the writers. They knew they were up to a naughty act, one that would humiliate Dan, and they felt a sense of guilt even before it was committed. And yet it was essential to feel they were part of a plot, conspirators dealing in the silent language of knowing nods, exchanged glances, something that had a not-quite-detectable undercurrent.

All week long there have been rumors of plots and counter-plots, late night telephone calls and secret meetings. And while some of these things have taken place, I want to make one thing clear, Dan. We come to you as friends of the Voice, people who really love this paper, or else we would not be here at all.

Hentoff—almost a brand name—was now speaking as one of

nine writers representing roughly fifty others. In keeping with his gentle face, Hentoff chose a kind, almost apologetic, and certainly conciliatory tone with which to begin.

Dan Wolf looked relieved, as though it would be easy if things remained on that level; he stretched more comfortably into the chair behind the large wooden desk, a bit oversized for a small man, but with a hint of handcraftsmanship sufficient to remove any feeling of corporate ease. It was still the room where each writer had come to discuss his work or had come when he had no work to discuss but only his blocks, which were accorded an equal respect.

Wolf, continuing to size up the situation, began to experience the same kind of sureness—something in his fingertips—that enabled him to spot a good writer and wed him to the right topic before others zoomed in on the same territory. Yes, he could take on this crew; its efforts were nothing more than a harmless attempt to embarrass a father. With the grace of a small but quick man, Dan reached for a clipboard on a nearby shelf and began to read off a list of names, continuing for a minute or two before looking up at the faces across from the desk. "If you people are not happy here, these are just a few of the writers who would give anything to have their work printed in the pages of the *Voice*. So go, start your own commune or whatever it is you want. And just wait. See what happened to *Evergreen,* to the *East Village Other,* if you believe in overthrow, to say nothing of the *Herald Tribune* and far more substantial publications, you who believe you understand the finances of publishing. But go, go, I don't want anyone working around here who is unhappy. Start your own paper; let's see how far you can get on your own."

He had let the lid off, and now some of the hurt was leaking out. But it didn't matter because the initial strategy was a brilliant one, right down to the prop—the clipboard—making it seem as if there were two thousand people lined up at the corner of University and Eleventh just waiting to replace a bunch of ingrates. He had, despite his whine, regained the upper hand.

"I love the *Voice*," Robin Reisig whispered aloud, responding more to the hurt inside Dan than to the threat. "There's no place else I'd like to work. It's just that I can barely manage on the money I make."

"First, Dan, where's the Scotch?" said Joe Flaherty, who had been called forth from the Lion's Head Bar. Dan produced a bottle with the same ease he had produced the clipboard. Joe took it, poured himself a drink into the glass Dan gave him, and then handed the bottle back with a nod of appreciation. "Now what kind of bloody meeting is this, everyone going on with love songs about the *Voice*, how they come as friends and other confessionals? You're not in church, you know. You're in the fucking office of management, and you don't carry on with how much you love it when you want a raise." And here he paused to take another sip. "When I was on the docks, the bosses would have had a good laugh if anyone went on like this. I've never heard of anything like it. Look, you go in, you present your demands, you give Wolf a certain amount of time, and then you get the hell out. But none of this stuff about how you love the place. It makes me want to puke, telling him that, when all you really want is a paltry raise. I mean I don't even have to be here; I'm on leave writing a book. But I wanted to back this group here if you're talking about pay. The pay is miserable. I have nothing to gain because I'm on leave, like I said, writing this book, but you just say, 'Now look, Wolf, the pay here is rotten. We've had enough. Here is what we want.' And then you get the hell out."

Dan was smiling, for although everything Joe had said was true, it was also true that he was saying it to please Dan. Joe was putting on his tough working-class on-the-waterfront act, which had almost as much appeal as a fancy family name to a small balding Jewish man without much brawn. By spelling out the strategy that people with guts would adopt, Joe was pretending to be invulnerable to Dan, forgetting that people who are serious don't spell out their strategies in front of "management" unless it is "management" they want to please. Joe, by being a sloppy, drunken court jester, distracted all the others. All, that is, but Dan, who had taken the brief period of entertainment to figure out his next move. And it was a fine follow-up to his first.

"Now you, David Gelber. Don't speak to me of injustice. I remember the time, the one and only time, we asked you to go cover something. And all you could do was lament you couldn't get out of town that day. So, you, you, who have had all the freedom to write on anything you choose, on the one day you're assigned something can't come through, haven't a strong leg to stand on."

"But you don't understand. I really was busy and I couldn't get away. If I had just a bit more notice I would have been glad to go."

"And you, Paul." And here Dan spoke in softer tones, Cowan being one of the writers Dan felt he had birthed. "I can still remember the time I printed something of yours I didn't like just because I knew you cared about it so much. I couldn't hurt you by not running it."

"What was that?" Paul asked with curiosity.

And when Dan told him, Paul laughed. "I agree. It wasn't very good. I wouldn't have been hurt if you hadn't printed it."

"You can say that now, Paul, but you forget how much it meant to you at the time. I know it would have been devastating and I didn't want that. It was more important to encourage you even if it meant printing something I didn't much like."

Dan was now completely in control, using the techniques that had worked for years, those of the kindly father-therapist, making exceptions for his favorite sons while making sure they didn't forget the indulgences, of which Dan kept a careful inventory, just in case there was a sudden audit.

And when Dan had reminded the last member present of the ways in which he was an ingrate for daring to come to him as part of a group, his face was no longer marked by a tightening but rather a triumphant sparkle. "I sent them out like puppy dogs with their tails between their legs," Dan remarked, ready to grant a $25-an-article raise when the writers were ready to come to him as individuals. Quite a coup, it was, to restore his position so rapidly; almost as if there were a return to the old days, when Dan was first getting the *Voice* started.

The time was the early fifties; no one was paying much attention to alternate life-styles; few had them and none knew the term. Along came a small Jewish man with scanty credentials in the way of family or learning but with a feel in his fingers, in his guts, in his blood, for Bohemian life. Intuitively, Dan Wolf had a sense of it; he knew Mailer and a few others who were hanging around the Village at that time, people who had a way of sifting the world through their own psyches and emerging with something that was later to be called the New Journalism: a concern with atmosphere, ambience, style—all the external surroundings essential to map out one's psychic geography.

It was no accident that Dan teamed up with a therapist, Ed Fancher, a shy, retiring man (on the surface) who came from a family of some means and who was not Jewish. Dan was more Maileresque: in part, a frigid Jewish woman susceptible to the charms of the alien, whether it be Wasp or Negro. But unlike Mailer, Dan was not a half-drunken Irish cocksman. Except vicariously.

From the beginning there was a vision of an empire, but one on a modest scale, befitting a small man. And so starting with almost nothing but a gutsy idea, Dan founded *The Village Voice,* a newspaper that would deal with the fears, insecurities, fantasies, repressions that psychologists wrote about and relate them to the sociology of everyday urban life, where politics, people, neighborhoods mingled harmoniously with nervous breakdowns.

Dan turned out to be a genius as an editor; he had an extraordinary talent for spotting talent and then riding out the bumps of development through patience, encouragement, understanding. However, he wasn't a gambler or bold man by temperament and he insured himself with margins of safety—getting people with established reputations or their children to write for the paper. (There were the Kempton kids—Sally and Mike, children of Murray; Max Lerner's boy, Steve; Dwight Macdonald's son, Mike; Susan Goodman, daughter of Paul; Steven Schlesinger, son of Arthur.) Thus, Dan made it clear that the *Voice* was a place where writers (or their children) wished to be published and would be only if Dan thought they were good enough. With a few "name" writers on hand, Dan could take risks with unknowns, discovering people like an impresario, but one whose pleasure was derived from the shaping and molding of individual talents rather than their mass marketing.

And then, as sometimes happens, there was a fortuitous coming together of talent and time. By the sixties, Dan had proved to himself and others that he could spot a nascent talent and help it come to term (and thus the frigid Jewish man could prove his womanhood). But he couldn't have known that the sixties themselves would be a talent, that the era was a creation, feverish with flower children rebelling against bourgeois backgrounds, against parental authority (a hint of things to come?), Villagers going on vigils for peace, mothers standing on town squares chanting, "Not our sons, not your sons, not their sons," upholding the theme of family, while all along leitmotifs announcing the family's decay were in the background like noise pollution. Yes, time itself was as ripe as a young talent.

And the paper could claim many firsts: the first systematically to cover all the civil rights demonstrations (after all, was it not Mailer, an original *Voice* writer, who had prophesied the love affair between whites and Negroes before it was even a reality?). And the *Voice* was there to cover the long funeral of the civil rights movement as it slowly shifted into the antiwar one.

And Dan was there as attempts to counter the culture became less lugubrious and flowers began to sprout long before organic farms in the psyches of sons and daughters of people like Dan. Believing the defiance of authority to be more psychological than political, Dan gave writers this perspective with which to view the world around them. And thus came the voices of Don McNeil, Sally Kempton, and others whose analysis was never doctrinaire, the writers being far too idiosyncratic and insecure ever to surrender themselves to one idea, their need to work out an identity never getting buried in the chaos of events. Hence the funny uneven quality of the *Voice,* with some of the best, original writing, and some of the most indulgent, sophomoric, as if the need to develop required regressions and unevenness, carelessness itself as much a trademark of the Bohemian tradition as an old garret room.

With the same kind of capriciousness that made the sixties themselves a talent, the seventies showed up with fatigue—the flower children were wilting in the wake of overdoses, the Diggers at work on their own grave, the demonstrations dying as the Vietnam War proved to be the most stubborn of terminal cases.

But most crucial for Dan Wolf was the way in which the whites' love affair with blacks had atrophied. What did it mean to be a Bohemian if you now were as afraid as any good burgher (might be) to walk the street of your native "village"?

Dan Wolf no longer could consult his fingertips with confidence about Bohemian life-styles. If the "counterculture" was on its way out, so was its sympathetic coverage, for Dan understood that both had grown out of the same roots—a gentle and confused rebellion on the part of children against all that seemed deadening in their parents' lives.

But now Dan was not sure of his readership. Simultaneous with the demise of the movement in its more conspicuous and media-rich manifestations was the blossoming of other papers and magazines which were beginning to cover the counterculture (semantically upgraded to alternate life-styles), and over a period of time not only was the turf that once belonged exclusively to the *Voice* undergoing its own erosions but others were beginning to invade the narrowing strip.

Psychology, in all its fads and failures—head trips, body trips, drug trips, encounters—was being reported on regularly in *Psychology Today. Rolling Stone* was stealing the young readership from the *Voice,* a theft Dan accepted in the same way he accepted the fact that he might get mugged any moment on the streets of the Village. The young were no longer to be pursued so avidly; he was now more interested in people like himself—affluent New Yorkers who wanted to live well and for whom politics and psychology were columns in the brain along with restaurants and rock.

It had been the genius of *New York* magazine to take the how-to formula and apply it to the existential problems of urban living. And no matter how many times Dan or other Villagers might raise a supercilious eyebrow at the "slickness" of *New York,* they could never knock success, and *New York* was now a success, and a growing one. What's more, it was a competitor for the same market. It, too, wrote about the politics of the city; it, too, covered alternate life-styles (only with the added illusion that it was giving you a guide to copying some of the chicer ones instead of an ironic way of feeling superior to them, as the *Voice* had at one time done).

Damn it, how did Felker manage—giving New Yorkers the illusion they were getting a guide on how to "do" their lives better in the city. What a vulgar assumption that there's a way to "do" your life! What kind of creature can convert existentialism into a repair book manual?

But Clay could do it. He was just that kind of creature. And not by making his readers feel superior to success. No, Clay was onto something profound. He knew people have a need to experience regret—all those bittersweet emotions that accompany the roads not taken in life. But what kind of coarseness could take moments not seized, loves not pursued, life not lived fully and convert such notion of loss into brownstones not grabbed, restaurants undiscovered, and bargains not bet on until pronounced best by *New York*? How dare he translate regret—so rare and delicious an emotion—into something vulgarized, trivialized, and concretized. How dare he so accelerate an emotion that by the time he had finished packaging it, you still had not had a chance to experience it. Didn't he know that the bittersweet emotions had best be left to *The New Yorker?*

But he wasn't even dealing with regret anymore—Felker. When he had finished, all that was left was envy, pure and simple. You felt crummy about your life after reading his magazine, as if you didn't know how to "do" your life. Still . . . what genius to make his readers think they could learn how to live better by reading his magazine. All they were doing was feeling a cheap flash over every opportunity they decided not to take because they were scared, because they couldn't afford risk, vision, mortgage. Vinyl regret. Oh, where was Norm? He understood such things; he even thought the *Voice* was too safe, too square, too straight. Why did he have to go off and make millions writing books? And why didn't Felker become some fashion lord? King of Bloomingdale's, that site of original sin in New York where everything is boutiqued so tastefully. Now *there's* an empire. Why did Clay have to mess around with writers? Why couldn't he have dealt with real fashion? He would have been brilliant. Opera is out, ballet is in; opera is a way of thinking of six months ago. Dan could just hear Clay's mind at work.

But it was tricky. For despite Clay's vulgar sensibility, he had hit on something. He was right; it was time to tap the roots of urban dismay—all the negative emotions people in a pent-up city feel—the need for escape and, yes, even envy. But to trick people into believing that they could change their lives by knowing the latest trends, instead of just telling them that life was becoming tougher in the city; or to have them believe they could change their lives by reading *New York* . . . Well that was just unfair.

Dan himself was now a rich man. The $3 million sale of the *Voice* in 1970 to Carter Burden had made him a millionaire. And although he remained as Editor of the paper after the sale, he was receiving a salary of $72,000—a far cry from the old Bohemian days of indifference to money. He now had various interests to defend, and property and possessions to protect. People, he sensed, were fearful, anxious to hold onto whatever they had; everything was changing, all was image, illusion; the old values, the Bohemian ways, might be suitable for nostalgic export but not for the pages of the *Voice*. It was time to cultivate a new readership.

A tone started to emerge from the pages of paper that resembled a whine—the muffled cry of those who feel they are being neglected, sacrificed, no longer getting their fair share. It was time for the eternally tolerant to stand up; Villagers, vegetarians though they may be, worshipers of the sun, sex, and insanity at selected moments . . . nevertheless did not like dog shit. It all started there.

Then following the get-tough dog shit stand, which Clark Whelton introduced, were revelations that welfare hotels were ruining the Village, that the Washington Square Park was now being taken over by blacks, and that the Villagers did not like them any more than they liked dog shit.

Then along came Attica—the perfect opportunity to put on a white gown, long gloves, and officially debut. But time for preparation was skimpy. Word had just come through that the inmates who were rebelling had killed the guards, and the paper was due to go to press in a short time. It was the moment for the *Voice* to show courage, to act; and while betraying the once liberal roots, those at the paper knew they must not appear shaky—go all the way or hold off. And the *Voice* decided to go all the way. After all, the inmates had threatened to cut off the balls of the guards who were white, according to the latest bulletins. Clearly, things had gone too far. The love affair had been dying, and now it had turned into open warfare. Even Mailer would understand.

But no sooner did the *Voice,* in a passionate piece written by Clark Whelton, come out defending Rockefeller's decision to send in the National Guard, than the news arrived that it was not the inmates who had killed the guards but the men whom Rockefeller sent in. There was panic; the piece would kill off whatever radical readership remained as surely as the bullets had destroyed the men. The article, like the decision to open fire, *mis*fired.

The *Voice* had to do a quick about-face, but not one where they would appear sniveling. How could anyone have known the news was wrong? Had the black inmates actually cut off the balls of the white guards, the *Voice* would have had an article that people would be talking about the way they once did (before *New York* hit the stands, at least). And, too, Dan believed that if he could feel terror of blacks (and here he was not alone), why wouldn't they, in turn, have every desire to castrate those who were trying to keep them out of their schools, parks, neighborhoods? And perhaps even those who gave coverage to such sentiments.

For the first time in *Voice* history, two pages were set aside to run without any advertisements; writers were rounded up and asked to contribute a piece on Attica *from a radical point of view.* The pieces were treated with an uncommon respect for the visual—

they were not cut up into many fragments. A statement was being made that came as close as possible to an editorial retraction of the Whelton piece, making it look like the thoughts of an individual gone astray.

It worked, leaving the *Voice* safe for a moment. But the whole incident was an omen that Dan could no longer act on his instincts; they had become dulled, those of a man who fears he is about to lose something and begins to fight back by flailing out. *"No,* New York *magazine, you cannot have my readership. I will show you, I will get another one all my own, the way I did the first time."*

"The Next Moment in History Is Ours," Vivian Gornick proclaimed in one of the earliest articles about women's liberation. Dan took note of the hundreds of responses. The *Voice* had a sudden gush of life left like a school of squid washed ashore who send up an inky squirt before they collapse and become transparent corpses.

Dan, like most Villagers his age, couldn't personally respond to the tide of feminism he felt mounting; the rights of blacks (before they threatened him)—yes; young men sent off to fight an immoral war—yes. (He had even courted a West Point graduate, Lucien Truscott IV, seduced as much by the numeral after his non-Jewish name as by his political awakening.)

In the same way that Dan had understood intuitively how to start the *Voice* and make it grow, he knew that he must now hand over some of his authority. But only to one who would not challenge it, someone weak, in search of a father figure himself. It is likely that Dan did not even know that the man he had in mind had lived through his own father's suicide and was not about to challenge whoever was the head of the household.

The Gornick piece had given the *Voice* new blood, and it would be Ross Wetzsteon who would direct its flow. No one realized that under the gentle, almost saintly, exterior Ross's own blood was gushing; what was noticed instead was that Ross seemed different from Dan, someone whose intuitions were more in line with women's than men's. Bearded, patient, gentle, someone who could deal with women in a special way. Dan, of course, not only dealt with women writers but had also discovered many. The *Voice,* in fact, could be proud of its early record of women writers who would later become some of the best known—Sally Kempton, Susan

Brownmiller, Jane Kramer, Stephanie Harrington, to name but a few. But the moment was not yet theirs when Dan worked with them.

In contrast to Dan, Ross was a fellow sufferer (one might almost be tempted to call him a "sister" were it not for the ways he made you feel labels were anathema to anyone with sensibility). With Ross, you had to worry as much about him as about yourself—the way he cared, the way he himself was overworked, and the way something in his eyes told you that all was not well in the spiritual sense, the existential, if you will. But he wouldn't tell you! For once again, he would be the first to admit the pretentiousness of such talk.

When you were in his office, he made you feel that he was interested in you as a writer with a woman's sensibility, never as a woman *per se*. Here was someone literate who cared about words and not what you looked like or felt like in bed. He didn't even try to mind-fuck you the way Dan did.

No, it was language and style he cared about in writing, and complexity and nuance in life. Nothing could be pigeonholed and given glib labels without destroying the individual perspective on which the aesthetic sensibility depends. Which is why he did not want anything defined; there were to be no strict borders, especially when it came to that most treacherous border of all—the line that separates women from men. Ross was ready to concede it was a combat zone (bannering the very title "Combat in the Erogenous Zone," before it was used for a book), but it was one people of courage dared to cross. The alien was no longer the black, it was the woman.

And so, he encouraged explorations into the areas of combat, and for a year or two, the *Voice* gave consistent original coverage to the women's movement. Again, the writers were pioneers, from the first piece proclaiming the movement's "moment" to the subsequent ones chronicling its phases, its battles, its victories.

Just as the *Voice* seemed to be recapturing its identity, competition started to rear up: *Ms.* appeared on the scene, along with a growing number of feminist publications. The *Voice* was caught in the middle. And Dan, tired, was locked in the middle of his own life. Not even Ross, who felt forty zooming in on him, could take seriously any separatist talk except as a gimmick (which is how the paper seemed to regard Jill Johnston).

The *Voice* did not want to print pieces filled with primeval rage; let the feminist papers do that, and let the *Voice* find women who still felt possessive, jealous, and who were, if the truth were to be made known, still in search of romance and the right man (after, of course, the right analysis). Feiffer and Freud, like Papa, know best.

Skirmishes were of interest as long as they ended in bittersweet resolutions—man and woman going off together into the combat zone aware of its dangers, its complexities, the dartings, the piercings of the emotions. But never quite a stroll into a fading sunset. No, sentimentality was to be avoided almost as carefully as raw anger. Either simplified life, which, according to the guiding principles of humanism, liberalism, and high art, had to have contradiction. It was too simple to say men oppressed women or that they were pigs. The phrases lacked drama. For a long time no one questioned Ross's taste.

Then something odd happened. Fugitive Jane Alpert sent a piece to the *Voice* from somewhere in hiding. It told how she really felt about men, that the earlier piece she had written containing a reverential portrait of her lover, Sam Melville, published after he was killed at Attica, was a lie. This piece was the truth; it was only with women that she could feel solidarity, and that was the real lesson of being a Weatherwoman. Ross turned the piece down.

Off Our Backs, a small feminist publication, rushed it into print. On the day it appeared, all copies of the paper were sold out in New York. *Ms.,* which had also received a copy, printed it as quickly as possible. The piece elicited more responses than any other the magazine had ever run.

Given the historical importance and commercial interest of the piece—a combination irresistible to any publication—why did the *Voice* decide to turn it down? You can't write about a man's sexual performance once he is dead and has no chance to defend his honor, Ross explained. It was the first revelation about Ross.

There were uncomfortable parallels with the Attica piece—that is, an omen of things to come. With Attica, Dan had been quick to recoup. But because the Alpert piece was not published, it took an accumulation of pieces done over a period of time to show that the *Voice* was beginning to do with the women's movement exactly what it had done with the blacks—cater to a conservative backlash and hope for the best.

There started to appear from time to time little parodies of the movement. Clark Whelton, who was by now well established as the house reactionary, having gone from dog shit and Attica to defending the Canarsie people who stoned black children bused into their neighborhoods, wrote a satire about women under a pseudonym.

And then came the writers who had too much pride not to use their real names, ones who considered it an assault on their manhood to do anything nasty and *not* sign it, and who, it seemed, took some delight in knocking women. Several, predictably enough, were sportswriters. Joe Flaherty wrote a satire that had no bite; Nick Browne wrote a nostalgic piece about the good old days, when guys drank beer and eyed pretty chicks out on the island. Joe and Nick came out of what one might call "The Lion's Head School of Journalism," where the tradition of maleness and alcohol leaves little room for "wenches" except in a soggy bed.

Something was happening; the men whom Dan had discovered and put on staff—those who chose the swagger as their stance—were now being given an outlet for their woman hating. But not by Dan. By Ross, the man who would have been labeled a feminist if he didn't see the absurdity of all labels.

In a desperate move to kill off the competition, Ross tried another tactic: assign a woman to write a piece about *Ms.* It was time to put the official organ of the women's movement—and a mere upstart of a magazine at that—in its place. As a separate and gratuitous bit of insult, the *Voice* printed a Sorel cartoon showing a grossly distorted Gloria Steinem. And then to indicate that the paper hadn't lost its sense of humor, or its openness to criticism (as had the women's movement), it printed a letter criticizing the cartoon, headlining the letter with the sought-after pun: "Mourning Gloria." After all, she's still alive.

Although it was never officially spelled out, Ross had his writers and City Editor Mary Nichols hers. Diane Fisher dealt with the critics who wrote for the "back of the book." From its inception the *Voice* had been divided into three areas—the political, the psychological, with the cultural zooming in from behind.

For example, on February 4, 1971, the front page of the *Voice* contained "New Ideas for Old Jails" and the "Politics of Rape—a Selective History" as its two feature stories. Sandwiched in between were the beginnings of "lesser" stories—"I Witnessed the Beatings" (in a Queens jail) and a filler entitled "SoHo Saved." The two photographs, taking up roughly half the page, were, with charming irrelevance, about Central Park: one showing the skating rink full of people and another a seal amidst much ice, looking for all the world as if he were awakening to an everlasting midnight sun in the Arctic. On top of the *Voice* logo was the banner for the week, "Sarris: Taking Sex Straight—p. 5." Although an arbitrary choice among issues, February 4, 1971, seems fairly typical of the late sixties-early seventies period, when Dan was doing less and Ross more.

Corresponding with these divisions in subject matter were the various categories of writers. Fourth-floor people, who worked under Mary, were primarily reporters. They got assignments, went out to meetings, and wrote them up. Ross, up on the fifth floor, dealt mainly with people who were more "writers" than reporters, the creative troubled folk traveling on internal odysseys whom Ross had inherited from Dan. Except for the one or two Dan kept for himself until the very last moment—like Ron Rosenbaum.

On the fifth floor—that which housed Ross, Diane, and Dan— the rivalries simmered and festered; on the fourth, they were all out in the open like a bonfire, ignited by the perpetual friction between Jack Newfield and Mary Nichols. Who, each wondered, would assume ultimate command of the political reporting? Mary, as City Editor, had a considerable lead over Jack, an Assistant Editor. And just to underscore the titular differential that appeared on the masthead, Mary also had a large office with a young male secretary outside to screen calls, cut out clips, and do anything else essential in keeping Mary's enemies "runnin' scared." Jack worked in a tiny cubicle, crammed with letters and papers which could be used by anybody when he was not there. And although most people at the *Voice* had a disdain for titles—a mere aristocratic mannerism—titles nevertheless defined not only decor but salary. For while it was Jack who was doing most of the serious muckraking reporting that gained the *Voice* its reputation and Jack who had written three books, it was Mary who earned $18,000, and Jack, $10,000.

To know Mary Nichols' former husband is to understand a lot about Mary. Bob Nichols, a dark and moody anarchist of independent means, sneered at power, upheld failure as a major virtue, and often wore two different-colored socks to prove his point. Bob wanted to restore a sense of "community," as if the world were a run-down brownstone. An architect who landscaped the mind, he could work unencumbered by spatial limitations.

It is said that the two finally split over elevators; Mary wanted to move from their old South Village tenement into a new building with an elevator; Bob could not bear to live in a place that symbolized the evils of technology. So Mary moved out, lusting for the literal (and some peace).

Mary did not anticipate it would end that way when she, a beautiful young woman from Swarthmore with milky skin and long blond locks and a good Philadelphia family, met the dark, brooding man straight out of Harvard who already resembled a youthful Bertrand Russell. Filled with ideals as well as beauty, brains, and money, the two settled down to live like Bohemians in a neighborhood inhabited by "real" people (which seemed to mean those who did not attend Harvard, have trust funds, or any choice about where they lived). And in anticipation of the dropout culture, Bob worked only on projects that interested him, while Mary had babies. And who could have known as she sat in the Park with her three kids that she secretly craved power? Not even Mary, it would seem.

Only when the children were grown would Mary realize how many of Bob's notions were totally cerebral; what a difficult and childlike person he was and how she longed for the freedom to go after the power of which Bob was so contemptuous. As if to prove that Bob's philosophizing—the kind that led to many wasted years in Mary's life—was wrong, Mary began to follow the ins and outs of petty politicians, bureaucrats, just the kind of thing that Bob considered "schlocky." It was so compromised compared to his kind of work—using bits of discarded tires and other rubble to convert old vacant slum lots into little slum parks, preserving the natural resources of the ghetto with a purity unknown even to environmentalists.

While Bob settled down to domestic life by marrying and moving in with writer Grace Paley, Mary spread herself out in the huge apartment which wrapped around the corner of the thirtieth floor of a stunning new building, using the elevator with abandon. With windows for walls, Mary could see every bridge into the city; at night, the helicopters flying over the harbor looked like lightning bugs. Mary's habitat in the sky made the city seem transcendental.

It was in this setting that Mary held her thrice-monthly

Thursday-evening soirees (the fourth Thursday having been set aside for the meetings of the Village Community Board of which she was a member). Thursday at Mary's was as secular an affair as can be imagined, where the only rituals accorded respect were part of that most urban of religions—patronage. No pretensions of a literary order! Salon became saloon as soon as the "boys" arrived. The beer—lots of it—was in the kitchen "fridge," and one was free to help one's self. There would be some talk about what was going on in City Hall until somebody interrupted to ask who would dial a joke, one of the many services offered by Ma Bell.

Mary let everyone carry on in an atmosphere both jovial and strained. For who could know *for sure* if the right thing was being disclosed; that is, something that would rate a favorable mention in Mary's column, "runnin' scared."

Mary had gained weight and seemed to be indifferent to seducing men sexually, but power—the promise of a good word in her column—was a more tantalizing offer than physical favors.

Not only were there the Thursday-night soirees with their curious mixture of city bureaucrats, reporters, tipsters, and beer-drinking chums all seated around a big comfortable coffee table on orange and pink Pucci-like (another dig at Bob?) upholstery of the couches, munching on celery and radishes and gossip about less favored colleagues who were never invited to Mary's, but there was also her life at the *Voice*. Mary practiced the kind of patronage that the paper would be the first to expose. Elsewhere, that is. Mary had her writers and she trained them well. Those who reported what she assigned found that they were put on staff, particularly if they were men. There was Lucien Truscott, and Clark Whelton and Howard Blum. And then there were the young boys who started out as her secretary before advancing to higher positions.

Alan Weitz, a quiet, smart sort of person who always wore dark glasses, had come in off the streets. But it was Dan who had taken him in and made him Mary's aide. Even though he later went on to become Associate Editor (Mary eventually had him elevated to Senior Editor), he could not forget Dan's original act of human kindness. Less than a year after Dan was fired, Alan quit his job.

David Tipmore, a big blond fellow who had a more outgoing personality, seemed to enjoy being Mary's secretary. He would sit outside her office clipping out things of interest, kibbitzing with other writers, and tending to the nuisance calls as Mary sat in her office, her feet on her desk, answering phone calls from City Hall and other sources with hot tips like a bookie taking bets. David expanded into a writer, with Mary's encouragement, turning out pieces about fag hags and the like.

For a person interested in serious investigative reporting, Mary was probably the best person under whom to work. She was generous with her disciples, giving them leads wherever possible and helping them to follow through on a story, particularly if it embarrassed somebody. She herself had been an excellent investigative reporter on community affairs for the paper and she had a good record with those she trained. No suicides and few nervous breakdowns.

People who worked under Mary advanced. For she seemed to believe that anyone who stayed at the *Voice* too long without a staff job was an "unemployable." She had a distrust of the creative writers, as if there were something germ-ridden about them. Anyone, she assumed, who would accept such exploitative conditions without in turn exploiting them had to be slightly diseased.

In more subtle form, this philosophy was shared by everyone at the *Voice,* although it was never discussed. On the other side of the pride in independence, there was shame. For it was hard to work at a place that had a worship of success and that paid so little (was it not the original philosopher-king of success, money, and sex—Mailer—who had started the paper along with Dan and Ed?).

Mary was one of the few at the *Voice* who was straightforward about money. She thought it wrong that the writers were paid so little, although she never seemed uncomfortable with the fact that she was earning more than anyone else except "management." Significantly more. The young and onetime jobless men who worked faithfully for her she took care of. But she couldn't do the same for the women. Not in her chosen position as one of the boys. Which may explain why Mary opposed Bella Abzug's election so strongly, favoring at first the dying Bill Ryan and then, once he "passed on," his quiet, inexperienced widow. Anything seemed better than a noisy, yes, pushy, yes, aggressive, yes, woman. ("Jewish" would have to be whispered, the way rumors of Ryan's terminal illness were.)

But Mary's antifeminism came in spurts. When it was turned off, she might secretly try to get a woman more money or advise her where else to publish her work. Once she even handed over the city editorship to Mary Breasted while she went on vacation. But you had

Dan Wolf   *Fred W. McDarrah*

Fred W. McDarrah

Mary Nichols

Jack Newfield

Fred W. McDarrah

Mary Breasted

Fred W. McDarrah

Nat Hentoff

Fred W. McDarrah

Joe Flaherty

Fred W. McDarrah

Paul Cowan

Fred W. McDarrah

Bartle Bull

to be very special for that, someone who could be groomed for bigger and better things than the *Voice* had to offer. Breasted subsequently moved on to *The New York Times*.

Generous toward her followers, Mary could display meanness, malice, and spite if she sensed you were not with her and would not get out of her territory. Ross was no problem: he handled the psychological, the life-style, the "head" pieces; and Diane Fisher could do whatever she pleased with the culture reviews. But Jack. He was another matter. Almost as bad as Bella.

Both Jack Newfield and Mary Nichols were interested in power, but it seemed as if Mary had a sense of it only by identifying with those who had it. Jack, whose lust was no less, nevertheless could not betray Bedford-Stuyvesant entirely. He chose to write about those without power or how they were being hurt by those with power. Which did not mean that Jack *identified* with the powerless. On the contrary. That would be too painful for one who could still smell the sweat from the subways he took while commuting to Hunter College and could still remember the gaucheness he felt when he came into contact with people whose class had given them more grace. He knew what it was like to be fawning; flattering and conniving were basic skills for anyone with ambition, especially if he had to start out on his own. This Jack understood just the way he understood—in his gut—that most people in power had gotten there not because of their talents alone but either by an accident of birth, connections, or both. He knew as much about cronyism as Mary; but if a rotten marriage breeds a sense of spite and goads one into going after power, the humiliation of being thought grubby produces something other than spite—a sense of outrage and anger.

Jack's coming from a poor family was not his fault any more than was his father's fatal heart attack, when Jack was four. Yet the world rewarded those with money and classy educations as if they were something one got because one deserved them. Jack knew better. And yet he wanted the privileges, the recognitions "they" got; he wanted to socialize and be seen with the powerful. But he knew early in his career, when he was rejected for a job at the New York *Post* after a brief tryout, that he would have to work very hard to get them.

But somewhere within Jack's jungle view of the world (as distinguished from Mary's, which might be of a well-managed zoo), there was compassion. He knew that he was lucky to have learned how to fight his way out and up, and that insight saved Jack from being smug, no matter how many people he falsely flattered or how many others he inadvertently snubbed. Life was still a subway even in a limousined car.

Jack enjoyed seeing those without power gain it (if they deserved it), while Mary liked to watch those with power lose it. It seemed as if Mary were more interested in embarrassing people than doing away with injustice, and whatever spoils of power came her way in the process she kept for her pals and herself. Jack, of course, was no stranger to cronyism; he had often benefited from knowing the right people in the right places. One had the impression that if he were faced with a choice between principles and friends, he would compromise. But only up to a certain point. Purity in politics was for Jack, a luxury, and Jack could not afford luxuries.

By choosing to respond to personal situations in a nonpersonal way (neither Jack nor Mary ever wrote confessional prose) and through politics, the two were fated to clash. Jack also wanted to use the *Voice* as a vehicle to express his beliefs. And while they were more radical than Mary's, the two ultimately had more in common ideologically than not. It was in temperament that they differed, Jack lacking the confidence that a well-to-do Wasp family had given Mary.

But clearly if any one reporter on the paper was to be identified with muckraking, it was not Mary Nichols or Breasted, nor Lucien, Clark, Howard, nor *any* of Mary's disciples. It was Jack. Even allowing for his sloppiness with facts, his overall record was outstanding. Once he hit upon something, he did not stop hacking away at it, and thus turned the savagery of ambition into a useful tool. Jack was the first to expose lead poisoning in slum areas. Because Jack had grown up in the areas which were now decaying right down to the poisonous flakes of falling plaster, his writing reflected an outrage that the most poisonous piece of gossip that Mary might hunt up about political boss Meade Esposito could never have. It did not titillate Jack to know that children in the slums were dying from lead poisoning, welfare hotels, or the rotten prisons they graduated to when they tried to make their way up and out of the jungle. Jack knew that were it not for his skin, he, too, could have wound up behind bars, for, in more subtle ways, he had been penalized for the crime of growing up poor.

Although not a stylist, Jack could write movingly. When Jack wrote an open letter to Mayor Lindsay in the pages of the *Voice* asking him to change, to become the person Jack had believed he was going to be, it sounded as if he had been personally hurt. When Jack wanted to know why Lindsay appointed more marshals—the men who come to take away the few possessions the poor have accumulated when they default on a payment—as one of his last acts in office, Jack seemed to forget how integral patronage is to a politician's life.

Perhaps Jack turned away from politicians who had held out hope because he wanted to avoid another disappointment, another death. In the sixties, he wrote a book on Bobby Kennedy. And his book on the New Left, *The Prophetic Minority,* could still employ the language of vision. But the seventies were different, and with corrupt judges there would be little risk, corruption being as eternal as the tides. When Jack's 1972 *New York* magazine piece on the ten most corrupt judges in New York was reviewed by an august legal body and found to be substantially accurate, despite lawsuits by the judges and slurs by other reporters, he still did not receive any of the prizes the journalism profession bestows on its most talented members.

So it must have hurt to hear Dan turn down his request for a raise, $25, a token request really—for at last, because of his growing reputation and a marriage to a woman from a wealthy family, he no longer was dependent financially on the *Voice.* It was pride, pure and simple, that made Jack ask for more money. He listened as Dan explained that Jack was a nobody when he came there and the *Voice* made him into somebody and if he was not satisfied, he should move on.

Jack was done with begging; it wasn't necessary anymore. The psychology of the orphan no longer informed his behavior. But . . . Dan must be punished. There was only one way to show Dan that Jack was no longer intimidated by him and that was to intimidate Dan; to go over his head to the man who now owned the paper—Carter Burden—and threaten to strike. Jack was convinced there could be no greater humiliation for Dan than to have the writers take a dramatic step without even consulting him.

And what an embarrassment for Carter, who paraded as a liberal politician, to have people at the paper he owned striking because of shamefully exploitative working conditions. How many people in New York knew that *Voice* writers were earning less than $100 a week in the 1970's? That people as well established as Nat Hentoff and Jill Johnston received $90 a week, without benefits? Or that the *Voice* was the only paper in New York which did not use union printers? How could it be that a paper that was so good at pointing the finger at everyone else had such messy laundry at home?

Jack understood the power of exposé; it had worked with lead poisoning and a host of other issues. If he could get the "heavies"—people such as Feiffer and Hentoff and Johnston—to threaten to strike, Carter would consent to a raise. And the one thing Jack knew with certainty was that all *Voice* writers were in agreement that they were paid too little. Writers on other papers were starting at $20,000, and a free-lancer could get several thousand for an article in certain magazines.

Yet Dan was still carrying on as if the paper had no money. Just one look at the number of ads would prove otherwise. Who was getting all the money? Where was it going? Into Carter's pocketbook? Dan's? No writer seemed to know and none even thought to question it, so convinced were they of the privilege of writing for the *Voice*.

Dan took the questioning of finances as a personal insult. It was none of the goddamned business of writers. *He* was the one who had to worry about money in the beginning and now *he* would be the one who would look after where it went. Was it not *true* that the writers were nobodies when they came to him and it was *he* who made them into sombodies by giving them a chance to appear in the pages of his paper? Of course, it was true.

But it was also true that it worked two ways: that the *Voice* was a "nobody" when Dan first started it and that the writers helped to make it what it was. And what's more, they helped to make Dan a rich man.

And now, in December, 1971, sufficiently irked, Jack called a few close friends at the *Voice* to talk about the possibility of a strike. A strategy was worked out—to get as many *Voice* writers as possible at one large meeting and find out the number willing to go along with a strike.

At first, the evening had the feeling of a costume ball where a by-line came dressed in a body. Many *Voice* people who had been contributing regularly for years had never seen what anyone else looked like. Who's the one in a veil and chiffon scarf who came in late and is standing by the entrance to the room? So *that's* Blair Sabol. And who's over there, sitting near Feiffer and Hentoff? Marty Washburn? I see.

All speculation was interrupted when Mary Breasted announced she had an objection. What were outsiders, people who didn't write for the *Voice,* doing at the meeting? Especially when Mary Nichols was not invited.

Like who?

Hentoff's wife.

Nat explained that Margot had in fact written for the *Voice* for quite a long time and had stopped for a while precisely because she opposed its exploitation. Besides, Nat pointed out, it was nice just to meet each other in this informal way. It had never happened before, this chance to meet outside of the *Voice,* and it felt good.

Mary didn't agree. Meetings were bores; she had little interest in unspontaneous socialization. Nor did she care to discuss now or in the future the direction the paper was taking. She was here for only one reason—to talk about getting more money. And that was it.

The meeting then got down to strategies. Paul Cowan, at whose comfortably spacious apartment the meeting was being held, brought up the question of health insurance, pointing to the Band-Aid on his chin, which covered the still fresh surgical marks made to remove a skin cancer. Since he was not then on staff, he had no health insurance to cover the cost of the operation. Perhaps Dan could think of a way to get nonstaff people coverage in the future.

Jack still believed that the group should ignore Dan and go directly to Carter. *Let's use our power as media people—every paper in New York would love to expose the* Voice. *Carter knows that. Imagine what a picket line outside would look like for Carter. We could even shut down the paper if enough people go along.* But Jack didn't think it would come to that; the mere threat of publicity would get Carter to increase the pay.

Mary was adamant. She would not be part of any move to go above the head of Dan, particularly when he hadn't refused anybody anything yet. Only Jack. Which is why Jack should not be the one organizing this. His motives are totally suspect. They're strictly retaliatory. And they don't have anything to do with money, she protested.

Others pointed out that it didn't matter what Jack's personal motivation was. He had gotten everybody together, and nobody before him had even thought to organize. So forget the personal crap, Mary was told, or they'd never get down to the issues.

Each person went around the room and introduced him/her self. A lawyer, experienced in labor arbitration, explained that he had been invited on a friendly basis by Paul Cowan and his brother Geoff, who was also at the meeting. The first thing that was apparent was that no one had any idea of what to ask for because no one knew how much anyone else earned. People learned that staff writers received $125 a week whether or not they wrote, and nonstaff writers received $125 for an article only if it was printed. Hentoff thought it unfair that columnists, who were paid only $90 a week, should be penalized for the "privilege" of appearing regularly in print, which in other terms meant doing more work for less money.

The critics then started to speak up. They had a more complicated system of pay. There was $50 for the first play reviewed and $25 for each additional one reviewed the same week. But this system, with its many variations, favored short, empty reviews. Arthur Sainer pointed out that if he wished to write an in-depth review of a single play, he lost money. And at the rates the *Voice* paid, he couldn't afford to. Looking sad and hollowed like Ichabod Crane, he said he would like one amount, no matter the number of plays, so he could put all his energies into his writing rather than serve up a pleasant smorgasbord.

Marty Washburn, an old classmate of Ross's, who was primarily a painter, announced that he felt good to get paid at all, considering what crap often went into the paper; no one else would even print him, let alone pay him for what he did.

However, most felt different. While granting that the *Voice* gave writers freedom to do as they pleased—a freedom that all conceded was rare in journalism—they felt exploited. What they did was good, they were good, and they deserved more money. But going over the head of Dan left them a bit uncomfortable. Was it really necessary? Couldn't one first try to deal with him before subjecting him to that sort of insult? Mary Breasted made it clear that she would not be part of any plan that insulted people. And others, following her lead, agreed to give Dan a try.

The angrier writers wanted to draw up a list of "demands" as part of a "get-tough" policy. They were fed up with Dan's paternalism. Finally, some accord was reached. Each reporter should get $25 more, bringing the minimum for a normal-sized article to $150. The longer pieces should receive $200. "Off-the-head" pieces that required less legwork should receive less money. Joe Flaherty objected. Sometimes little pieces that come from the head are the hardest of all to write. Anyone can go down and cover a press conference, but a good little piece takes more effort even if you never get off your ass once.

It was agreed that writers should get expense money and a kill fee for pieces that were assigned and never make it to print. (Some people, it was learned, were already getting expense money, but it was never established as policy.) Others wanted to be able to work on longer pieces and get paid extra amounts for doing that. Dan, they thought, should have the right to decide whether he wants a long piece and then the individual writer should negotiate the amount. But who would present the demands to Dan?

No single person.

A group.

But who?

Representatives from all groups—one from the columnists, one from the reporters.

Don't forget the critics. We're always left out.

One from the critics.

Finally, a vote was taken and those present elected a team of nine—touching the tender hearts of those who grew up with Pee Wee Reese, Duke Snyder, Gil Hodges, and Jackie Robinson. Mary Breasted once again brought up the subject of Jack. His motives were untrustworthy, and she didn't want him on her "team." Others, however, felt Jack was essential. Jack himself made it clear that he did not want to do anything that would hurt the rest of the people present and offered to resign from the group, but his offer was rejected.

It was decided that the delegation, *including* Jack, would meet at Mary Breasted's the night before the meeting with Dan. Afterward, everyone would reconvene to share the results of the negotiations. People thanked Paul and Rachel Cowan for the use of their apartment, and there was a lot of warmth as the evening came to an end. Most people seemed convinced that they were working to build a stronger *Voice,* and despite the missionary sound of such a sentiment, there was a warm and relaxed glow as people mingled in the elevator and shared taxis home.

Already word had gotten back to Dan that the writers were up in arms—fed up with earning $100 a week—and had held a meeting at which an attorney was present; they had even called Carter Burden with threats of a strike, Dan was told. It became clear that someone was spying, someone who had attended the meetings and now was reporting what happened to Dan, even false things like the call to Carter. An atmosphere of paranoia started to creep into the office. Who was it that felt a greater loyalty to Dan than to the rest of the *Voice* writers?

Ross was torn throughout it all. Part of him still identified with the writers. But another part knew that he was being groomed for Dan's job. There were calls in the night from Ross begging to know at whose house the meetings were taking place, who was there, and how people felt about him. That was what was most important. The issue of money was secondary. If he ever got to a position of power he promised he would see to it that the writers—all the regulars, not just the few on staff—got sick leave, vacation time, health insurance, and more than $100 a week for an article. But what do they *now* think of me? he wanted to know. "How much money are *you* now earning?" one writer asked Ross, sidestepping his major concern. "But you can't ask that. It's like asking a man the size of his cock." No matter that most *Voice* writers would tell you that, or better yet, write an article about it that Fred McDarrah might photograph.

The night before the meeting with Dan, the writers assembled at Mary Breasted's house, a strange corrugated shack hiding behind a loft building located on the lower West Side of Manhattan. To enter, you had to walk through a narrow dark alleyway, reminiscent of a scene from a Dickens novel. Inside it looked like a hippie pad, with a few posters, two mattresses on the floor, and a couple of sprigs of dried flowers in a wine bottle turned vase.

Mary was eating when the group arrived. There was no apology that she hadn't set up anything to serve; Radcliffe and class oozed from the whole setup. You could see Jack taking it all in, knowing that only someone who had choices of fancy new apartments or old country houses would elect to live in this place. And it must have galled him that she was capable of seeming so unpushy, so cool, so confident; her long-legged body athletic and angular, but not quite horsey. She seemed not to care about looking seductive.

And yet . . . it was rumored all over town that she was having an affair with Carter Burden, the owner of the *Voice,* proof for Jack that Mary was hardly as indifferent to power as her surroundings might indicate. There was some fun in imagining Carter coming down, walking through the dark alleyway, and spending the night on a mattress on the floor, chauffeured away from all that Louis Quatorze that Amanda had pushed on him. Some said that he really liked this; left on his own, he would opt for the simple life of books and a mattress on the floor.

Perhaps. But teaming up with Mary Breasted was not exactly slumming. She came from an old distinguished New England family, and if it was not as financially prominent as the Paleys, it made up for the difference by its intellectual distinction—a grandfather who was a well-known Harvard archaeologist. It was all pretty classy to a Brownsville boy. Jack understood that Mary could afford to look indifferent to money; her cold New England looks revealed her background as well as a listing in a social register. Jack also knew that despite appearances, Mary did not lack ambition; she just knew how to make hustling look classy. She was as anxious as he to be recognized. Harvard did not make an ego disappear; it just made its "sons and daughters" act on its demands in a more direct, even economical way. It was a lot like money itself—coolness: if you had some, you could easily get more; if you had none, you had to pay to get any. The kind of confidence that comes from class gave you a reserve that made it possible to accumulate more without begging, without filling out emotional forms or standing in line.

Mary finished her meal as unself-consciously as if a group of ten people were not waiting in her house. And then it began. Mary again accused Jack of forcing himself on the group. Jack again offered to get off it, but Mary wouldn't relent. She continued, accusing him of secretly meeting with Carter Burden, evidence of his foul play in the whole matter, a charge loaded with irony since it was Mary who was said to be meeting, eating, and sleeping with Carter right in the very place. Since the affair was not yet public—she was still to appear at the annual *Voice* Christmas party with Carter and give a joint party in the shack that Mary Nichols would attend—Jack could not point out the arrogance of her accusation.

How clever of Mary Nichols, who understood it was a good move to be on the side of the owner of a paper (particularly if he happened to be a politician, as well) to have one of her disciples do the dirty work. And Mary, the younger, had learned her lessons well. How easy to be one of the boys by sleeping with the most powerful, her seductiveness all the more alluring since she camouflaged it so well.

Jack did not fight back. He once more offered to remove himself from the group if the others present thought his own history of controversy would interfere with their chances of getting more money. Nat Hentoff pointed out to Mary the graciousness of Jack's offer, but Mary slammed back, as if the remark were a tennis serve, that it wasn't gracious at all. Jack didn't know what graciousness was all about; he simply had no choice, and that's why he offered.

Mary couldn't be held back. The battle was on; it was strictly class warfare. Had it been on the streets in a ghetto, it might have ended with a stabbing. At one point, it looked as if Mary was ready for physical combat with Jack. It had nothing to do with actual sex (except that Jack understood that she was able to use her neutral-looking gender to seduce the powerful). It really was a war between the Gothic spires of prep schools and Harvard on one side and the sweaty corridors of Hunter College on the other. It was a warfare between someone who summered at the right places and someone to whom summer had always been a time when the streets were unbearably hot and everyone sat out at night to cool off, where people never "summered," "wintered," or got away at all. And summer was always a noun.

Both Jack and Mary cared about the same areas—prisons, city politics, municipal corruption—and hence were vying for the same assignments; it had many times irked Jack that Mary could, by virtue of her stony, bony appearance, seem to have more integrity. She could even be more careful with factual details in reporting since what informed her work was a theoretical concern for justice, in contrast to Jack's gut one, which allowed for the sloppiness of the intestinal tract. Jack took no pride in the kind of perfection one might associate with scholarship; purity in reporting was a luxury like 100 percent pure cashmere, and besides, it was too close to gentility. Didn't the Wasps who went mad from time to time always remember to put on their gloves before they were carried off to McLean?

But right on the other side of the fine manners was the callousness that recalled the robber barons. And Mary was as vicious, when she wanted something, as any kid in the street. And now she wanted some of the power and recognition that Jack had gotten through his own labors, not because he had gone to the right schools or been born into the right family. His lineage, so to speak, was all wrong—which is what finally made Jack retreat and remove himself from the delegation. Intimidated by Mary's class, he agreed not to attend the meeting with Dan.

What a costly omission that turned out to be. It's hard to imagine Jack handing Dan verbal Valentines after being insulted by him. He was no longer someone Dan could intimidate, even quietly. He wasn't Lucien Truscott or Clark Whelton, who refused to attend a meeting because of beliefs in "rugged individualism." Jack understood that rarely did ideology alone dictate strong passion.

Besides, Jack understood Dan in a way that few others could. Jack knew what it was like to have little money, to live with a mother who had no husband to support her. And because he knew what Dan had been through, he also knew how wrong it was—how unjust—to use such historical deprivations as a basis for exploitation. How dare Dan convince the writers that he had made them into something when they were nothing; that they were all cripples, unemployables, who but for the grace of Dan . . . That was the ultimate psychological hold—dependency—that had to be broken before one could have any self-respect. And although Dan had given Jack a home at the *Voice*, Jack's loyalties were shifting. They would always be with the *Voice*—the paper where he had been able to pour out his heart, his guts—but he was learning how to detach the *Voice* from Dan. And in so doing, he managed to cut the umbilical cord he was beginning to see had him in a stranglehold.

O.K. Dan had done a remarkable job of building up something from nothing. Jack was willing to grant that Dan was probably one of the greatest editors of all time, that he had both discovered and developed from fifteen to twenty first-rate writers. But Jack, too, had built up a career from nothing. It was the self-made quality of the two that allowed for a mutual respect and antagonism. Dan could no longer feel superior to Jack in the way he did with writers just starting out or in awe of him, the way he did with Mailer and others more firmly established as literary figures. And

Jack suffered from some of the same shame about himself that Dan did.

Unlike Mailer, Jack never went around advertising how small and Jewish he felt against patrician Wasps; Jack's writing lacked the flamboyance of the confessional, and for Dan—with his voyeuristic flair—this meant there was not that much to see.

Jack, like Dan, did not seem to think of power as an explicit means of sexual freedom. Neither appeared to lust after money and fame in order to have any woman in the world at his sexual command. Dan seemed afraid of open sexuality and, were one to judge by his life, preferred a woman who was conventionally dependent in all ways, including financial. (Neither Ed Fancher's wife nor Dan's worked; both stayed home and had babies, although there was plenty of help to get them through.)

In contrast, Jack chose an independent woman as a wife— Janie Eisenberg, a photographer—and was not put off by the fact that she had more money than he. And it was Jack who fought to get a woman writer on the staff when Dan left and a year later succeeded in getting Felker to rehire Vivian Gornick (whose name Felker posted on the masthead although she was not technically a staff writer but a writer with a retainer's fee). During Dan's peak period, there wasn't a single woman on staff. (Vivian, the only one, had been let go when she took time off to write a book, although no such punishment had been handed out to Jack or Joe or the other men who did likewise.) It is true that when the *Voice* paid almost nothing, there were several women on staff. However, the *Voice* has always been owned and controlled by white middle- and upper-middle-class men (there's never even been a regular black reporter), which isn't very different from any of the other power structures the *Voice* so self-righteously sneered at.

And if anything is to prove that women are innately no less corrupt than men and that it is only lack of opportunity that accounts for any semblance of purity the sex may have, it is the behavior of women in positions of power at the *Voice*—women without a feminist bone in their bodies, although much bile for having had to wait so long to obtain any influence outside the home.

When word of the abortive organizing efforts leaked to the media, it was Mary Nichols who spoke to the *Times*, giving the reporter the impression that the feuding was the result of a desire on Jack's part for a "new left" take-over. (Mary was the first to admit in conversation that, prude that she was, she found reactionaries such as the Buckley brothers more to her liking as people than radicals whose abrasive style repulsed her.)

Yet it was Mary who hinted that it was hardly Jack's good looks that got him invited to Jay Kriegel's wedding, which happened to take place the weekend of Attica. Mary made it seem as if the two events had been planned to coincide in order to build her case that Jack was so shoddy a character, even his politics could be sacrificed to his career.

Unlike Mary, Jack never pretended to be pure, merely to have limits. That was one reason he could not accept the politics of the counterculture; they seemed like indulgences having little to do with class oppression and more to do with psychic growth. Yet there was a decency resembling innocence in Jack's code of ethics. It's hard to imagine him writing that Mary may have thought she was being invited to a fancy wedding because of her thin figure. Jack was capable of sarcasm, of nastiness, and of verbal sniping, but he was not vicious with things people were born with (or without); nor did he bring in personal addictions. Dirty politics were one thing; gratuitously hurting somebody by poking fun at his looks gave Jack no kicks. He was more generous than that.

The day after the meeting at Breasted's, Jack arranged to have lunch with Ross. Now that he was no longer part of the delegation, Jack wanted to find out where things stood. Would Mary be given ultimate control if Dan were to retire and Ross take his place? Would she then convert the paper into an instrument to accomplish her own political ends?

Ross wanted to reassure Jack; he knew that there was a rivalry between Jack and Mary. But at the moment, it seemed more important to know if the writers who had been meeting secretly still liked him. What did they think of him? Please say they liked him, loved him, needed him and, of course, he would do anything. Jack seemed unconvinced as Ross picked up the bill for lunch and, with some hesitation, charged it to the *Voice,* just the way he had seen Bartle Bull do it.

Bartle Bull. Never has a name been more perfect as this animal entered the scene, nostrils wide for the stench of family, of human relations. Concern for such relations was not a way to run a business, and he, Bartle Bull, was not interested in anything as petty as manipulating individual psyches, nothing as small-scale as the shaping and molding of ego and talent. The world of modern finance had little to do with individuals and their baggage of psychic history that Dan had taken such pains to shoulder. The time had come for the *Voice* to be evaluated with a cool eye, one trained to look at an operation as such, not as a family or an outpatient clinic.

In a position of power from the 1970 sale of the *Voice* (which he, along with Carter, now owned, each having sufficient personal wealth to use as one might in a Monopoly game), Bartle Bull thought it was time to expand. The era of the family candy store was over: it was perfectly sound, in fact, ingenious, to pay writers the equivalent of jelly beans, to keep them from knowing the business end of the paper right down to how many beans each received; but for those now in charge, a new vocabulary was mandatory, one that included words like "conglomeration," "expansion," even "empire."

One of the first attempts at expansion was to revive the *Voice* books, a publishing venture that those before him had never been able to get going. Bartle appointed a relative, Alexander Cockburn, to take charge.

Bartle Bull began to expand his own "creative" powers as well. Whenever he felt the urge, he wrote a column on ecology called "Ecofreaks." Whether he traveled to wild lands in Africa or some about-to-be-bulldozed local areas, he jotted down notes and then served them up.

Columns themselves were largely a Bartle Bull import; while they served his own needs, they also made the paper more contemporary, less scroungy and arbitrary. You knew exactly where things were pegged if you categorized them, put them in boxes or columns. Hadn't *Time* and *Newsweek* realized that long ago? And now with *New York* the real competition to kill, he began to copy the magazine more and more. "Centerfold" was instituted in an imitation of "Best Bets" so blatant as to cause some to blush. But not Bull. Along he went, starting a cable TV show called "The Voice with Bartle Bull," just as *New York* had one called "New York." Bartle the Bull was "into" copying the one that was number one, with no apologies. Those who would work with him would go far; those who would not could be killed off as mercilessly as big game animals.

There was no need for petty sniping, the kind that married couples engage in so skillfully; no petty feuds of the kind that Jack and Marys older and younger had waged. Wars among individuals were inefficient. Of course, in order to end them Bartle perceived that he would first have to kill off the family structure. And that might take some time to do—Dan would no longer be head but beheaded. A perfect *Voice* pun. And punning was popular with *Voice* readers.

Bartle was leaving nothing to chance. In the age of modern technology and high finance, instinct was to be left to the animals. Publishing people were no different from anyone else who had something to sell.

If surveys showed that readers bought the *Voice* because they wanted to know where to go for kinky sex, ads directing them where to go were to be printed even if you had to call them massage parlor services. And even if it meant creepy people hanging around on the ground floor of the *Voice* building, which housed the classified advertising section. Concerns about what kinds of people came into the *Voice* building were those of a prim scout mother. Which, as it turns out, Mary Nichols was.

Not that Mary didn't want money; she would be the first to admit she did. But not at any price. Mary had enjoyed the *Voice* when it felt like a family, *her* family; even the feuds were part of the fun, the way it had been in the old South Village between the Italians and Bohemians, who learned how to live with each other. To make the *Voice* sleazy contradicted every value she held. She did not want a paper that was cold and impersonal. And she certainly didn't want a tabloid, even if that was what sold. Dan would have known it was wrong of the *Voice* to run a front-page picture of Joan Kennedy with a caption, "An image of faded glamour. No magic of yesteryear could look more tired than the wounded features of Joan Kennedy . . ." especially when there wasn't even a story about Joan, merely about Chappaquiddick and Ted. How close to yellow journalism could you get?

And there were other things that were beginning to bother Mary—rumors, whispers, that certain offices of the *Voice* were being used as casting couches. The *Voice* had been free of *that* under Dan, who, as father of the family, respected the dictates of the incest taboo. And while Mary might oppose Bella and hire young boys as her secretaries, and then put them on staff, patronage was never based on any real sexual give and take.

In print, yes. She loved to get at the movement, particularly those elements she found offensive: the young women, oh so shrill, who were constantly screaming about orgasm and who disdained going after the pleasures to be found in power, or at least those derived in wresting it from men. And the people of both sexes who were interested only in their own were equally distasteful; she had no qualms about saying that she did not want her children to grow up homosexual nor to see such perverts walking around her neighborhood, which set up a conflict on the paper, since a good part of its readership consisted of just the people Mary was trying to oust from her neighborhood.

Patronage for friends, in the form of a favorable mention in a column after someone had given you a hot tip, was one thing. But to hold out the promise of publication, no matter how indirectly, in exchange for the opportunity to have relationships was wrong. Morally wrong.

Then why were all those recently divorced young women streaming into the office of Ross? It was a question which upset Mary, although she did not see the irony of her role in the general takeover of testosterone at the *Voice*. As for Bartle, it didn't matter if one converted power into sexual currency as long as circulation increased. If Ross could get better writers by propositioning them, fantasizing about them, or even just listening to their tales of loneliness and then encouraging them to write them up *for the Voice,* so much the better. Moral scruples on that level were part of an amateur's operation.

If anything, Ross was a useful person to have around. So absorbed was he by his own insecurities (which he might or might not choose to work out through his job), he would never question a major shift in power even if it included purges. That is, Bartle understood, not as long as Ross's own position was insured.

As in earlier times, when Ross decided to side with Dan instead of his fellow writers, Ross would, if necessary, side with whoever was in charge, even if he suffered a bit. Anguish, he could tell himself, nourishes the soul. So Bartle let him have his fantasies; they were petty. He wasn't demanding any big piece of the financial pie Bartle was hoping to bake. Ross, like the other writers at the *Voice*, shared the mentality of the beggar—grateful for whatever crumbs came his way.

When the coup finally came and it was decided that Dan (and Ed) were to be offed, Ross did not resist. The rest of the children, sensing their inability to stop things, wanted it known that their loyalties still were with Dan; in some ways, they would always be. As they were to write themselves in the paper, "Over the years other publications emulated the *Voice*. None succeeded in capturing the essence of this newspaper. Because for 19 years its soul was Dan Wolf and Ed Fancher. We are their children. . . ."

Ross, questionable at best as a leader, and traitorous and tricky to at least a few, was accepted with a minimum of embrace. Ross was, like Alexander Cockburn, an upstart, ready, even eager, to ingratiate himself with whoever turned out to have the most power. But there were others who could not shift alliances with such grace. Yet their regrets over the ousters of Dan and Ed were strikingly naïve in one respect. Had they had the courage to stand up to the father when they had the chance, they might have been able to prevent his overthrow. It was they, the children, who, out of love and fear, and all the complex emotions that make up family ties, created the vacuum which more calloused, less caring creatures were now to fill.

The Daughters Speak

Abner Symons

"If I could think of anything to say to them, I would have. But I don't have the words to express how I feel because I want to kill them."

Diane Fisher

Better Annie Fisher than Diane for a girl growing up amidst the West Virginia mountains, where "the difference a single range can make is amazing." As a young girl, Annie used to go down to the newspaper, where her father was the Sports Editor; it was a daily, and there in the newsroom she picked up the sense of excitement a paper can offer. But somewhere there was a dream to escape the reactionary tone of the whole town, to get away from the mountain ranges that divided the miners from the more respectable folks. She had heard about a place called Greenwich Village; it was a kingdom made magical by reversing the order—where *not* being respectable (at least in the way her father was) turned out to be the ultimate in respectability. That is, people respected you if you smoked and had sex; there was no need to drive to a secluded mountain edge. You could do such things right in your own home. If you lived in Greenwich Village, that is.

And what revenge—to run away—for a father who had himself left a family behind when he went off to the war and Annie was only six, returning almost a stranger as she was on the verge of womanhood. "It would have been better if he had stayed overseas. You know, someone doesn't have to really be dead not to be alive for you."

When Annie finally came to the city after graduating from West Virginia University, she couldn't immediately fulfill her high school yearbook prophecy that one day she would be an editor of a Greenwich Village newspaper. "I couldn't think beyond secretary. I was so intimidated by everything I had read."

66

The year was 1958, and Diane was a striking woman—high cheekbones, big brown eyes, long light brown hair tied back, more natural than severe, more simple than stylized, as if a bit of the mountain range were incorporated into her face. But it was her body that gave her homeland away—the limbs that had room to swing freely, never needing to knot themselves up as they carried adolescent dreams of escape. Her ambition quietly accumulated over the years—to carve out a life as different and distant as the mountain ranges of her childhood.

On the surface Annie, now calling herself Diane, seemed at ease with the world. It was easy for her to land a job at the largest advertising agency, J. Walter Thompson, where she worked as a secretary for four years, going in each day, marking time until she was ready to be released from the straight world and realize the dream she had never once forgotten.

"I was convinced the *Voice* was so hip and I was so square I'd never get a job there." By hanging out on Madison Avenue, Diane acquired sophistication, but she didn't care because she wanted something else—something "meaningful" that had the integrity of her bone structure.

Slowly she began easing into the Village scene. "I was living with someone, so street-smart." That was the key—in West Virginia they didn't have streets, not the kind she saw in New York, at least, where there wasn't a single tree and only your "smarts" kept you out of trouble. To the daughter of an Army officer, there was something exciting about city streets filled with potential combat.

"The man I lived with lived in a different world. That was what I thought the *Voice* was like. I didn't know then that the *Voice* was a lot more like me than it was like him. But I still didn't have the nerve to approach the *Voice,* even after I left advertising. It was, you know, a classic case of what that woman at Radcliffe [Matina Horner] said about women fearing success. I often think of that."

Finally, in 1962, Diane developed the nerve. She called Ed Fancher to see if there was any typing work. "If I could ever get into the paper, the light that was hidden under the bushel would come out." There was no typing work, but Ed had a need for a part-time receptionist in his office, where he practiced psychotherapy. " 'If there's anything I'm not interested in, it's being a part-time receptionist but I'll come in,' I told him." A bit of the semi-Southern ladylike sense of duty arising alongside an intuitive sense that she just might be able to see the light of the *Voice* by entering through the door of a therapist. And Diane was right. Weeks later when she called Ed to remind him that she hadn't been paid, he told her about a part-time job as a receptionist. But this time it was at the *Voice*.

On Halloween, a day encased in costumes, Diane stepped out of her high school yearbook dream and started work on a Greenwich Village newspaper. It was only temporary, Ed told her, but then three weeks after she began, the New York newspaper strike came along. It was a lucky break not only for Diane but for the *Voice* in general. People who might never have been inspired to pick up so local and offbeat a periodical, addicted as they were to *The New York Times*, were caught off guard. If the paper that had provided reassurance merely by being there every day and looking, on the surface, the same as every issue dating back to when one first started reading it could suddenly disappear, then why not take a chance on something totally unknown, like *The Village Voice?* Just for the heck of it.

Dan knew it was the moment to start moving. Quickly. The paper doubled in size, and suddenly there was loads of work and only Dan and Diane to do it, Jane Kramer having just left. Dan told Diane she could write fillers, the little boxes that went in between columns and were later to become so important to people who skimmed through the *Voice* as a habit. Diane turned out to be good at it—not only doing fillers but at being a filler, and for the next six months she worked at anything, doing editorial on Monday and Tuesday, billing on Wednesday, and the front desk on Thursday. On Friday she often took off to go sailing.

It was a life of intimacy at the Sheridan Square quarters of the *Voice*, with people sitting in everyone else's lap. You couldn't help but know everybody. And yet, Diane reports, "I was really intimidated. I mean always. I never asked for anything, including money." But with her cheap apartment, Diane could get by on the $80 a week she was earning. She would have worked for even less; there are few places that can accommodate the loner seeking intimacy, and the *Voice* was one. It was easy to remain anonymous; the atmosphere provided the personality.

When the *Voice* first started, Jerry Talmer had been in charge of the back of the book—the part containing the cultural reviews. To be a part of the back of the book implied no slight; the

Voice had never a high regard for ordinary sequence, nor assumed that what was first was most important. There just may have been enough of the Talmudic in Dan to realize that the back of the book was an important section. Jerry was followed by Michael Smith, and when he, too, left, the only person around to do the editing was Diane. Not that she ever asked to be made an editor officially. "Everything that happened to me happened by Dan coming down and suggesting something. It seems typical that the way you got anything at the *Voice*—and everyone wanted something real bad—was not to indicate any interest."

As the paper continued to expand and Diane assumed more of an editor's role, a need arose for another person to do proofreading. Sometime in 1966 a young literate man showed up who seemed willing, even eager, to be given the chance to peer over periods and commas in the back room.

At first Diane accepted Ross Wetzsteon. But as he began to accelerate his activities, no longer confining himself to correcting punctuation, Diane found herself repelled by Ross. There was something about him, a way he had of hovering, that Diane could not abide. It was as if all the uncertainties and fears Diane knew how to conceal in herself stuck out with Ross. Diane, with her attraction to the warrior, did not trust insecure people. There was even a hint that, suffering and sensitive though Ross might be, his vacillating steps would lead him into direct competition over jobs. Daughter of an Army officer and Sports Editor, Diane was no stranger to competition. What she did not know at the time, however, was that Ross, like herself, had been abandoned by a father and that the real competition was not entirely over jobs.

Ross was told by Dan that one day he would succeed him; he now had a dream to make come true the way Diane had done with her high school yearbook prophecy. But Ross knew that now he would have to plan all his actions; not a single thing could be left to chance. It was something Diane understood when she was on a sailboat: that is, it might seem as if you were letting the wind take you where it would but in actuality you were always directing it—adjusting the sails, coming about, heeling. You took an active part in controlling the forces around you when you were at sea.

Back at the *Voice,* Diane drifted into things, becoming a generalist of sorts, doing a little bit of everything. Ross, on the other hand, began to specialize, choosing theatre as his own area.

Acting, posing, adjusting one's persona were not forms of behavior unique to the theatre; they were part of the drama of everyday life.

Ross began to write a column called "Theatre Journal," taking the name from Michael Smith, who had written the column before Ross. As if exhilarated by the notion that he might one day inherit Dan's position as Editor of the paper, Ross began to advance his own editing career with dizzying speed.

While the *Voice* was located at Sheridan Square, Diane could still feel on the same level with Ross. For she was. Literally. Everyone had access to every part of the place; everyone could hear what everyone else was saying and see what everyone else was doing. Although the space was cramped, it did not define people, and Diane liked the hodgepodge quality. Even that the floors leaned and squeaked; it made her feel at home.

But then in 1970 came the move to University Place and with it separate floors and separate offices and elevators and even a receptionist's desk—a miniature replica of the corporate world of Madison Avenue, from which Diane had worked so hard to escape. Still, it was in the Village, within walking distance of her pad, and it had once housed the now defunct Evergreen Press. So there were hopes that the stratification of corporate life could be avoided even though the new owners, Carter Burden and Bartle Bull, were part of that life and aliens to the little lean-to quarters Diane had loved at Sheridan Square.

Once ensconced in the solid new building, Ross began to act upon the dream that had seemed too distant to take seriously at Sheridan Square. And when it came to a choice of offices, it was irresistibly difficult not to think which room would be more fitting for a future Editor of *The Village Voice*. Diane, who had been at the *Voice* longer than Ross, was given the first choice of rooms on the fifth floor, which was the editorial floor, housing Dan, herself, and Ross. The floor below, the fourth, was for the reporters who were under the command of Mary Nichols.

Clearly, the top floor was the top floor, but who was to have the front room, the one with the large picture window, Ross or Diane? (Dan had already taken a room which was distinguished mainly by its inaccessibility.) Diane bypassed the large front room, choosing instead one that was small and looked out on a side street, a final statement, she hoped, as to what she thought of status and the concern for the outward signs of success. It was a cozy little room, resembling that of an old but sturdily crafted sailboat, and Diane fixed it up with a few simple Mexican fabrics which hung from the wall and a few to cover a tiny cot. Ross's room had a big view, a big desk, and a battalion of sharpened black pencils standing upright in a big mug.

"He took it so seriously in a status sense, in the whole 50's sense of making it. That never meant anything to me. He told me once that of all the people at Cornell with him, Dick Schaap was the only one who had made it. *That* was success to Ross."

But Ross didn't find Diane's choice of rooms as much a statement about success as it was a statement about herself, indirectly announcing that she *chose* to be less conspicuous, less important, less visible; that she was more comfortable with something modest not because she disdained success but because she wanted to be in hiding. With those attitudes, how certain could she be of her position at the paper?

Although Ross and Diane had come to the new location with roughly equal rank, shortly after the move, Ross received a raise. True, it was only a paper raise—a change in titles on the masthead without any more money—but it was sufficient to show Diane the direction of the future.

In Diane's world, it had been the men who had gone off to war, not the women, and as one left behind, she did not know how to fight, only to retreat, which made her appear remote and even a bit forbidding. Ross, who seemed so unlike a warrior, nevertheless stayed out front, looking always as if he were about to crouch but always remaining visible as the first serious sibling skirmish was erupting.

On the surface, Diane remained calm, never making an issue of anything while secretly harboring feelings of hatred for Ross and feelings of hurt as she began to realize that her choice of a room had made a great psychological difference, yes, even at the *Voice,* where office politics were becoming knottier than those at J. Walter Thompson just because all communication was through symbol and metaphor instead of through words. Again Diane began to retreat.

At about this time there happened along a young man named Lucien Truscott IV. Attractive in a brash sort of way, Lucien became a link to Diane's past, a partial return to the home-

land she had left as the *Voice* and the Village became a dream
turned sour. There could be no one more suitable to tap Diane's
roots than a young West Point cadet who was turning against the
establishment under the direction of Dan Wolf. For Diane, who
had left the home of a father who had once gone off to war, leaving her and her mother, Lucien easily came to be her father and
herself in one.

And besides, Lucien had a little boat he was living on that
he docked on the New Jersey side of the Hudson because the city
was so foul. An ultimate display of street smarts for one inclined to
appreciate them. In fact, when he used to come down to the Village
and show off by speeding around in crazy circles in front of the
harbor traffic and the Villagers loaded onto the Morton Street Pier
for the purpose of sunning themselves, it was hard not to be impressed. Even Mary Nichols managed to maneuver her way off the
rotting planks for the purpose of teaming up with Lucien and
taking a spin in the Hudson River. Lucien was probably one of the
few urban sailors who could spot a corpse floating in the river
while bucking the strong currents and then write about it for *The
Village Voice*. But for Diane, Lucien was the onetime future general turned hip writer for a Greenwich Village newspaper who
could still retain a touch of arrogance more in keeping with a com-
mando operation than a kooky river excursion.

Diane had never felt at ease with those she thought of as
New York intellectuals.

"I never made any issue of anything. I really felt I was alone.
I had never talked to anyone about anything. I was kind of scared
of them and I gave off an aura of 'don't bother me, I'm too busy'
because I was scared of them. It wasn't until long after I was at
University Place that I began to talk to people and I found that
Jack Newfield wasn't that way just with me."

But nobody knew Diane was scared because she looked cool
to the point of contemptuousness. Her choice of Lucien as a lover
reinforced the impression that she had little use for the intensity,
the talkativeness, the emotionality that were at the heart of her
silent terror. Only Ross might have known the truth. But he was
too busy to notice. By now he was virtually running the paper,
along with Mary Nichols.

Each Thursday, Mary would barge into Ross's office, by-
passing Diane. In her hand would be a list of articles she was ex-

pecting to come in, a list based on the articles she had assigned. Ross had the unsolicited pieces before him as well as the ones he had assigned, and between the two, a rough skeleton of the next issue could be constructed. The entire business took a few minutes, and that was the Thursday "conference," a word used mockingly by Ross, who was quick to recognize the pomposity of such a description. Only later would he strip the word of quotation marks and see to it that a conference became just that, complete with agenda, attaché cases, a closed door, secretaries, and discussions of expense accounts, famous people to be interviewed, cover themes, and a host of concerns that were not part of the emotional vocabulary of Dan, Diane, and Mary. For the time being, Ross could go along with the vocabulary of the makeshift because he saw things were shifting in the direction he was pining for. With Dan's unofficial abdication of editorial duties and Diane's further withdrawal, Ross felt a growing confidence. Even his therapist (who happened to treat his wife and Diane, all three participating in the same group) was setting precedents of change by separating from his own wife. The future seemed to be opening wider for Ross at the same time it was closing in on Diane.

Ross felt comfortable with the new owners of the *Voice;* he felt that Bartle's way of thinking was closer to his own than was Dan's. Diane could not talk with Bartle at all. She did not see the need for change. As far as she was concerned, a paper had managed to get out every week for the nearly twelve years she had worked on it, and in the beginning there were only two to do it— Dan and Jerry, then Dan and Michael—and then the duo stretched into a triangle with Dan, Diane, and Ross, and as Dan eased himself out of the picture, Ross and Mary became the duo again, as if Ross were fated to always have a woman with whom to compete.

Then came the change that made it possible for Ross to shed the self that had put up with irksome conditions—the *Voice* was sold to *New York* magazine in 1974. For the first time Ross was in a position of power. But before he could realize his dream, he had to destroy the reputation within the *Voice* as the man who had betrayed the workers to side with Dan and the Ross who had betrayed Dan to side with Clay Felker in exchange for fame, money, women—the American dream-nightmare that Annie had been trying to escape all her life and thought that only at the *Voice* would it be possible. Annie had to go. Annie, who had known Ross when . . .

Annie, who had always despised him, had never seemed to need him, who in no way identified with him, who never confided in him, who sneered at his vacillating obsequiousness, and Annie, who hated him for holding up the mirror in which they could see themselves through each other and be forced to face the secret deformity of insecurity.

Diane had seen some of the changes coming; she had seen how the size of the paper and the place had changed the soul of the *Voice;* she had seen how the ratio of advertising to editorial content was beginning to change the feel of the paper; how it had doubled in ads since Bartle and Carter took over. And although they had scrupulously kept their promise not to interfere with editorial policy, Diane felt that by increasing advertising drastically, they had done more to destroy the character of the paper than if they had run editorials in support of their favorite candidates, or even themselves.

But she was not prepared for the final blow. Nor was Ross prepared to do it all on his own. Direct action had never been his path. Ross first convinced Mary and Jack to go to lunch with him so that he could use them each to support his case. Dan immediately told Diane about the lunch, whereupon she became enraged and immediately confronted Mary and Jack for going behind her back. Each apologized. For a moment it backfired on Ross, who had to explain things to Mary and Jack.

Then Diane disappeared into the hospital for a minor procedure. When nobody at the *Voice* could track her down, her boyfriend, who also worked on layout at the *Voice,* was called in Connecticut, where he lived to be near his sailboat. He waited for Diane to get out of the hospital before he broke the news to her.

Diane then summoned her pride and went to the *Voice* early Monday morning knowing it would be torture for Ross to announce he was firing her, although by now he had told everyone else. There was a perverse delight in waiting to watch Ross squirm. It was just like that coward, Diane thought, not even to have the guts to go out and get rid of someone on his own.

It was September of 1974, one month short of Diane's twelve-year anniversary at the *Voice.* How appropriate, she thought, it would be if Ross could hold off until Halloween. A trick instead of a treat.

But Ross was too impatient, although he would have appreciated the playfulness of the phrase. But he could not wait; it had been building up too long, and now he was in a position to get rid of the woman who had hired him, the woman who had remained faithful to the father figure he had just helped get rid of, the woman who had always rejected him in favor of men who made Ross uncomfortable—the macho, the swaggerers, even though he was now elevating them into major positions on the paper. Oh, it was all so confusing; life was so filled with irony!

Now, though, was the time for blood. Ross would act with the guts Diane thought he lacked. He would show her for once and for all that he was not such a coward; he had balls; he would just go right to her and do it. But even if he had balls, he still had a heart, and so he began by saying, "There's no painless or tactful way to do this."

"Cut the crap," Diane interrupted. "What's the severance pay?" It was as if the ability to at last tell off Ross had opened up some instinct for job survival in herself, enabling her for the first time she was at the *Voice* to ask a question about working conditions.

For twelve years nothing had even been spelled out, or even spoken about. She had never signed a single contract, never known exactly what would happen if she should lose her job. For the *Voice* was her life, what she had always wanted to do, a childhood dream come true, and she had accepted it for better or worse, till death do us part, asking no questions as she accepted the vows that she had managed to avoid in her personal life.

"Ely [the *Voice* accountant], Bartle, and I decided your severance pay covers any vacation," Ross reported. Diane was beside herself. Thirteen weeks of severance pay (she was being paid until the end of the year) for twelve years of work and no vacation. She was speechless. It was only later that she reflected, "It put me so beside myself I was paralyzed. I couldn't do a thing about it. If I could think of anything to say to them I would have, but I don't have the words to express how I feel because I want to kill them."

Fred W. McDarrah

"I love running to first base and forget about second or third or getting home. I'm in love with first base. The rest doesn't seem as important."

Barbara Long

Long she was not, but rather short and chunky. Her face was a bit puffy, but when she smiled her deep dimples and dark eyes filled her round cheeks with a gypsylike beauty of fire and strength, all of which came from the waist up. For Barbara, in contrast to other *Voice* writers who felt crippled metaphorically, was the only one who was crippled, whose legs could not support her weight without a cane, having been damaged by the polio she contracted as a young girl.

Born into a family of poor white Russian peasant stock, Barbara knew she would have to exile herself one day if she were ever to develop. After college, in 1960, she made the move across the river from Jersey into the big city, alone and crippled and with the thought, less shaky than her legs, that she was going to be a writer.

She started work in a small printing firm, where she earned $80 a week—enough money to enable her to rent a cheap tenement apartment in the East Village (where she still lives). Then along came the 1963 newspaper strike. It was as lucky a break for Barbara as for Diane.

The *Voice,* in the absence of other papers, decided to print a special book review supplement which inspired Barbara to send in a ten-page critique of an author she admired—Calder Willingham. A few months later, after the strike had ended, *Newsweek* listed one of Willingham's novels, *Eternal Fire,* among the ten best of the year, and Ed Fancher, who had read Barbara's piece, found her judgment all the sounder after it was echoed in *News-week* and gave her a call in the middle of the night to announce that her piece would appear in the *Voice,* convinced that if Barbara had been ahead of one of the country's largest national news-weeklies, the *Voice* would do well to ferret out this unknown critic. Barbara was invited to drop by.

With an appropriately eerie intuitive sense, Dan suggested that Barbara write a review of *The One Hundred Dollar Misunder-standing.* When the *Voice* ran a clever put-down of the book, Robert Goover wrote a letter requesting that Barbara never be given an-other book of his to review. She, in turn, high on her first encounter with instant feedback, responded that she thought it was obvious that he had nothing to fear—in order for her to write another re-view of one of his books she would first have to read it.

Barbara had been reviewing intermittently for the *Voice* for three years when Dan looked at her one day and said, "You know you're not getting any younger. You're twenty-eight years old. It's about time you started writing. Whenever you come in you talk about the fights. My readers don't care about them. I don't care about them, but it's all you ever get excited about. Why don't you cover the next fight and write it up for the paper?"

Again Dan's brilliance was at work, recognizing a subject that would arouse the writer in Barbara and at the same time stir up reader response. That the first woman to cover boxing did so in the pages of the *Voice* was no insignificant feat for a relatively new paper bent on attracting attention. Dan liked Barbara's way of dealing with her deformity; perhaps it reminded him of some-thing within himself that enabled him to believe, I may not look impressive to you, world, but I'm going to surprise you. Just you wait and see. I'm going to produce something you never even thought someone like me could do.

By offering Barbara the kind of encouragement essential to her development as a sportswriter, Dan had called the shots as perfectly as Cassius Clay had thrown the punches. Barbara was the only reporter present who saw the knockout punch in the second fight between Sonny Liston and Cassius Clay (as he was then called). That was important at a time when there was controversy over whether the fights were fixed. Dan got the story he wanted and delivered it to the world with a banner headline, "The Lady Saw the Punch."

"It was as natural to me," Barbara remarked, "as embroidery is to other people. I love it—the male atmosphere. I grew up in a house full of uncles who protected me from the women. I thrive on male atmosphere. I also see nothing unnatural in fighting." Barbara, like Dan, knew that to infiltrate the world of glamour without an easy entry, one had to do something spectacular, and that required an enormous output of energy, which was a form of fighting itself. Perhaps that's why it was natural for the man who was capable of stabbing his own wife—Mailer, one of the original voices of the *Voice*—to respond immediately to Barbara. "No other woman has invaded the male psyche and felt so comfortable there," he told her.

It all happened quickly, afterward. Dan contacted her to report that the "big call" had just come in. Barbara thought it was the White House inviting her to join a gathering of well-known American artists. She would go even though Arthur Miller had just refused an invitation based on the politics of that domain. It isn't the White House, Dan said, it's even better than that. It's a call from *Sports Illustrated*. The Editor always wanted a woman sportswriter, a natural, not one who had just been taken off the lipstick beat.

Barbara was wined and dined at the private bar with all the editors of *Sports Illustrated*. "That is, senior editors, male of course, in a terrific opening to a career." Maybe it was too terrific; no story ever made it to press. But Barbara did have a chance to preview male attention and found it rewarding. Although Dan had encouraged her writing with great generosity, he was paying her $20 an article some three years after she had begun writing for him. Barbara managed to get by financially with the aid of an illiterate polo player who liked the idea of giving her money. Designating him a "patron," Barbara must have felt more authentic as an artist whenever she wondered why, if she's as good as Dan says she is, does he pay her so little. However, "there was great exposure and getting invited to lunch by everyone."

Salutes to her talent came quickly and furiously. A call from Mailer followed a story she wrote on a white comedian at the Apollo theatre in Harlem. Go back to the Apollo but leave out the white comedian, then give it to *The New Yorker*, he told her. Barbara, following Mailer's advice, sold her first article to its editor, William Shawn. But somehow the follow-through on such a dazzling start never took place; as with the *Sports Illustrated* assignment, *The New Yorker* one never made it into print, although she was paid handsomely for it. Then came a call from Byron Dobell at *Esquire,* asking her to write a profile for the magazine. At last she succeeded in going all the way. Within six months of her debut as a sportswriter on the *Voice,* Barbara had a profile of Truman Capote in *Esquire* (June, 1966).

It was all happening so fast, there was no time to ask what it was doing to her. It was only years later that Dan told Barbara of his misgivings that she had jumped to the major leagues so quickly. He felt she should have written more for the *Voice.* Barbara thinks he was right, in retrospect. At the time she took her chances, chance being so chancy itself. Afterward, you make your mistakes look like existential errands instead of errors.

When the call came from *Time* asking Barbara for biographical information for a piece being prepared on her as the first woman sportswriter, she declined the honor. "I had a feeling that it would be very destructive and I refused because it would have been a gimmick. Everybody was being Something-of-the Year —Baby Jane Holtzer, Gloria Steinem—and I didn't want to get into that."

Barbara already was that. What, it seemed, she could not risk was an unfavorable comparison with other women. Barbara instinctively knew when there was no fight, when the competition was too great. Writing about men and being compared to men posed no threat. In fact, it was a way to insure something she might otherwise have missed. Never had she forgotten the baseball player from her hometown whom she had had a crush on and who rejected her. Ultimately he got engaged to the "dull girl next door" and Barbara got hurt, giving up forever on baseball and baseball players. "After all, if you can't trust a baseball player, you've got to give up on the game."

Dan understood that Barbara's bombastic self-advertising was superficial, that underneath a writer was struggling to break out. And for all the hyperbole, Dan saw that Barbara was a restrained person. Like himself, she was not self-revelatory; she told only what she chose to tell, and it was rarely confessional. He respected her need to think of herself as a professional sportswriter instead of someone compensating psychologically for a physical condition not of her choosing. He knew, too, that no matter how pedestrian was the clinical view, Barbara would be the first to appreciate the irony of a cripple becoming an expert in boxing and bullfighting.

What neither seemed to notice was the total dependency on Dan Barbara was developing. Every time Barbara had a manuscript, she would taxi over to the *Voice* at Sheridan Square and spend time alone with Dan discussing it. He knew how to play with her combination of strength and weakness, juggling with the grace of a magician so she always felt strong momentarily.

"Of course, it was a love thing, a family thing. I'm not a joiner. I'm not a feminist. I wouldn't belong to an organization, a union, a club. I don't go to panels, symposia, so O.K., Dan was an important father figure. I just thought how clever of me as a young writer to hit upon a great editor as a Daddy. How farsighted of me. I knew Dan genuinely cared because he cared about writing, which meant he cared about me because that's what I was. He cared also about the direction I could take. He realized the freaky quality of my subject. I could have become a celebrity. He knew how dangerous that was."

It was strange to hear how Barbara, for all her perceptiveness, did not seem to understand the ways Dan encouraged the big-time recognition both he and she sought while making her so dependent on him it became impossible for her to have the confidence to gain it.

"Dan always knew I had a hunger for reality. I could talk about wild fantasies, about celebrities, ambition, power but he knew it was meringue. When I was finished spinning out the fantastic for him, I had expelled it and I could settle down and get back to writing."

Dan the exorcist. Dan enabling others to exorcise themselves. He was never direct, never active; at best, he was a catalyst, suggesting something, offering something, directing by orchestrating the neuroses of others, as he himself was supposed to have said.

"One thing Dan knew about all of us. We were all hungry, ambitious, competitive young writers. There's nothing trickier than to be an editor and friend and mentor and to handle a group of some of the most hot-to-get-going talented young writers in New York. All in one tiny office. He had to deal with all of us. That's a lot of ego. We all wanted his attention and love and got it, but not all of us realized that Dan's first love in all these sibling rivalries was the *Voice* and *that* was the baby, not the writers. We were just the arms and legs of the baby. Whatever love and attention he gave us was in the interest of the baby. It was like a classroom with thirty kids raising their hands. Me, me, me. We were terribly hungry. We wrote for Dan. I still write for Dan. No matter what the publication, I'll probably always write for Dan."

After the first explosion of opportunities, the responses and the calls and the letters dwindled. The gimmick was over; one is tempted to say the "game" was played out. And there was anger because underneath the gimmick, the game, and the much sought after glory was a real writer. With a transparency that she would spot instantly in anyone else, Barbara rationalized.

"The writers earning $50,000 could never write for the *Voice;* they are too professional, too slick." But no sooner would she sneer at slickness and the rewards it brings than would she start to salivate. "As soon as the big money was waved at me, I went for it." It wasn't for the money itself, she claimed, but the recognition the money represented, the one form of attention she could never get from Dan. Whenever something celebratory like a check came through, Barbara's first response was to phone Dan. "I had a terrible need to be loved. I needed people to give me gifts, some concrete show of love—money."

One hot summer night when Barbara was lying in bed in her tenement, burglars broke in. Barbara was petrified; she didn't have her crutches nearby. After managing to escape physically unharmed, she rushed to call Dan. He asked no questions, but offered to go to the bank as soon as possible. It was worth more than a six-figure salary to her—the immediate response, the personal touch.

"There aren't that many people in my life who will give me money when I show up battered and bruised, and Dan is one. He just said, 'I'm sorry they did that to you.' He understood."

It was as if some psychic synapse were missing. Barbara seemed incapable of connecting up the facts that if she were paid more than a pittance she would not have to live in so vulnerable a place. Or more important, she might not feel so dependent upon a father figure, confusing love and money in such a way as to forget she had some real need for protection. It was impossible for her to believe she could protect herself. When you were down and out and your ego was in tune with Bessie Smith, Dan came through, showing you it isn't so that no one wants you.

It was at these moments Dan came to resemble the parent of a schizophrenic child who withholds love all the time and just as the child is about to figure out the parent has no use for him he comes through lovingly, throwing all normal perceptions askew and forcing the child to accept a world of contradiction. And so it was with Barbara, who could say in one breath: "Money is about the least important thing. Yet I needed people to give me one-hundred-dollar bills—the beauty of those zeroes in crisp new bills. And then I felt a little bit of safety, for when the burglars broke in it was like a squirrel having his winter supply taken away."

Barbara, caring so little for money, actually disdaining it, rose above her lower-class origins by adopting the aristocrat's indifference but was never able to transcend the insecurities that come from having been poor and having always to hustle; yes, to be a squirrel and hoard—hardly an aristocratic image. Yet Barbara the writer was always present; even when describing pain and humiliation, she could focus on the particular—the zeroes on crisp $100 bills, the zeroes fading into flames as they had done when a famous bullfighter used $100 bills as paper for rolling joints in front of lots of guests. And when the party was over, Barbara the writer could mold the concerns of status into images which she would share with Dan and both would be cleansed of the gore and glory of others and the need to live their lives vicariously.

If Dan took money out of his pocket only in times of crisis, it was Ed who occasionally came through with a spontaneous act of largesse. After Barbara had been burglarized, he offered her the use of his penthouse apartment on Fifth Avenue for a couple of weeks when he left the city. "It was like a summer vacation, moving into Ed's lush apartment for a couple of weeks. To me, it was the same as a vacation."

Something was happening to Barbara's work: it was getting harder to produce, and when she did manage to get something onto paper it wasn't very good. One afternoon she went to Dan with a piece she had finished. "I'll publish it if you want, but in terms of your overall work, it's slight." It was a good adjective to use—"slight"—conjuring up images of lightweight champions. Once again Dan's genius was at work, enabling a writer to believe that she was so good that something "slight" would disappoint her large and loyal readership, which he was willing to do, making her feel the decision to reject the work was hers, not his.

It was a very supportive and severely undermining tactic. What Barbara needed most was to see her name in print even if it meant giving up the notion that she was to be compared with Tolstoy. Barbara tried again, this time with a piece on Frank Gifford, who evidently was not as suitable a subject as Levin for a complex character portrayal. "I'll publish it," Dan said, "but you haven't written in a long time. And while this is a pleasant piece, your readers want something special from you." Consequently, again there was no piece and Barbara was forced to create rationalizations instead of copy.

"The size of the audience wasn't important to me. It was *who* the audience was." For a while a letter from Alger Hiss saying Barbara was the best writer he had read since his friend A. J. Liebling wrote soothed the wounds of the ego. "You know, at the *Voice,* the better you are, the smaller the response," Barbara would say, which was important for her to believe as her sole audience became Dan, and then only an aural audience, as one might have with the Pope. "Many *Voice* readers feel more comfortable with writers who are no better than they; the readers like bumbling people. They're not turned on by a well-done piece."

There was some truth to that observation, no matter how psychologically convenient it was for Barbara to believe it. If the *Voice* ran something silly or sensational or outrageous, there was sure to be an outpouring of letters. However, what Barbara could not acknowledge was that the outpouring was not limited to crap; the well-turned-out piece also received responses. Often dozens, and occasionally hundreds.

As fewer and fewer people recognized Barbara's name, she began to yearn for a larger readership. Where were the early days, when editors from all over town were calling and Mailer was urging her on? Now there was only Dan. "On my deathbed, I'm going to think of some end of an article that never got read because it got caught in a sandal ad," she would joke, adding immediately that it was preferable to having a piece caught between two Givenchy gowns as happened in *Vogue.* For the world of Givenchy gowns belonged to women, and from her early days Barbara had wanted to enter the man's world, the world of power—it was one way of finding love, and if not love, its substitutes, status and glory, which, after all, were not lacking in glamour either.

For someone who had to make it on her own from the moment she crossed the Hudson into New York, the world of power held a greater allure than love, partially because it seemed more accessible. It was only one step away, one more spin on the merry-go-round before you could grab the brass ring; the important thing was you could see it and know where to reach for it every time you went around. Dan kept alive such fantasies. But he did not offer her a staff job, pretending she was too good for that, too much of a stylist to be a mere reporter, or so Barbara chose to interpret his withholding of a staff position.

However, Barbara could not bring herself to criticize Dan, who had helped her when she was nobody and when she was bruised and had narrowly escape being beaten. So it was the *Voice* that she started to question. "I was angry that the *Voice* never pushed, never advertised my bullfighting series. There were millions out there in the country who would have bought the paper had they known it was in there." And again the sad refrain of one who has been hurt turning the bitterness into grandiosity—"millions out there" who would have run to their nearest newsstands if only they had advance notice that Barbara Long was back in print, a stunning comeback, as they say of the sports figures and of the singers who spend years as alcoholics before they return to the world of the floodlights and an ecstatic audience cheering the courage of self-willed recovery rather than the performance.

"It was either Dan or Ross who said, 'We've always acted very cool about having the only woman in the world writing about boxing and bullfighting.' " Now Barbara could add, "That's nice," for she was among the first to appreciate "cool"—it was classy, but the style didn't work toward enlarging readership.

"I had reached a point where I wanted publicity. I was no longer in danger of becoming an overnight success. By the *Voice* being so cool, I missed out on potential readers. Oh, Feiffer listed my name in his ad for the paper even when I hadn't written a single piece for two years. But still I think that somewhere I lost out . . . somewhere between the wisdom of my saying no to *Time* and the *Voice*'s coolness. Somewhere. Much of it was my fault. I wish we would have hit on something. But I didn't take the initiative. The one area I'm not aggressive in is taking care of myself in personal finances."

Quite innocently, almost by chance, it happened—Barbara spoke of taking care of herself and making money, not needing a patron, a pimp, an outlaw, a father figure, or whatever, to fall back

upon. But as soon as the connection between decent pay and independence was hit upon, Barbara the writer was at work, weaving
metaphors to explain it away, not listening to her own words, which
contained a lot of truth, not paying attention to the literal, to the
"taking care of myself."

"I love running to first base and forget about second or third
or getting home. I'm in love with first base. The rest doesn't seem
as important." If ever there was an eloquent summary of women's
fear of success, that was it. Was it because getting to first base was
so hard or, as it seemed in Barbara's case, because it had been so
easy? It didn't seem real; it left a lingering sense of fraudulence. And
although the men who were there said it was real, their behavior
contradicted that message: they didn't give out the rewards handed
to others who get to first base; it was as if they didn't really expect
her to get all the way home. And so she accepted other things from
them, all along blaming herself for the ways in which the men were
being unfair.

"I'm such a bad business person I never criticize others or
judge anyone else in business matters." Though Barbara felt the
Voice shortchanged her by not publicizing her work more, she could
not bring herself to question any way in which Dan had played
into her own sense of helplessness, the one which she had brought
with her when first she came to the *Voice*. That would entail the
tampering with the anchor, the one person who believed in her, the
one father she had found. While sons might be able to overthrow
the father, daughters have a harder time even on a symbolic level.
Perhaps they should play chess.

By "orchestrating the neuroses" of his writers, by "editing
people, not copy," by being the head of "one big unhappy family,"
Dan won the everlasting loyalty of countless writers. They came to
believe it was Dan who gave them their talent. Even the most
perceptive could speak as if Dan had a hand in their genetic makeup,
according him omnipotence because he understood the side that
had always made them feel like freaks, outsiders, aliens. Only Dan
could nurture the secret self, making it grow to bizarre dimensions
until the writer finally prayed to get out of his own head, turn off,
walk into a pond, get stoned, whatever.

He would tell each writer about the others he *never* read, the
others who were not good enough for him to worry about. It made

you feel so goddamned chosen that there was no way you could ever blame him for anything, especially if you lacked a core of confidence to begin with, as did most of the people who were attracted to Dan— the ambivalent people who were strong and not strong at the same time, the emotionally androgynous people for whom Dan would become whatever they needed him to be.

"To interest Dan, you had to have something special going. A writer had to be original and exciting. And for the few of us like that, he pampered us. Dan is not an exciting man. He enjoys exciting people. He likes originals. If Dan and Ed called, starting a new publication, I would go back to writing for them. They made me feel respected for my work. I would still write for very little money if it was for Ed and Dan."

Barbara never questioned money with Dan and Ed—how pitifully little they paid her. As usual, she had interesting and convoluted things to say about the subject. "Advances are not good for me. I get money mixed up with love. I can't understand it—if a person loves me enough to give me money, why does he want me to produce as well?"

With rationalization as immediate a response as a tic, Barbara had no trouble convincing herself that the only way she could produce was to have Dan and Ed withhold the real proof of love—money.

One suspects that Dan shared some of her feelings about money—that it was a substitute for all the early childhood deprivations each had experienced. If the historical sense of deprivation is profound enough, all the money and love can never fill in the cracks of a broken ego. Even when Dan was no longer poor, he acted as if he still felt poor. But Barbara not only felt poor, she was poor—and while all around her others, with less talent, were getting rich and famous.

With the dawning of the seventies, old Aquarius himself was no longer around to guide Barbara, although Mailer had suggested she do a follow-up to a story. It was for *women Sports,* which meant being ghettoized in the one place she had always regarded as a slum —the world of women. All her attention had been directed toward men, all her work had been written for men. So involved had she been in the man's world that she had overlooked the struggles of women to end the division of the world based on gender. Having been kept, in one way or another, by a man—be it her patron polo player or Dan's sporadic largesse—Barbara was convinced that the only means of support in the world came from men.

When Barbara had first embarked on her career odyssey, leaving a household of women who did nothing but hound those around them, she had no sense of women who could use their strength in the outside world, women who could take on a cold alien atmosphere. All the warriors of the world, all the strong people who fought (as she knew she would have to do) were those of a different sex. Who were the fighters in the pioneer days; who took on the Indians and had rendezvous with death at high noon? Not women, according to the books she had read and the movies she had seen and the home she had grown up in.

Those of her own sex were either wives or aunts, nurturing and anonymous, or the brothel owners, who handed out a different kind of nourishment. For all her writerly appreciation of the icons of America, Barbara did not realize that she had allowed her life to be dominated by them; she had become, or had at least been striving to become, the partner to the outlaw—the brothel owner, the barmaid, the woman living in the man's world for the man.

The decade of the seventies was no kinder to Barbara than it was to Dan. Using her frame of reference, one could say that time delivered a punch below the belt; as she was coming into her own, riding the crest of the sixties, feeling for all the world like Clint Eastwood coming into town, the alien-outlaw-outsider (be it black, boxer, bullfighter, bandit) she was toppled right off her horse by the seventies and replaced by a rider who had gentleness, softness—all the qualities women were seeking to elevate along with themselves; elevating, promoting, and cashing in with more vengeance and fight than Barbara had ever seen in a boxers' ring.

Even the men were beginning to write books about the evil male machine. Machismo was theoretically out; there was no market for it. To be the sole woman writing about it in the early seventies meant to be alone, without the support of even men. For it was men who still controlled the commerce of movements and were able to package them as they came and went.

Dan had foreseen that. But Barbara couldn't get angry at him for leaving her stranded; no, her anger, like that of the women she had always known, turned on other women. "The women's movement cannot deal with a woman who did things for herself only. Pioneers have a different mentality from the women in the movement." And then converting the anger, with characteristic pride—the anger and hurt at being left out—into the solace of the loner, she said, "I don't need them," the way Dan had done when the *Voice* writers—his children—ganged up on him for the first time and the way he reacted when Carter and Bartle "took away" the paper he had sold to them.

"No, movements may need loners—the Didions, the Sontags, etc.—but we don't need movements," Barbara continued, elevating herself into rather celebrated company. True—its stated members had been loners and pioneers, but they were successful. And more painfully true—they had better credentials with which to impress society. They did not have to wage class war as well as women's war. Nor did they do their pioneering alone. Both had been or were married, and one had a husband, the other a permanent lover. No matter the sex, the partner provided them with big houses and creature comforts, so if anyone came marching in during the middle of the night, they were not alone. They did not have to contact the one man they knew who would respond to vulnerability. And that made them less vulnerable.

Neither Didion nor Sontag, according to their writing, is a joiner; like Barbara, they share a distaste for sloppy language, a suspicion of movement rhetoric. But Barbara did not have their crutches, only her own, and that, alas, was no metaphor.

"My readership is male. I was accepted immediately by Mailer, Plimpton, Hamill, Larry Merchant and others on the basis of my seriousness and knowledge. Still nine or ten years later I encounter women who will say to me, 'You're a very good writer but I never read you because of what you write about.' And I say, 'too bad, that's your loss.' Gosh, blood is real. It's as if all the work I had done forcing readers to accept my knowledgeability about esoteric subjects suddenly gets wiped out by their fucking revolution. How could a movement dedicated to mediocrity, as all movements are, respond to quality. It was men who went to see Hepburn, not women, and men who like Didion and Sontag, not women. The movement women are very good at becoming celebrities but they are not talented. They have nothing to do with the written page or culture. And yet they're going to become a problem for me. The *Times* will assign a woman to review my book but she'll say 'this is not a work about liberation, it's not ideological' and I'm going to get a bad review."

It was painful to hear someone who really cared about writing, who could describe the joy from writing as one "so great almost no one deserves to have it," worrying about the review of a book not yet written, consumed with bitterness and anger that something had passed her by, something to which she was superior. How she tried to pretend she didn't care; that her lack of success was caused by a conspiracy of the yahoos, who had taken over the craft most indigenous to America—public relations.

Again, there was truth to what she said, but it was only partial. The women's movement, like all others, has a rhetoric, a party line, which may run counter to a concern for individual expression. Nevertheless, there was a vision, one where women could help each other provide that very network that Barbara had correctly perceived among men when she started work—how they naturally teamed up, beginning with the days when they played stickball and baseball together. Yet she felt more betrayed by the women than she had by the hometown baseball player who had broken her heart when she was young. There was no one now with whom to bond, and it was difficult to be productive feeling so alone.

"Either way, I'm going to lose. If they send a woman to review my book, she'll say it's not ideological and if they send a man, he'll say, it's not really about bullfighting because I'm too much of a writer. I never have been merely a reporter the way male sportswriters are. But I'd rather lose to a jerk sportswriter than lose to a woman. If you're not going to send me flowers, don't trip me either. If you're going to ignore my work because it's about men, stay out of my way."

Now Barbara was taking on the women's movement, huffing and puffing with anger, and just as she seemed on the verge of wearing herself out, a mellowness, a rationality, set in that must have moved Dan whenever he saw it.

"I accept the fact that I have hard dues to pay. My writing has come out of struggle the way all hip has. It's a style that makes me pay more for everything I get. It is a great joy to have a distinctive style, to know that no one has ever put together a sentence in that way. It's a joy so great almost no one deserves to have it."

And yet . . . one felt that Barbara deserved to have it.

"There I am alone with 18,000 men when I'm reporting a sports event at the Garden. And I love it. I love it. That's a lot of attention I know I'm going to get." This from the same person who could describe sitting home Saturday night after Saturday night, her fantasies of going out to the movies and having an ice cream soda afterward revived from teen-age years and woven into the conversations she had on the loneliest night of the week with her only companion—her typewriter.

Had Barbara only let herself grow . . . But that would have meant to learn to trust women, and she had scanty opportunity for that; living alone writing about sports and then going over once a month or so to see Dan, arriving in a taxi, all part of a charade to conceal her poverty, never wanting to acknowledge that she had little money. Dan was touched by the way she strove to be above her condition. She did not beg or grovel. ("Ask" or "negotiate" were words missing from the vocabulary of either for indeed they were incongruous with an afternoon tête-à-tête between a great editor and a rising talent.) When Barbara emerged from the taxi in a fake fur coat, her cheeks rouged and her nose powdered, for a moment it was a grand dame arriving, not an aspiring writer. Even when she was down and out and came to Dan, she did not see that as anything but an act of human elegance.

"I wanted it that way. I wanted him to be the person who would hand me money without asking questions. He played it out the way I wanted him to, needed him to. And that's not paternalism to me."

There was the by now all too recognizable combination of uncanny perceptiveness (the acknowledgment of will, the element of choice that made a person feel free, the existential errand) and blindness (the inabilty to see how fleeting the element of choice was, how only the more pedestrian worries of getting contracts and advances and staff positions—the getting from first base back to home again—would ever make her comfortable, would ever free her to write her great book rather than worry about spiteful, conniving women turned furies).

"With the movement, we're back to zero, as if no advances had been made by the pioneers." And by now the refrain was so stale it required no translation. Suddenly, however, there was a new rationalization somewhat Maileresque.

"If men go up against a strong-willed personality, they walk away. It's like slipping a punch. But women can't. They feel they have to respond. Some of it is sexual. Energy comes across that way. Some women writers may be uncomfortable with that vitality. I don't know. They don't tell me the truth. I think they're too embarrassed."

Only a woman who had resisted the seventies could conclude, after the endless discussions, rap sessions, consciousness-raising groups devoted to talk about sexuality, orgasms, that women were "too embarrassed" to confront Barbara's sexuality. It was all topsy-turvy; it was Dan who had seemed repressed about confronting sexuality and who had enjoyed the excitement of others and in so doing had made it impossible for Barbara to come to honest terms with herself. As she herself put it, "I've always been my best material, but I haven't always used it. I was afraid to admit I was interesting."

Robin Reisig, between Karen Durbin (left) and Judy Coburn

"I just wanted something that would really last, almost something connected up with my teen-age feelings about religion. I didn't care about huge sales or money. Just some sense of wanting to endure. That seemed a goal. Now my goal is immediate happiness, not success. Compared to a scale of Shakespeare and Ibsen, any journalism success is small."

Robin Reisig

For a wisp of a creature who wished to pretend it was always spring, who seemed never to notice the bluebirds and blackbirds—to say nothing of the Bartle Bulls—ready to undo her nest, she had the right name: Robin. Robin Reisig. Small, soft, with long reddish hair, hers could be a Renoir face were it not for the worried look that didn't sit right in a setting of sun and picnics and outings on the river Seine. No, Robin was a bird for prey. But instead of worrying whether those bigger than she would threaten her survival, she worried whether they would like her, respect her, think her strong-willed, as if fighting for survival were some sort of "going all the way."

Robin came from a clean, comfortable suburb of Detroit, went to private schools in Bloomfield Hills and then on to Wellesley, where she was taught that the world belonged to those who are good and true, a state of character located somewhere between nobility and martyrdom: that is, one where the arrogance of *the* nobility is bleached out, leaving untainted the saintly self-sacrificing aspects of the noble *person*—she who does not think of her own needs first, she who lives with an integrity, a wholeness. In other words, the Wellesley girl with boy scout ideals.

As a Midwestern Jew, Robin may have felt something of the outsider at a New England Ivy League college, but she seemed determined to believe that one could transcend such parochial barriers. While a student at Wellesley, she'd had summer jobs at newspapers, working for the Detroit *Free Press* one year and a suburban Boston paper another, the *Patriot Ledger*. And, of course, good patriot that she was, she worked for her own school paper.

After graduation, Robin, right in line with the tradition of Wellesley girls, wanted to experience something different from what she had known at home or school and choose to go down South and work on the *Southern Courier,* where she was able to cover murders and other local events. (There are many variations on the noblesse oblige tradition fostered in Ivy League schools, and one is to be of service to those in society less privileged than oneself. That is, if the locale is exotic and time put in is temporary.)

When Robin was able to get quotes from Southern sheriffs that eluded more seasoned male reporters, she thought it was her dedication that got her the hard to come by facts; never did she think that a Southern sheriff might not take her as seriously as a tough-talking, tough-smoking male like himself. While on the *Courier,* "I didn't cover the things women usually cover." It was a junior year abroad of sorts, and Robin liked it because it was permitted. Furthermore, it was respectable, even admirable, to do something that was *not* expected as long as it was for a limited period during which one could grow and widen the horizons that rose straight out of the Seven Sisters college catalogues.

After her fling in the South, Robin returned to the life of a student at Columbia Journalism School. Emerging confidently at graduation, she was firm about two things: no job at a straight newspaper and only journalism that gave her a chance to do real writing as well. "I felt I could do anything." And why not? She had the right schooling and, as it turns out, the right connections (the one the result of the other). Her friend and entry to *The Village Voice*—Mary Breasted—had also gone to Columbia Journalism School, worked for the Peace Corps (called Vista on domestic territory), which gave her a chance actually to live in Harlem after graduating from Radcliffe. Mary, who was already writing for the *Voice,* had become a pal of Mary Nichols'; she suggested Robin as a writer to the older Mary, and Robin, equipped with the right introduction, called the *Voice.*

Nichols suggested several stories that she might consider, and in August, 1969, Robin made her debut into New York journalism with a lengthy piece on the telephone company. It was a good story, the kind that only arduous hours at the typewriter can produce. Robin received $75 for it. "I was so grateful just to be published, I didn't care about the money."

Robin's next story was lighter—a piece about women liberating the bars which keep them out. Mary Nichols, in particular, enjoyed it, having devoted much energy to becoming one of the boys and invading their turf once she had finally disposed of her husband. Robin seemed at home writing about the very things she did not do in real life—for Robin was no more inclined to drink in a male atmosphere (or any for that matter) and whistle at men in the streets than she was to commit murder in the South.

Within a year, Robin was up to $100 an article, which might not have imposed much of a financial strain (she had a cheap apartment and good health) if she would write more frequently. But the kinds of articles she took on required research. She did not feel comfortable until she had checked and rechecked every fact and every quote; it was something that her education had taught her she was morally obligated to do. The *Voice*, sensing it had a reporter who was willing to work hard, willing to be thorough and accurate (even though it was at her own expense), started to assign her long investigative pieces.

Robin knew these kinds of stories took more time, but she liked the idea that she was doing the tough ones, the challenges, the stories that not everyone could do. It didn't seem to occur to her that many were stories that free-lance writers *wouldn't* do even if they could. Few people who did not have the weekly paycheck that comes with a staff position thought it noble to cover something that, although deserving of coverage, had marginal reader interest. Most *Voice* free-lancers, sensing the showcase value of the paper, were not interested in spending weeks working on one story, letting time and space go by without having their names in print. Such indulgences were unwise for anyone serious about becoming a writer in New York; it was just too tough and competitive a profession for that kind of attitude. And then, too, there were practical concerns: why work on a long investigative piece when short ones, which could be produced with greater frequency, earned the same amount of money?

Robin, however, seemed to be flattered when Mary or Ross came to her and said, " 'This is a tough story. We thought you could do it.' They even apologized that they couldn't pay me as much as it was worth." It was as if the acknowledgment of the injustice excused it, and Robin, knowing that they knew it was a wee bit unfair, seemed willing to work all the harder. Accepting less glory for something that consumed more time and energy than it should fit right in with that Seven Sisters notion of nobility. No one could accuse her of being a hustler, a careerist; perhaps someone might even observe that she was just the tiniest bit purer than anyone else, although if confronted with what she took to be a compliment, she would deny it.

With time, there were small adjustments. After Robin had been writing for four or five years and the *Voice* ran a piece about cable TV—one of the first on the subject to appear in print anywhere—she was paid $250 for the three months of time it had taken to research and write it rather than the $125 she would have been paid if it had run in one installment instead of two.

By the time she was working on the Beame mayoral campaign in 1973, she was rewarded $200 for research time during the two months she was following him around, and when the piece went into print, she received $350. "Theoretically, on the Beame piece I should have gotten $100 a week, but I didn't." Again, the acknowledgment, even though it was a token one, that she was being underpaid enabled her to accept that fact in a ladylike manner—nobly rather than noisily. As it happens, there were free-lancers who were receiving a regular research fee of $100 a week all along. But just as nobody told Robin about it at the time, Robin was not willing to say who they were when she found out, somewhat in keeping with the dual traditions of secret societies and good manners, traditions encouraged at prep schools and Wellesley.

As Robin was approaching thirty, her *Voice* annual income for the year of 1973 reached no more than $4,500, supplemented by $1,200 from outside work. Something was wrong. Even though she had been singled out for all those difficult assignments that only she could do and consistently handed in excellent work, she wasn't moving. If she was so special, as such communications implied, then why wasn't she given the one recognition of worth the paper could offer—a regular paycheck?

Robin had a hard time dealing with things boldly, nakedly. "I felt that most of my experience at the *Voice* was a very positive one. I loved writing for the *Voice*. I was able to write about subjects I cared about in the way I chose, and that was what mattered to me. It may mean I didn't earn much, but I knew that and made that choice consciously."

Of course, if you're special in that special way that the Seven Sisters schools specialize in, you're above the concerns of money; after all, are they not the concerns of those who belong to the world of the hack rather than the Ivory Towers enshrined by time and

old school ties and reminiscences and rich fathers, followed by husbands and endowments and trusts? No, one well endowed was not
to worry about money; it was there and therefore not to be of concern; a well-bred woman rose above the concerns of mundane everyday life; others took care of them so she could volunteer her energies,
her gentilities, her sensibilities, and above all, her honor, to nobler
causes. And to ask for a fee for performing service, well, that was
already getting close to the world of the fallen woman—the prostitute.

Which is exactly what Robin did. But once again, only in
words as she explored the subject related to a real-life taboo. In
fact, it was her coverage of the prostitution hearings and speakouts
that earned Robin the greatest professional recognition: a mention
on one of *Esquire*'s one-hundred-most-powerful-men lists, except it
was the three-hundred-and-one-most-influential-feminist media list.

Why was the *Voice* withholding a staff job? Robin had done
all the things reporters were supposed to do: she had covered a wide
range of events, she had even written the mandatory going-home
piece about a trip back to Wellesley. And, as a product of an all
girls school, she had gravitated to the woman editor—Mary Nichols—
as her mentor.

"The only people who got to know Dan were those who went
in; I was too shy to do that. I was too shy to go in until I had been
writing for a couple of years."

But now Robin had the courage; she wanted a staff job. There
was a considerable difference in pay, and unlike a number of writers
on the *Voice*, Robin didn't have any large independent means of
income. Before the sale of the paper to *New York* magazine in 1974,
staff writers, all of whom were men at the time, were paid anything from $200 to $235 a week. (It was a big secret who got what
within that range.) Once on staff, a writer could produce at the rate
most compatible with his temperament, which meant anything from
a short article more or less every week to an occasional longer one
every month or six weeks. But no matter what the frequency—
whether you were Jack Newfield, who enjoyed writing regularly and
did so, or Joe Flaherty, who preferred to hang out in the Lion's
Head Bar and come up with less than one piece a month—the paycheck was there every week. So were the health benefits, vacation,
and sick leave periods. A free-lancer such as Robin received none
of these.

But there was something else about a staff job—something one could not measure. It was a recognition that the *Voice* thought well of you, that they wanted you around, that they respected you. You were no longer on trial every week, waiting, the way one did after one met somebody at a Harvard-Wellesley "jolly-up." It was security.

How difficult, though, to care about security and respectability, as did Robin, and yet to have a secretly rebellious, even stubborn, offbeat streak that makes one want to thumb her nose at the whole straight world in order to be free—not to get drunk and spend all afternoon in a den darkened by booze, but to be able to contemplate a host of daffodils on a hill or anything related to nature and poetry and all the other things that would assure one of a smidgeon of immortality, an ode to one's oh so secret self: the ego buried within. It was to live with an unbearable split, to feel both superior and inferior all the time, to both need and resent the outer trappings of success, to want and disdain recognition.

But Robin was beginning to need it. It was getting hard to live on $5,000 a year, and even then an uncertain $5,000, subject to well-being and rent control. One wasn't so free after all, always having to worry about being behind in the dental bills, especially if one enjoyed being punctual in paying one's debts. In fact, it was no fun to be indebted, and it didn't get your bills paid, your apartment cleaned, and it didn't allow for the purchase of new clothes that you might need to reduce the psychological deficit.

The time was long overdue to ask for the staff job. Robin thought of the men who had them. "Well, Ron is different because he's a genius, almost a Tolstoy." (A variation of the generally accepted description of Ron Rosenbaum as the Dostoevski of the *Voice*.)

And then there was Paul Cowan. She could accept his being put on staff when she was not because "he's so terrific." And Phil Tracy "because he's so prolific." But Howard Blum, now that was another matter. It was wrong to put him on staff, Robin thought, because he was no better than she. Robin still clung to the vision of a world where things are as they ought to be.

Never mind questioning whether it is just that some people are born into families with lots of money, such as Paul and Howard, and therefore don't even need a staff job except as a balm to soothe an ego. In fact, if jobs were handed out on the basis of justice they should go to people who need them, as Robin herself had argued when defending a staff position going to a man with a marginal income who has a family to support rather than to a woman who has none. Child of the sixties that *she* was, Robin found it easier to identify with men. It was different, however, from Barbara Long's lusting for their power; Robin lusted for their powerlessness. "Paul needs the dignity of a staff job," she said, in response to the observation that Paul does not need the money. Never mind that she needed the staff job not only for "dignity" but also to buy some shampoo so her hair would not get horribly matted, something she could accept when she was young and fresh and just out of college and working in the South. But years of working without job recognition had done something to the spirit.

Robin finally asked Dan for a staff job. "We don't have a specific need now." She approached Ross; his answer was more complex. "He knows me better." After Dan was gone, Robin went to Ross again. She had just been through a difficult year emotionally, she confided to Ross, who told the rest of the *Voice* people. A deep, dark love affair had left Robin wounded. Believing women have to be perfectly composed, she thought her brief "fuck-up" was a proper reason for her not being hired on staff. Were not women expected to make noble sacrifices for their careers in the tradition of the serious lady writers she had read and taken to her bosom at school?

When it was pointed out that men, too, occasionally "fuck up" at work because they are going through a rocky emotional period, she nodded sadly. "Don't ask me why it didn't apply to others. I know I'm as productive as others." And when asked what she did with the bitterness and hurt that that knowledge must produce, she said, "The bitterness I internalize."

It was difficult for Robin to compare herself to Howard Blum because she came out favorably. Occasionally, there were moments of lucidity, moments when she seemed to perceive a relation between the injustice of her situation at work and how she felt about herself.

"The thing about being young is important in more ways than one. I'm tired of always being in debt and worrying about paying the dentist's bill two months late." But it was elusive—the anger—weaving in and out of the conversation.

"I felt logically, if I were in power I would take Paul and Phil on staff before me. But I felt they should also take me. I began to feel not being on staff was depressing. Like many writers, I'm both very conceited and very insecure."

Echoes of Barbara Long, before her, and preludes to Marlene Nadle, who followed, all three unable to grasp the ways in which outside recognition prevents the vacillations between fierce conceit and insecurity from swinging too far apart. It's one thing to stay home and write poetry, but to go out as a working reporter flings the writer into a tough, competitive world. Emily Dickinson might have trouble with a press conference were she seeking to interview a newsmaker and had as her inner belief, "I'm nobody. Who are you?"

"I like Paul and Phil very much. I couldn't feel mad because I like them so much." And now another factor is introduced as a criterion for a staff position: how Robin personally feels about the people. If they are her friends, she cannot compete. And although her boy scout sense of honor would make cronyism a sin if used in her favor—that is, to ask someone to do something for *her* because he (or she) liked her—she nevertheless could not do something for herself if it were at the expense of somebody she liked.

But it was something more profound than the boy scouts, the Seven Sisters schools, and other distillers of true-blue ideals. To become a woman reporter is hard work, and few manage to do it without personal sacrifice. (At the *Voice,* almost all the men are married or live steadily with someone, whereas almost every woman is unattached.) Writing becomes the love affair; it may be the same for men who live with someone, but they do not feel the vulnerability that constant living alone, broken up only by the jagged rhythms of writing, imposes.

Under such circumstances, it becomes scary to risk fighting, to risk angering the people who provide one with the comic relief from work. If one has no nest to which to return at night, and one is injured after an attempt to fly, as Robin was when she took a chance at love, women like herself believe that the momentary lapse will, quite properly, be held against them. In contrast, most men *expect* a base line of security as a given in a work situation. When they do anything special, they expect increased recognition. But the base line is not negotiable; a rotten affair which leaves them emotionally drained does not demand a sacrifice. They do not have to pay for it with their job security. But women, "so grateful just to be published," to be taken seriously, to be given a by-line, a "voice," feel they must perform continuously on a dazzling level lest they risk losing what they initially consider a gift.

The one time Robin "fucked up" she thought it perfectly

natural that she be punished. Guilt over sex? Over men? Over romance? Perhaps. But if a job becomes one's life (to be only sporadically interrupted by romance), then it is as fragile as love with an unsteady man. Making demands may mean the end. Robin could wonder why she didn't get the job she was convinced she deserved, but she could not fight for it.

"I'm as productive as staff writers, but I don't push it as much." Were pushiness to be the basis for getting a job one deserves, most women would lose out; most *do* have a harder time asking for what they want and what they deserve, particularly when they are alone in a work situation (as well as a home one) and when it involves pushing for something gross, crude, crass, like money, and one is, at heart, a lady.

"I had the misfortune to go through my one huge emotional crisis at the time they were taking people on staff. It's a coincidence that I wasn't at my best when they were taking people on. I didn't feel betrayed." And then right after: "I didn't feel angry until they took Howard on. I don't want to go into that because Howard's already so angry." Again Robin hesitating to talk about an injustice because the person who benefited is already angry at her for questioning the decision in the first place. It's almost back to the old days of faking orgasms so that the man won't feel incompetent. To suppress anger can become a vocation of its own: the constant turning inward can a poet make, but more often it produces a shrew or a bitter, weary woman.

When first Dan and then Ross turned down Robin's request for a staff job (and none of her male friends on the paper made any effort to fight on her behalf), it would seem natural that Robin approach the one person who had been a source of support from the beginning—Mary Nichols. However, knowing that Mary liked her and was responsible for giving her a start on the *Voice,* Robin could not go to her. Would not such an act hint at getting something because of friendship or asking to be given something out of kindness? It was merit that was to be the basis of her appointment. Only for men could it be extreme need, or the ability to fight.

"I think something's being missed here. I don't think women should be supportive of women more than of men. If I were an editor, I would take people on staff impartially. It isn't that people are discriminating against us because we're women. It's just that we're not shouting and screaming and being aggressive."

It was almost as if Robin had said, "It isn't that they're discriminating against us because we are women but merely because we behave like women." True. Many women have not been taught to fight for their rights (they have not even been taught what their rights *are*). Hence, it's all the more reason not to make the ability to fight for a job a basis for offering one.

Listening to such counterarguments, Robin would become wistful. "I didn't feel at first that it does make a difference to one's self-confidence to be taken on staff. I now do." But then the contrapuntal play would begin when Robin was reminded that it was family wealth that gave Paul a certain kind of confidence whether he were to have a staff job or not and that perhaps he needed "the dignity of a job" less than she. But that was going too far, stripping away too many of the protective layers she had wrapped herself in for years, believing that it was truth, goodness, or at least the wanting to be good and true that makes a person win out in the end.

"Dignity and self-confidence apply equally to poor and rich alike." Anyone—let alone a *Voice* writer, a political writer, a person who has gone down to the South and reported on the poor— who could come out with that statement was revealing how deeply blinding is an upper-class education or how hopelessly naïve was she. It made one want to shove the world in Robin's face and show her that it is not just, it is not fair (or else she wouldn't be in the position she was). But no, one begins to think that there are certain women who will be masochists no matter what. Women like Robin inspire a liking, even a craving for evil.

"No one," Robin continued to protest, "likes to think he's not earning his own living."

"But Paul isn't."

"Well, now presumably he is."

"Oh, come on."

"Paul's a friend. I hate to talk about it."

No one was attacking Paul personally. What was being questioned was an unfair system—the class system—the injustices of which Paul himself explores regularly in print. Which may be one way a person who happens to have been born rich and who has developed a concern for justice sincerely tries to work out the conflict about having so much more than others.

Then followed a litany of apologies for other men. "If it" (the matter of Ross's using his position to meet other women by holding out the offer of publishing their work) "happened, it happened in one short period. Most people go through fucked-up periods, and I gave them some leeway. I don't know what happened and I guess I don't want to know." Indeed. Were only the world (or at least Ross) as tolerant as Robin, then he would not have held her "fucked-up" period against her.

What about Dan? How did she feel about all the money he was paying himself?

"I have enough things to be upset about. Like not being on staff. I would have been happy to make $10,000, so I can't care as much as some people if someone makes $70,000 or not."

When it was pointed out that if everyone had cared about what each person was making, the salaries of others, the basis for increases—the ordinary concerns of "workers"—Robin (as well as Dan) might be in a different situation now.

When pressed to consider that it was immoral for anyone to be paying himself $72,000 when he was paying his writers a wage they could barely get by on, Robin said, "Of course, it's not immoral. Of course not. I said, 'Of course not.' I'm not sure of that, I'm taking back the 'Of course not.' "

Not wanting to go on record too strongly one way or the other once again. God, what do they teach you at the "J" School, or wherever it was that Robin learned to be such an equivocator? "It was just the weirdness of the disparity of salary. I don't know what I think."

Weirdness? Damn it. It was plain unjust as well as immoral. And, of course, it was the ultimate in liberal hypocrisy.

So. She couldn't be mad at Dan, who had turned her down for a staff job. She couldn't be mad at Ross, who, with greater understanding, had done the same thing. The only group she could see as a possible threat were the women at *Ms.*

It all came about when Ross was trying to figure out a way to engage the magazine. Having seen that a lot of women whom he would have liked to see writing for the *Voice* were preferring to submit their manuscripts to *Ms.* (one also suspects he wanted to see the women, too), and knowing the power of the pen, Ross turned to the one woman who would agree to write about a competitive publication although she had no security at her own and had been told she was not to expect any in the near future. With Robin, Ross could feel assured that the piece would not sound bitchy, that it wouldn't seem informed by spite or revenge or anything nasty. The *Ms.* women would trust Robin once she explained that she was not out to do a hatchet job. And it worked.

The *Ms.* staff allowed Robin to sit in on its meetings; she took notes and interviewed people, and then she checked her quotes. When it was all done, she rechecked everything. Trying to straighten out a contradiction between two parties, she started to call people back to confirm facts, ferret out rumors. In her anxiety not to print anything unfair or untrue, she began to drive people crazy.

In the meantime, the *Ms.* staff was wondering exactly what she, or the *Voice,* was up to. And Robin was encountering the largest writing block in her life, second only to one she had in writing the story about Wellesley, which it took her almost two years to complete. Friends suggested that Robin drop the piece; many thought she was a fool to cut off a possible source of publication.

"It's pernicious to consider the consequences of one's work," she countered. As long as one is true to one's own sense of things and tries as hard as it is humanly possible (making humble allowances for human fallibility), one must not worry about the results. One must accept them as a good soldier. When reminded that to worry about survival was a reasonable concern for soldier and civilian alike and that only martyrs and masochists shared an indulgent indifference for self-preservation, Robin didn't care.

Unknown to herself, she was acting much more like a reckless gambler, risking her health, her reputation, and her survival, only to realize over a year later, when the *Ms.* story had not run, that she was scared. She was told there was still time to ask that it not run at all. But she argued that not to run it wasn't fair to the people whose time she had taken. When it was pointed out that the people at *Ms.* would view it as courageous to say, "I don't want the story to run; it would give way to distortions of the magazine and hence be a disservice to women," she could not. It was wrong, immoral, not cricket. But it wasn't immoral for Ross to have assigned it, to risk her reputation with potential allies, particularly when he was withholding the recognition at the *Voice* that he had the power to give her. (It is an interesting aside to note that two other Nichols disciples wrote pieces about *Ms.*—Stephanie Harrington for *The New York Times* and Mary Breasted for *Saturday Review*—

but only when each had job security either through her own or her husband's work. Robin's piece never ran at all.)

"I'm sort of scared of the way those people—I hate to use that phrase. I just have this terrible feeling of having a lot of powerful people angry at me and I try so hard to be fair whenever I do a story, and for them to talk in negative and inaccurate ways about me scares the hell out of me. Well, it doesn't scare the hell out of me; it's just profoundly depressing."

Back we go. Whenever there is a strong emotion—fear, anger, resentment—we wind up with depression, the one-way trip for women. Robin, after being exploited in countless ways at the *Voice,* could defend everyone responsible and then see as the only fearsome ones the women at *Ms.* Like Barbara, she found it impossible to get angry at the men in charge. But unlike Barbara, she couldn't even sustain her misplaced rage; all she could feel was "profoundly depressed."

If one starts out believing the world is right and just and true (rather than the jungle, as Barbara perceived it), and then one winds up without much credit, it follows that there is something wrong with one's self, not the world.

"I feel, for whatever reason, less confident now than I did five years ago. Whatever has to do with the *Voice* has undoubtedly to do with not being taken on staff. It's very oppressive not to make a living. It grinds one down. I don't want to overstate this—'my spirit is ground down'—it's just a small, subtle effect."

What is surprising is that someone who covered the women's movement, or at least certain key issues, could benefit so little personally from it. "When I first started, I was certain I could write almost anything I chose. Maybe feeling less self-confident is a part of getting older. I just wanted something that would really last."

Both Barbara and Robin: grandiose and insecure in the same way, concerned with immortality rather than with day-to-day gratification, but furious at not getting the latter and blind to how the deprivations—"the grinding down of the spirit"—make it hard to write the masterpieces that would insure the immortality each were seeking.

Robin has changed her goals, and at twenty-nine she sounds defeated. "I just wanted something that would really last, almost something connected up with my teen-age feelings about religion. I didn't care about huge sales or money. Just some sense of wanting to endure. That seemed a goal. Now my goal is immediate happiness, not success. Compared to a scale of Shakespeare and Ibsen, any journalism success is small."

Robin Reisig is now a reporter for *The Real Paper,* a small underground paper in Boston.

Fred W. McDarrah

"A male friend drove me to the airport. As we were going to the gate and he was holding my hand, I had a sense of a very visible pull. The hand seemed to be holding back. My hand, his hand . . . I wasn't sure. But somewhere when I was thousands of feet above the city, I realized that I was tired of saying good-bye to people, to men, and that, goddamn it, I was going to work it out—the woman-versus-writer thing."

Marlene Nadle

Marlene, like Diane, like Barbara, like Robin, was another refugee who had come to the big city to find herself. There was a softness about her—something in her voice; it was slow, none of the speedy big-city rhythms, a very believable girl from Buffalo who had quit her job as a teacher to seek her way as a writer.

But the outward appearance was deceptive. It would have been hard to deduce that the first thing Marlene would do, upon arriving in the city, was ring up Dan Wolf of *The Village Voice* (a paper she had kept in mind when once she chanced upon it in her Buffalo College library) and tell him that she planned to cover a demonstration in Washington. And it would have been impossible to predict that when Dan Wolf said no, he had his own people, she would do it anyway.

Marlene bounced into his office after the demonstration, finished the piece in front of his eyes, and handed it to him. It is not hard to imagine Dan thinking, "That girl has guts," and admiring her for them. It probably predisposed him to liking her writing even if it hadn't turned out to be as good as it did, good enough to be picked up by Mailer and quoted in *Esquire*. Dan had a new star in the works.

But the star was not prepared for stardom, and when it happened so quickly, Marlene essentially stopped writing for a year. Oh, there was a second piece—a story on the House of D (as the former detention house for women was called)—but all Marlene could see in this "O.K. piece" was the discrepancy between it and the first. "Every story was the test of whether I was writing at the Mailer level. I looked at the second piece and said, 'This isn't going to be read one hundred years from now,' which is the level I'm usually operating on."

When Marlene was unable to clear her way out of a court story, she never once looked around to see what was blocking her —that she had never covered a court case, that she was unfamiliar with legal technicalities, that she was dealing with a subject less flamboyant than a demonstration. Marlene did not give a single thought to the fact that she had no real foundation to just go out and do a story on anything. Instead she settled for the verdict that it was the good stuff that had been the fluke, the miracle, the fraud. For all the Mailer influence, she showed scant appreciation of training.

Like Barbara, Marlene had come from a working-class family rooted in a small city; only by becoming an exile did she believe she could avoid the destiny of a woman in the provinces, the destiny of the wives and mothers who had done nothing with their lives. She was interested in adventure and courage—fighters for justice moved her the way fighters for their limbs moved Barbara, and in the early sixties they, too, were all men. The message was clear: cast your professional dice with the opposite sex. "I didn't then and certainly don't now have a model as a writer. When I started writing I called it the age of innocence. This was simply something I was going to do."

About a year later, Marlene was ready for another round, and went to interview Malcolm X, just like that, although she had never interviewed anyone before.

Dan played on the contrast between her strength and her weakness, admiring the cockiness but worrying about the inability to follow through. "'You can't produce consistently,' he told me, while all along admiring whatever I turned in. 'That is, you do good things but you can't be counted on. You have to be able to do pedestrian prose. Those are the people who get staff jobs; the butterflies are those we use for color.' It was only very late in my relationship to the *Voice* that I finally heard from Dan that everyone louses up a story from time to time. For I had a very special relationship to Dan. Like Barbara, I was one of the chosen. I didn't have to kick ass."

Slowly there began to develop the classic woman's relation to Dan: the writer in search of a father figure—one who is kind, gentle, encouraging but somehow remote, there and not there, quietly undermining all along as he seemed to wonder whether a young woman who had not married, who had no means of support, who had not borne children could really be relied upon to be put on staff. There was enough in Marlene's own head to tap when it came to that question—whether she could be both a woman and a writer. Almost from the beginning of her career, she began to see the two as adversary and felt she would always have to choose between one or the other, woman and writer, a variation of the choice between weakness and strength. "Remember, I wasn't supposed to be doing this. I had a tremendous ambivalence about success if I allowed it."

Marlene continued to write for a while, mainly on the civil rights movement. "Unless a subject hits me in the guts, it's not going to work for me." At about the time she was producing with regularity, along came a Peruvian painter who invited Marlene to go back with him to South America.

"Actually, I'd been looking for a shrink to marry. Every time I'd meet one I'd think, uh-huh, now I'll become a lady writer. But the other side of that is should I find that miraculous Leonard Woolf, I would then fear I'd become dependent, and without him, I would not be able to write."

Anyway, the Peruvian painter wasn't a shrink or a Leonard Woolf; just a crazy nonverbal free spirit who asked her to "come back with me to the country." When she left for South America, she thought it would be for one month or so. Months later she still had not returned. Dan took care to sublet her Village pad. To this day, she thinks leaving may have been a way of avoiding the success she was on her way to achieving. For at last, she was showing Dan that she could be counted upon to produce with regularity, that she was "reliable." Although Dan had always made Marlene feel special—sending her to his dentist and offering her other signs that he personally cared—there was something he withheld, although she is uncertain as to what it was.

"He was very understated even in what he did appreciate. When I found out through a movement source and before anyone else that there were going to be riots in Newark, I called Dan immediately. His response was, 'So. There are going to be riots in Newark.' "

It was the Peruvian painter who supplied what Dan could not—emotion. Unlike Dan, he couldn't deal with words; he was a totally visual person. For a brief period, Marlene was happy. During this time, Marlene heard that the Debray trial was going on in South America. She knew that she wasn't going to cover it by staying up in the country with her lover, nor was he about to travel around with her.

"The thing that did it for me was I had the sense that I'd have to take care of him, and goddamn it, I wanted a mother or a father myself. I wasn't going to do it for someone else."

Marlene left for South America, where she stayed six months, covering the Debray trial and South American politics until she received a letter from Dan: " 'Goddamn it, we're not your real estate agent. Come on home.' That was Dan's way of saying he was tired of arranging sublets for me."

Before Marlene left for the States, she decided she wanted to speak with Allende. She went to the Senate, told him that she had been in Bolivia, seen Che killed, and was not sure what it meant. "Can I talk to you?" she asked. Out of the talks came a brilliant series of interviews with Allende which the *Voice* printed. Marlene, however, had no feeling that they were special or that it had been extraordinary for her to win the confidence of leading political figures who would spend time discussing politics with her. Maybe one reason they trusted her was that her aim was not to get a scoop, nor was it to become famous through them. "I had a lot of real political questions about the moral legitimacy of violence at the time, so I didn't measure what I was doing in terms of my career."

Most of the time Marlene was in South America getting previously untold stories, she felt very negative. "I felt unresolved as a writer in terms that it had cost me a man." There was even a stopover to see him back in Lima and a chance to shuck a career. Marlene left on the next flight, afraid that if she stayed on for a day, she might stay forever.

"I'm really not sure whether I did the right thing. The conflict had very little to do with the *Voice*. They did what I told them to. Rather it had to do with giving up the writing. Am I always going to lose people? I didn't know which way to go in terms of writing versus a relationship and I was just treading water. I saw that time as an intense conflict."

During the next two years, Marlene returned to South America several times, but always as a writer who supported herself by getting "adopted." "I had letters from people saying, 'Here, take her in. She's a starving child.' " Once she actually stole a small piece of cheese because she hadn't eaten for so long. Although she was writing, it was sporadic and the *Voice* was paying very little for her pieces. Despite all her political savvy about plantation owners and serfdom in South America, Marlene, like Barbara and like Robin, could not see how the chronic dependency in her own life, a dependency made necessary by the working conditions of the *Voice,* continually eroded her confidence.

In her mind, the conflict was between being a writer or being with a man, unable to see that the two might not have been pitted against each other had she any sense that she could support herself without a man, that it wasn't only the man who could provide security.

"I had a sense of running on one cylinder. I was treading water again. An on-and-off thing—should I be a writer or not. I don't know what to do in the big world without *The Village Voice.*"

The conflict unresolved, Marlene came home once again to what had become home—the *Voice.* "But there was very little satisfaction for me to be published at the *Voice.* If anything, it was a proof of failure. I was standing still there. They would publish anything of mine. There was no challenge for me. I was not doing any hustling. Which was necessary because I was afraid of it. It was one more test of my strength. The *Voice* was just home, family, and friends."

Just! But it was true that there was no woman at the *Voice* who seemed to have both love and a career at the same time, who had worked it out, and both Dan and Ross, two true Mailer disciples, were able to communicate what a sense of failure it was for a woman to have her womb lie infertile, unseeded, a hollow.

"If I was a writer, I wasn't a woman with love in my life. I think the turning point came when I saw a photograph of Dorothy Parker with the caption, 'Writing is torture but not writing is worse torture.' My favorite fantasy is to be a dumb blond manicurist. I wish I could turn off my head, but as Ross says, I'm condemned. I wish that weren't true. But I couldn't imagine myself if I stopped writing. There would be no contentment."

These words struck home. No matter whether women have gone off to Egypt in search of further understanding a man (as did Vivian Gornick) or stayed at home covering Abe Beame (as did Robin), all have sacrificed a steady love life.

"I basically feel I should be a person who is strong. I can be but am not. I get detoured by baggage. What does it cost me if I write? In my own head it cost me a chance for love. Men do not want women who are that strong."

Or at least not many of the radical men of the sixties who disposed of women as if they were paper plates. Of course, there was the Peruvian painter. But he, too, wanted a houseful of babies and Marlene to take care of them, the house, and him while he painted.

Almost as a joke, Marlene strolled into Dan's office one day and demanded that he send her back to South America. "I want to see Debray; he's just come out of prison." That was a big demand for a place that thought twice about underwriting costs to New Jersey, but Dan went along with it. There was something in the way Marlene presented it—a sassiness—that must have reminded Dan of the strong-willed defiant young woman who once walked into his office off the street with an assignment he had already turned down.

"I sort of felt the *Voice* would jump at my fingers if I just snapped them." She was right. Off again she went to South America, "adopted" this time by a conservative Latin-American writer in whose home she lived.

When she returned to the States for good, Marlene hinted at her readiness for a staff job. She could now do it, and it seemed from the expression on Dan's face that he might consider offering her one. But she didn't want to press the matter at the time because she had just signed a contract to write a book about South American politics. Then came word from home that her father, her real one, was dying of cancer. She boarded a plane and headed back to Buffalo, believing that she could stay with her father throughout and write the book.

It was the summer of '72, and for eight months she stayed with her father, virtually running the hospital. Then it was over; her father died. There had, of course, been no time or energy to write the book. Nor desire. While at home, she felt free of the conflict between love and work. A father dies only once.

In the spring, when she returned to New York, there was a restlessness; radical politics seemed dead, and it was hard to separate her sense of personal loss from what was happening outside herself. All she knew was that between Brazil and Buffalo, time had been totaling up and now she felt like a stranger in the city.

She didn't know people anymore and people didn't know her. All except one—Dan.

"I have to get out of town," she told him, again demanding a miracle, half as a joke and half because he always seemed able to come up with one for her. This time was no different. An airline had just sent a freebee to the *Voice,* and within a day Marlene was off to Thailand, her panty hose hanging out of her handbag.

"A male friend drove me to the airport, and as we were going to the gate and he was holding my hand, I had a sense of a very visible pull. The hand seemed to be holding back. My hand, his hand . . . I wasn't sure. But somewhere when I was thousands of feet above the city, I realized that I was tired of saying good-bye to people, to men, and that, goddamn it, I was going to work it out —the woman-versus-writer thing."

When Marlene got back to New York, her "home" was on the verge of being destroyed. The *Voice* had been sold and Dan was about to be let go. Something had to be done; Marlene mobilized herself the way she had mobilized the nurses and aides in the hospital when her father was dying. She organized other writers to try to save the jobs of Dan and Ed and that of Diane, who was about to be fired by Ross, it was rumored. Marlene had to interfere; she had always cherished loyalty. What else was courage and fighting all about? Even risks and sacrifices were part of a fighter's life, if one were to believe Mailer and other writers who seemed to understand such things. Strangely, though, they themselves never did have to sacrifice love, sex, family, home, security. But never mind. Now was no time to analyze. It was a time for action.

Coming so shortly after her own father's death, the activity seemed a way to resurrect him; he who had always been a free spirit, a wanderer thwarted only by real life and its responsibilities, and it was she, the only child, who had followed the road his life had not permitted him to take.

Then, too, organizing to save the jobs of Dan and Diane (another whom Dan had befriended when she came to the big city in search of something other than the life her mother had lived) seemed to revive the spirits of the sixties. Once again there were causes, action, enemies, allies. Passion became alive through politics.

Marlene became outspoken as she busied herself with getting people to share her sense of challenge. She remembered the lust she had known when she came to the city in the sixties and it was burning with brave blacks and their followers. What had happened to them all when she was off in South America treading water and writing about Allende and Debray? Was it all over now just when she was returning to a sense of herself?

The one thing that had bypassed Marlene entirely while she was away in Latin America interviewing radical heroes was the women's movement. Never had she had a sense of a woman as strong, as an ally, a fellow fighter, who could help her escape her mother's fate. There had been no one like that at the *Voice,* as far as she knew. Yet now she wanted to fight for Diane's job, not because she suddenly felt a surge of feminism. It was a way to support Dan, to tell the new people (and the old) who had gotten rid of him (and hence made it possible to get rid of Diane) that they were morally repugnant, that she had no use for them.

But without Dan and Ed, she could no longer snap her fingers and get results. When no one meeting at Mary Nichols' apartment would say a word about the change for fear of their futures, Marlene began to see that the *Voice* was an entirely new place; no longer a home where they took you in no matter what, but an arena where you had to fight your way in. It became all the more imperative to retaliate; when the enemy was in charge, you didn't consider whether you would lose your job. Marlene was ready to be part of a walkout; no one else was. "Maybe it was part of a fantasy that they would be forced to take Dan back."

Meanwhile, Ross was letting it be known that things would be different for those people who remained "special friends" of Dan; the meaning was clear: defend Dan and your words won't be welcome in the paper now that I'm in his place. But Marlene was not a person to worry about careerist concerns when a moral principle was at stake. Like Robin, she couldn't fret about job security. But unlike Robin, she knew what she was fighting for—for Dan, her father, her family, the people who had been good to her.

Outraged at the cowardice of others, she could not comprehend that she was alone. "I've been very lucky in never having to compromise because of my peculiar relation to the *Voice.* And the first time I was put to the test, I felt I was up against a principled stand I should be taking and simply couldn't rush in and kiss ass like Cockburn and Cowan and not say a word. Briefly, there was talk of a walkout at one of those hysterical meetings at Mary's house, and Cockburn and Cowan, mainly to head it off, set up a writers' committee. That deflected all action. I didn't want to be a member of ass lickers anonymous, which is what it turned into."

Not everyone shared her point of view. It was unanimously conceded that Dan (with Ed's backing) had been the "soul" of the *Voice* and its creator, and without him and even his neurosis the *Voice* never could have become what it was. Nevertheless, several people thought that Dan had been a greedy man, and were it not for his avarice, the situation he was now in could not have come about. To ask writers to risk their jobs for a man who had brought about his own downfall, at their expense as well as his own, was unfair.

At first, Marlene could see the situation only from Dan's side, and from that vantage point it was patricide. She could not conceive of writing for a paper that had killed off Dan. And so she didn't. She began the life she had wanted and feared—the challenge of making it on her own in the big wide world without a man for protection. It was hard. She started with a good project—an interview of Mary McCarthy, with whom she had already spoken. But every publication to whom the idea was submitted turned it down. When *Saturday Review* sent a curt note saying they don't take work by unknowns, it hit.

Marlene, who had done the first interview with Debray, who had been there when Che was killed, who had spent hours talking with Allende and writing about it for the *Voice,* exclusive after exclusive, which had been recognized by the likes of Mailer early in the sixties now to be labeled an unknown. And by *Saturday Review,* no less. As with Barbara, something had gone wrong; somewhere along the way, she had missed out. Like Robin, she had never put careerist concerns first. Unlike both, however, Marlene was a quick learner, and the strong side reappeared as promptly as the sun after a summer rain.

With time, the "offing" of Dan receded in the scheme of criminal acts. "Dan did not expect what happened, Dan, who has been praised by everyone for his psychological insights. If he could be so wrong about Carter Burden—and he himself admits that he totally misjudged the man—then maybe he could be wrong about me." It was a breakthrough, stronger than the sun, for it was a first— the first time Marlene questioned Dan's omnipotence.

The most important thing was not to be true to a man forever but to be a writer—that was the spiritual survival she had always chosen. Even though the new *Voice* had odious aspects, if she could still write in her own voice for it, as she had once done for the old, she would compromise. She would return. It made one a bit more humble about purity, that ideal of the sixties.

For the first time, getting published was a challenge. "My head is not a commercial head. It's a whole new process—thinking of ideas to market. I find by the time I go through the process, I couldn't care less about the piece."

The *Voice* was still one of the few places where Marlene could write about what stirred her. The only problem was to find out what stirred her.

It was no longer possible to write about civil rights and South American politics. It was woman as writer, woman as activist, woman as woman that she cared about. Until those issues were explored, nothing else could be. And now she was not alone; there were other people to talk with. One didn't have to rush to Dan; he wasn't the sole person in the world who could understand conflict. Could it be, Marlene wondered, that he had unintentionally and unknowingly encouraged her personal divisions (conflict always making more interesting psychic copy)?

Marlene, like Robin, wanted some personal happiness, and like Barbara, she wanted to write seriously. But unlike either, she was going to figure out a way—"goddamn it"—to stop sacrificing one's personal self for one's ideals. It was a farewell to the sixties and to the men she had known who had judged the world with a purity that made their personal lives look like scum. It was the final good-bye to good-byes.

My Own Story

Four women—distinct, different; and yet in each I see reflections of myself, hear my voice echo. What is it that makes us individual and yet one at the same time?

There is a part of me that wants to go with the wind and, like Whitman, Emerson, and Diane, "do my own thing," whether it is sailing, putting a paper together, or writing without concern for market. Freedom, in a word.

There is a part that cares about words and language, the joy of shaping thoughts and feelings and coming up with a sentence that has never been written before. The Barbara in me.

The part that wants to tell the truth, perform a service to humanity, to feel a sense of responsibility and integrity is the Robin in me.

And the part that wants to change the world, to fight injustices, to grab onto a vision of a just world, where people are more equal, loving, and happy is the part of me that is Marlene.

Thus, there are all sorts of ways in which this quartet of women serves as a mirror. But as I listen carefully to what they say—their words, their own voices—the one common denominator is money and our inabilty to fight for it. Fight for causes? No problem. But not for our jobs. As a result, all four are now without a job at the *Voice;* one, fired after twelve years of steady work by the man whom she hired; one, the first woman to write in a man's area— boxing; another covered just about everything with conscience and diligence; the last among that small group of women who travel the world alone and get to the figures who are making history. Not a single one is employed by the place to which they gave themselves so totally.

And the anger, the bitterness, the hurt, so often turned inward, becomes a mirror for us all. For what woman cannot recognize the patterns? The woman who turns to one man as the loved one who can do no wrong and simultaneously points at a third party as the betrayer.

All were loners and pioneers who left their hometown, hit the road, and came to the city to try to make it alone with the thousands of others like themselves, having to climb and claw but thinking women weren't supposed to do such things and deciding to identify with men. But never really deciding, just instinctively feeling that men could do it more easily. And then vicariously becoming men by writing about them and for them and—irony of ironies—for a man who was himself living in the worlds of excitement through his writers.

None could turn to other women, and because they were isolated from each other, they reacted to a work situation the way women react to romance. Which is no coincidence. All were forced to make personal sacrifices for their work and had to live through fantasy. Given a male editor who was kind and supportive, they overloaded him with emotional meaning, and if he was paternalistic as well, the Oedipal feelings were unavoidable. Women at the *Voice* were loyal to the father figure, fiercely loyal, sacrificing all; whereas the men, even those in open search of a father figure (to replace their dead one), were able to overthrow him when their job demanded.

Perhaps all four females who were identified in subject matter with masculine concerns were compensating for denying the "masculine" striving for money; they would have to find different ways to be one of the boys, to be a son, to please a father, since making money was out. But that seems farfetched; nice on paper, perhaps, neat—but not convincing. The kind of explanation an analyst might offer because it ties things up without his being concerned with whether it is so.

There are, I think, simpler explanations for why four women of exceptional talent and experience wound up in the situations they did. I believe they say something about all women, particularly women writers; as I listened to them speak, I experienced a disintegration of that line that had kept me at a safe distance. I no longer felt comfortable with the stance of the observer—detached, knowing, ironic. For the first time, "sisterhood" had a real ring; I couldn't mock the term as I was tempted in the past when it was used by strangers (and often ones hostile to me and my way of thinking). I no longer could write sharp vignettes, biting and insightful though they might be; the stories were too close and they hurt or made me angry. There were times I wanted to kick Robin as I listened to her get so close to something and then block it all out. But then I have only to turn to Barbara to feel compassion. It was Marlene, however, who moved me the most; she seemed the most anxious to understand what had happened, to explore, and to change. She seemed the only one who had not been permanently drained by the experience of the *Voice,* the only one who seemed capable of growth in the sole direction I have come to believe (based partly on these stories) will make it possible for women to avoid winding up where some of us did—to avoid reacting to a work situation as we do to romance, by having some sense of bonding with other women. Not because it will make it easier to gain entry into the man's world but because we can, by being strong among ourselves, make the man's world one that no longer rewards and punishes on the basis of our sex.

A pretty pompous introduction to an autobiographical sketch!

I was living in Cambridge, Mass., when my first piece for *The Village Voice* was published. I had visited New York in the fall of '68, when the New York City public school strike was going on. By chance I was passing a street corner where Nat Hentoff was addressing a group of parents planning a sit-in at the local public school, P.S. 41. He asked for volunteer teachers, and I offered my name.

Hentoff had compared the action of breaking into 41 with what was then going on in the Ocean Hill-Brownsville section of Brooklyn, where community leaders wanted community control. Out of curiosity, I decided to make a trip out to Ocean Hill-Brownsville and visit the school that had become the center of controversy.

What I found was entirely different from what I expected to find, based partly on Nat's talk. I wrote down my impressions. It was easy because they were strong and vivid. I slipped all eight pages' worth through the slot of the door at Sheridan Square and left town. I had said what I thought and that was that.

When a friend called the following Wednesday to tell me that there was a piece in *The Village Voice* with a by-line the same as my name, I ran out the next day and bought several copies. It was hard to believe. My behavior in New York had felt more like that of a fugitive than a writer. The piece itself was a critique of liberalism, Village style. I was particularly impressed with the freedom; not a single word, including a glaring grammatical error, had been changed.

Only now in retrospect can I see some of the other reasons why the piece may have appealed to Dan. It spoke knowingly about Village literati—there were slightly snide references to Barthelme, Grace Paley, and Hentoff himself—putting down their fey mannerisms while acknowledging them by putting them in at all. For Dan, that was equivalent to Marlene's strutting into his office and finishing a story right in front of him.

To be able to poke fun, albeit gentle fun, at well-known figures so fearlessly revealed a strength I suspect Dan found attractive. Also, it revealed a knowingness about the Village liberals, who liked nothing better than to castigate themselves. And here Dan had picked up something; I was not from a small town or some faraway province. I was a city kid who had been born and raised in the streets of Brooklyn. The *Voice* held out no hopes of salvation from provincial America, from plastic America, from patriotic America; the "c" had already been converted to a "k" by my parents, who were radical Bohemians. Being "villagey" was nothing new to me, nor was the Village itself an escape. Quite the contrary. Bohemianism always seemed a bit suspect—dropouts seemed to me less tolerant of others: they were constantly handing down judgments, although the snickering quality saved them from the charge of sententiousness. For the last thing they wanted was to pose as judge. But I knew that the greatest posture of all was to pretend to be free of one.

The Bohemian style of life—whether it is lived in the Village or SoHo or my own home—seemed woven in with a particular brand of narcissism that was not attractive to me. It is one of the reasons I was drawn to the sciences—they seemed to offer an escape from the self that was far more reliable than one or two crooked streets. I, too, wanted a refuge, but only if it could be found beyond the third ear, the eye in the back of the head, the antennae all over the body that picked up other people's vibes, no matter what. No coffeehouse, no matter how many variations of the bean it offered, provided me with the refuge I was then seeking.

Going out to Ocean Hill-Brownsville—a whole new world—

came much closer to removing me from my own confines. It was exhilarating to be able to take standard liberal rhetoric and hold it up to the light of experience. It made writing seem effortless—to anchor it in a social reality. I dashed off the eight pages in a couple of hours.

What really impressed me, however, was that you could get something published without any connections. There seemed few things in life that worked on the merit system. From the moment the *Voice* published my piece, I felt a respect for it. But it wasn't gratitude. I thought the piece was good. It was a surprise that for once the world was behaving as it ought to. I stress this because I think the initial trust was one of the things that blinded me later on in my dealings with the paper.

The following week, the *Voice* printed a piece about the school strike that opened with the line that neither the writer nor Hentoff knew what he was talking about; only Frankfort did. My feeling that the *Voice* was an open forum was cemented. If ever I were to write regularly, I thought, it would be for something like the *Voice*. I did not define myself as a writer at the time (although I had written a book about teaching in private schools, which was shortly to be published). I was then working as a researcher at Harvard Medical School and taking graduate courses in sociology at Brandeis.

When a check for $35 arrived from the *Voice*, it seemed gratuitous. I hadn't expected anything, even to be printed. No one had asked me for the piece, and usually dissidents are shut up, not given lots of space to air their opinions. I don't think I was yet so fully aware of the seductive quality of immediate feedback. Since many *Voice* writers were lionized after a single piece, only to be paralyzed for a year or so afterward, I think it was lucky that I hadn't planned this piece as my writing debut. It never would have been so easy if an entire career had depended on it.

The most effortless pieces have been those where I wasn't counting on anyone's response. It is easier for me to perform as a fugitive when I don't expect to be observed than when everything depends on my performance, an observation Masters and Johnson have been able to parlay into an industry. (I can easily imagine writers' clinics where one is told to do everything *but* sign one's name.)

More important than the psychological pressures that attend performing was the fact that my furtive behavior had spared me contact with Dan. I did not have the advantage of talking out a piece with him—the one thing that almost all the writers who worked with him considered of enormous value. I am sure I, too, would have benefited from having someone of intelligence and perception listen, taking a different point of view to get me to sharpen my own. But because I had to create my own antagonist with whom I could carry on a dialogue, I never came to believe that my writing was dependent on Dan or anyone but myself.

Although it was shyness, not conceit, that brought it about, I never would have had the courage as an unknown writer to go in and speak with an editor or demand an assignment. It would seem that one had to earn the right to be so arrogant by showing what one could do on one's own. This attitude was to have unfortunate consequences because Dan had little use for shyness. As an insecure person, he assumed one was avoiding contact with him because one didn't need him, rather than because one felt uncomfortable about imposing on his time.

Had Dan understood the reasons why I or Robin hesitated to approach him initially, I suspect he would have had little sympathy. He was attracted to boldness. Fortunately, my writing had been bold, and it was Dan who first printed me, although he didn't know me. Since I didn't know him, or a single other person at the *Voice* for that matter, I had no idea of what he looked like, what the *Voice* looked like inside, or how it was run. I just assumed that an editor was a person of power who had many demands on his time.

However, I also assumed that Dan was a man of courage and boldness himself to take chances on unknown writers and to print clashing opinions. I didn't yet know that it was the clash Dan admired as much as the opinion. I didn't yet understand how everything at the *Voice* was ultimately viewed as psychological, not political. Since my own bent at the time was in the direction of seeing the personal behind any public presentation, I was quite a natural *Voice* person.

But class origins have always been as much a part of a person's psychic load as whether he or she has had a dominating mother, a passive father (both of which I thought could be explained, in part, by class analysis), or whether the person was ugly or beautiful (which I also thought bore some relation to class).

To sum up my beginnings at the *Voice:* my first article was published in 1968, when I was thirty-two, living in Cambridge, working at a job as a researcher in social psychiatry at Harvard Medical School, taking graduate studies in sociology at Brandeis, and finishing a book—light and anecdotal about my previous experiences as a private school teacher. I had been divorced for six years and was then living alone in an old run-down house with enough hint of Charles Addams to give it style and make it a comfort that I had two dogs as companions and an electric heater.

What nourished me spiritually during solitary times—and they were—was an involvement—still only intellectual—in the social movements around me. I yearned to hook up with one of them in a way other than through reading. It wasn't money or fame that I had thought about when I hungered for involvement; it was the gratification of being engaged with something bigger than myself, although innate analysand that I was, I did not believe I could eradicate my ego.

But, but, but . . . it wasn't all so solipsistic. I was genuinely outraged by the injustices of the world, and it was these that moved me more than anything else. I also had a fascination for literary gossip. This I would indulge on cold evenings when I curled up with the *New York Review of Books,* the *Times Book Review* and *The Village Voice.* Together they provided a sense of what was happening, who was considered important, who was being taken seriously on the New York literary scene.

These dual interests can easily be traced to my own background. Until I was a teen-ager, my father owned a bookstore. It never provided much income, but it had once been a hangout for radicals of the thirties, most of whom became rich and reactionary (that is, relative to their early views). My father was radical and never became rich. Since he was well educated, his indifference to money seemed partly a choice.

My mother had been trained as a professional musician. Although she never pursued a career, we always had two Steinway pianos in the house. That was odd for a family that couldn't afford a car. We were an odd family, especially in Flatbush—a solidly nouveau riche Jewish neighborhood. I like to think we were the only Jewish family that can claim to be nouveau poor and downwardly mobile. (I like to think that to ease the still vivid sense of stigma I felt as a child who came from a family that was different from all the others around me.) My only sibling—a twin sister—seemed oblivious to these things. She chose paths other than politics and literature—she became an interior designer—to work out her sense of outsidedness.

Early on, I had arrived at an understanding of the relation between radical politics and chic (the first *Voice* piece was really about that). I, too, felt the extreme, the apocalyptic, was of greater appeal. But I knew that it was an aesthetic appeal above all else. I enjoyed reading *Commentary* in the late sixties just to watch the way people were squirming with radical politics. I did not believe that Jason Epstein's analysis of society essentially differed from Norman Podhoretz's, although certainly their posturing did. After all, I was then reading Marx and Durkheim and all the other -heims Germany had bequeathed to the world of ideas. It seemed that the *Commentary* crew feared they would have to disrobe, and they were ashamed. Here, too, I sensed it was a class thing—Podhoretz never having gotten over being a boy from Brooklyn; nor had most of the *Commentary-Dissent* crowd. I was convinced you could bunch people by class—where they lived, where they sent their children to school, whom they married, and for whom they chose to write. It was certainly true in Cambridge, where even a mutt was inbred.

There were two groups with whom I had contact in that college town. One consisted of radical professors from Brandeis, all of whom were "into" politics-as-theatre (it is no coincidence that Abbie Hoffman came out of Brandeis) and shared a profound cynicism (which I was later able to write about for the *Voice*) concerning society's ability to change peacefully. That eased their consciences about the rather comfy lives they led. For why not enjoy things if you can't change them?

The other group—mainly Cambridge poets and writers—were as profoundly romantic as the professors were jaundiced. They drank sherry, thought taking politics too seriously was New York and grubby; in fact, everything except poetry and rare books was a bit grubby to them. Refinement was all that mattered. That seemed to me another form of life-as-theatre. It was all aesthetics, different forms of posturing, one relieving the other, as Mailer understood.

My first taste of something different came with the Medical Committee for Human Rights. Although I had been involved in civil rights actions in the early sixties and in the Vietnam resistance, I did not feel part of either struggle on a personal level. The problem with the Medical Committee for Human Rights, which I *did* feel very much a part of, was that it in no way changed my perception of men. All the leaders were male, and they treated young radical women like myself as members of an amusing harem.

I stuck with that for a while because I believed in the politics. However, it gave me an everlasting distrust of radical male leaders. I saw how they were the stars of the sixties, and I did not want to be a groupie.

In 1969, when I returned to New York, my strongest connection to a world outside my own head was radical health politics. I became a part of a local health council which had been organized to effect change in our community hospital. I also worked for the Medical Committee for Human Rights as City Wide Coordinator—a nice title for a volunteer job that involved making telephone calls and filing.

When the members of the local health council wanted publicity for a demonstration we were planning in front of the hospital, I was called upon, since I had already had something published in the *Voice*. I continued to write occasional pieces about our efforts at change; it was hard work, though, because what we were doing was not very dramatic. I began to see how the media and the Brandeis intellectuals thought alike; I was not ready to make a world view out of it like McLuhan, but damn it, it was true: unless a building were being seized, there was very little interest in coverage. And it *was* coverage that influenced change.

Health is a boring as well as depressing subject to cover; this is partly because it is connected so intimately to economics. And there is nothing more depressing and dull than hospital budgets, particularly when costs are continually rising and money to run the hospitals is continually being cut. One reason why the nursing home scandal could go unreported for so long was that it was too boring (so it was thought) until it was presented as a great detective story filled with human horrors and points of incongruity—the principal thief a religious leader. Only then did it seem worthy of steady investigation. Stories such as Medicaid and Medicare abuses did not catch the public eye (although those in the field knew about them from the beginning) because they were not presented in a dramatic way.

Finally, in 1970, I went over to the *Voice*, which had moved to new quarters on University Place, and asked to have a conference with Ross, who was my editor. We were joined by Mary Nichols. I had just done a long piece on Lincoln Hospital which a group of radicals had briefly seized. It had been agonizing to work on because I did not want to sacrifice the action part, but I also did not want to leave out the boring stuff that accounted for the drama. After all, it's easy to write a story about emergency rooms, but there are no sirens blasting from the heads of bureaucrats who make the budget decisions.

Also, I wanted to present my own commentary, and it was difficult to do it all tightly when encouraged to focus on the take-over of a hospital building. I pointed out to Mary and Ross that such coverage reflected the health system itself—paying attention only to the acute and ignoring the chronic underlying problems.

Both were responsive; Ross went so far as to turn off his telephone. Mary had a natural interest in how city agencies run, so there was no problem convincing her that there should be coverage of their affairs, particularly since they usually involved mismanagement. Ross was not interested in Blue Cross hearings on rate increases, community board meetings, and the like, but that didn't matter; as long as the writing was interesting, he would have no difficulty accepting it.

It was Mary who asked what I proposed should be done about the poor health coverage. I answered that there needed to be regular coverage so that people could get some understanding of how the health system worked. She knew my thinking: that health was a big business and that the major goal of it was no different from any other—profits: if people happened to get well as a result, that was a good side effect; if they didn't, that was a bad one, as unintentional as the good.

Since this was "my" point of view, Mary wanted it to be identified as such, the way one might with an editorial. That was fine with me, although the *Voice* never struck me as a publication known for its objectivity in reporting the news. They told me they would need a few days to think up a suitable name for the kind of column I proposed.

The following week "Health Forum" was presented to me as what they had come up with. The decidedly unsnazzy name appealed to me, or, more precisely, to my perverse sense of snobbery. I liked the association of older people filing into the halls of Cooper Union, settlement houses, public school auditoriums where free forums for the exchange of ideas were held for anyone who could get to them.

I had nothing against self-improvement; in fact, I had seen

far too much snottiness among the Cambridge intellectuals, who assumed that everyone but a defective was fully formed by five. The associations were not glamorous—babushkas, galoshes, retired school-teachers looking for ideas that were free. But it was fine with me. And so "Health Forum" became the title of my column.

Nor did I feel it should be mine alone; I wanted a dissenting view from time to time, as Ross suggested. In fact, after I had been writing the column for some time, I occasionally would suggest that someone who wanted me to write something that I knew nothing about but that seemed important, do it himself, and offered my column for the purpose. People would immediately call and ask me if my column had been taken away. Perhaps it was my own sense of ego that made me proud to say that I gave it to another writer who was a "guest" columnist and that I derived a secret power from being in a position to provide space for others.

At the initial meeting where it was agreed that I would write the "Health Forum," Ross said that he expected it to run more or less regularly. When I asked for an explicit translation of the "more-or-less" part, he answered, "Oh, something like nine weeks out of ten, I would guess." Agreeing to write a regular column was the equivalent of accepting a job. I therefore had to know roughly how much money to expect: that is, whether I could count on the *Voice* to live on since hustling for other free-lance work had no appeal to me. I had a hankering for job security, and it seemed the best of all possible worlds to be given that plus the freedom to write as I chose.

The freedom part I knew about. But not the money. I had been paid $35 for the first piece; however, I pointed out, an article about a former professor's radical teaching methods (which turned out to be phony poses and which took me one hour to write) earned me $75 in contrast to the piece on Lincoln Hospital, which took me weeks of hanging out at the place and then down at the Health and Hospitals Corporation, in the library, and several days to put it all together—all for a paycheck of $60. It seemed quite arbitrary at the time. What I didn't realize was that exposing posturing was of greater interest to Ross, at least, than was exposing corruption in the hospitals. It was quite rational after all. The basis for pay, that is. It all depended on his interests.

We somehow agreed that I would not be paid less than $75 a piece. After several went in on abortion profiteering, which created a lot of attention since the *Voice* was the only paper with a decent circulation that was writing about the subject, I started receiving $100 per article. Besides, a series on profiteering in private referral agencies had been the basis for statewide hearings which ultimately resulted in a change of law. (When the *Voice* called to tell me that the office of the Attorney General was trying to reach me, I assumed I was going to be sued rather than asked if I would cooperate in handing over my sources so that hearings could commence.)

I was never informed of the raise, but I think the feeling was that I was writing a combination of reportage—that is, I was going out and covering events—and commentary. The reason the work didn't read like news stories was because I placed them within a perspective and took a lot of care with the writing. I enjoyed taking a boring event such as a meeting to discuss a hike in Blue Cross rates and trying to make it interesting and informative without succumbing to the all too frequent solution *Voice* writers chose—telling the reader why the event is something they do not wish to write about in lieu of writing about it. I tried to limit myself to one line of the sort, "It was a rainy, foggy day outside and I had a hangover from the night before." I fact, I tried to eliminate sentences about rainy, foggy days.

Each week, it was I who decided what I would write about and how; the only problem was I could never be sure my piece was being run until I bought the paper and searched for it. I do not think Ross ever knew what it was like to work all week and weekend on a story, to feel the wonderful drain that comes after completing it, to look forward to reading it in print (where it always seems much better than the scratched-out drafts one has gone over), only to realize it's not there.

Since advocacy journalism often involves timing—revealing something before a public hearing or justifying the confidence of people who are willing to confide in a reporter only on the condition that their information will be printed at a certain time—delays lessen the trust one builds up with contacts which are essential if one does not cover the usual events where the press is being courted and the story is practically written, with transcripts of speeches, factual materials, researched bios all put together in a neat packet. The other point about not having a story appear when I expected it to was that I didn't get any money that week since I was paid per piece, not a wage.

At the time, these were minor annoyances which the gratifications far offset. There was enormous feedback, which provided me with a sense of a readership. I was also surprised at the number of people who wanted to get things into the *Voice*—stories, announcements, whatever; it was one of the few places in New York where a single filler could make the difference whether an event or a new enterprise was a success or failure.

It wasn't unusual for me to get home late at night, the phone to ring, and a voice on the other end to ask if this was the health columnist for *The Village Voice* before launching into a story about a vaginal infection she had had for three years and the five gynecologists she had been to, none of whom were of help. Yes, there was a link with a lot of strangers! Which may explain why I did not realize how isolating working for the *Voice* actually was.

The only people I knew at the *Voice* for the first year or two were Ross and Mary. I had seen Dan once or twice on the fifth floor, where I would wait for Ross once a week to discuss my article. I had gotten into the habit of finishing it over a weekend, and late Sunday night, I would go over to the office and slip it under the door, just as I had done the first time I ever submitted something to them. Then I would take Monday off and sleep all morning.

This manner of delivery worked well at the old Sheridan Square office, which had a slot, and even at the new University Place quarters, which did not, for I was able to push the envelope under the glass doors. One snowy night, however, I went over at about one in the morning to slip my piece under only to find that taping had been stuffed between the door and the ground to keep out the drafts. For an hour, I worked on stuffing it through, losing bobby pins, breaking twigs underneath as I remained stretched out on the ground in an imploring position. The few passersby out at that hour had a comradely sense and stopped to see if I was all right. Finally, I decided to leave the envelope half in and half out, hoping that it would not be dissolved by the snow and a bit amused at the disappointment of anyone who spent the effort trying to pull it all the way back out with the idea of stealing something of value. Shortly afterward, the *Voice* got a mail slot.

I had still never had a word with Dan, and the only way I knew what he looked like was that I had heard him greeted once or twice when I was waiting to see Ross on the fifth floor. (Ross and I would talk about a piece early in the week; he would make one or two suggestions, and I would rewrite it and leave it under the door.) I looked forward to my weekly meetings with Ross—they were my real tie to the *Voice*. Once inside his office, I felt at home. It was all paradoxical because part of what enabled me to feel at home was a sense of Ross's discomfort with the world. I felt there was a kindred spirit there, someone sympatico.

Ross was an excellent editor. The changes he suggested were usually subtle but they made a difference; they were always in the direction of leaving things open-ended, something elusive, something nearly but not entirely consummated. His editorial skills seemed to reflect his view that life was complex, multilayered, richly embroidered; he liked to pull things together with an ending that says there is no ending, only a contradictory set of impulses.

An example: I had written a long piece about young radical doctors working at a desperately poor hospital—Lincoln, in the South Bronx. Although the piece had plenty of severed limbs thrown in (there was even a picture by Abner Symons of one spread across the front page of the *Voice*), its main thrust was an exploration of the contradictions faced by an elite group—white middle-class doctors—when they try to renounce their privileged position to become part of the people they wish to serve. Put another way, I was interested in finding out the role of privileged white professionals working for radical change in poor nonwhite institutions.

It was Ross's idea to add after my own ending a final paragraph that showed the irony—the contradictions, the yearnings, the disappointments of the whole experience. For the first time in five years of writing for the *Voice,* I sat down *at* the *Voice* and worked on an ending with Ross. I don't know how many drafts we made until Ross, with sharpened pencil, made the final change. I had written:

> For most of us, a hospital is a world unto itself—rigidly structured, orderly and separate from the outside world. But in the South Bronx, toward the end of the day, when the brutality of ghetto life sends out a call for action, and the victims of violence start arriving en masse at the emergency room—to encounter wandering junkies and security guards [a juxtaposition Ross liked], doctors in uniform and doctors in beads [another he liked]—Lincoln Hospital becomes a microcosm of the hopes, frustrations, and ironies of American society.

Ross suggested I change the last line to "ironies, frustrations,

and hopes of American society." It may have been edging toward
melodrama, but I think it did tie together the piece in a way I would
not have without his help. There are endless examples of this
nature, but the main reason I looked forward to seeing Ross had
little to do with his talent as an editor; it was solitary work writing
at home all week, and this was my one chance to talk with someone
about my work. The human contact was important. With time, we
came to talk more and more about ourselves, and as Ross went
through changes in his personal life, he became less interested in
discussing anything but personal relations.

Since Ross was sensitive, such talks always took on a dimen-
sion of a discussion of the human condition—the inevitability of
loneliness, incompatibility, fears, along with the yearnings and strivings. The "ironies, frustrations, and hopes that are a microcosm of
American life" were becoming a microcosm for Ross's personal life.
He hovered, he spoke softly; he seemed fragile. If a story didn't run,
he apologized; he made me feel that it had hurt him as much as me
(although I never for a moment believed it).

The one thing we did not speak about was money. Curiously,
I hadn't thought much about it myself; I had never had much, and
writing for the *Voice* was merely an extension of earlier days, when
I was a student or when I had low-paying research jobs with prestigious universities. As in the past, there was no need for an expensive wardrobe. I believe that one way to have wiped out half the
Voice staff would have been to impose ties and jackets on the men
and skirts on the women. Things like that never mattered at the
Voice. Besides, I was hardly ever *at* the *Voice*.

There were two fringe benefits that came with the *Voice*.
They had nothing to do with working conditions. Both were social
events—the *Voice* Christmas party and the spring Obie awards. Ordinarily, they would have provided an opportunity to meet some of
the other people who wrote for the *Voice* but did not hang out
there. The only problem with both events was they included not
only those who were associated with the *Voice* because they worked
there, but also all the local politicians, city planners, entertainers,
village literati, critics, artists, Bohemians whose sole accomplishment
was to remain eccentric despite computers. And although you needed
an invitation to get in, once in there were so many people, it was
impossible to locate a fellow writer unless you happened to be standing next to one.

It wasn't always that way; originally, the Christmas parties were held in Ed Fancher's apartment, but when the *Voice* moved to its new quarters, the party was scaled accordingly upward. It was on the unused third floor, where the crush of people assembled to make merry, which meant obligatory chitchat with the person nearest by (since movement was impossible). Sometimes the stranger turned out to be someone whose work you had been reading every week for the last ten years.

The year following the third-floor affair, the entire ritual was moved outside the family to the large barnlike room in the Judson Memorial Church. There the crowds assumed their proper perspective; it was a noisy party, with live music and a general sense of being lost in a purplish gym, where the lighting had gone amok and the food had disappeared. Still, it was manageable for me because by the third or fourth year I had made friends with a couple of other women who wrote for the *Voice* (we had contacted one another independently and seen one another outside the *Voice*, in keeping with a clandestine affair). All that sufficed for comfort at a *Voice* party was knowing one other face.

After the sale to *New York* magazine, the party was held in a chic SoHo gallery. One room was for dancing; that is, the music was so loud that it was impossible to talk, although the less noisy room next to it was not much more conducive to conversation. There were too many faces somewhat along the lines of those seen on the "Bloomingdale's people." There were fewer community leaders, and the event seemed suitable for stargazing. There was a lot of food.

The Obies, initiated as a way of recognizing achievement off-Broadway when nobody else was willing to do it, naturally had a lot of theatre people present. The first years I attended were fun because there was good entertainment. The presentations were held at the Village Gate, where there were tables and chairs and a stage. Since the Obies had a purpose, there was little need to hang about wondering whom, among the hundreds of people, to talk to. Elaine May was the host one year, and quite by chance I sat in the one vacant seat left near the stage. Only when I recognized Alfred Hitchcock on one side of me and Elaine May's husband on the other did I realize I had chosen the seat set aside for Elaine May. No one seemed to fuss, and Alfred Hitchcock seemed benign enough as he laughed along at the jokes.

As the seventies inched along, the Obies became a bit stale. One generally left with a headache and a sense that off-Broadway, along with blacks and flower children, had seen better days. But even if the avant-garde was no longer located in the Village, the effect of both *Voice* functions was the same—to keep the majority of *Voice* writers isolated from one another at the two occasions at which they were all assembled. Theatre fads could come and go, but relationships at the *Voice* remained modeled after that of the therapist and his patient. Never were they intruded upon by an audience.

Although *Voice* writers were anxious for human contact, the competitive atmosphere made it hard to start friendships. Having an attraction for loners, the *Voice,* in turn, reinforced a sense of alienation. At least among the women. Several *Voice* writers hung out at the Lion's Head, but they were mainly men. And then only a certain kind; one would not expect to find Ross spending his spare time there drinking; nor did Jack go there to get drunk and talk about wenches; he went there (and other reporters' hangouts), but he didn't hang out. Bar life was not entirely comfortable for him; one sensed he disapproved of spending afternoons getting pleasantly drunk; and if he didn't disapprove, he himself preferred to hunt down stories than carouse under the head of the hunted old lion which hung over the bar.

Most of the social patterns of the *Voice* people I understand only in retrospect. At the time I was first writing regularly for the paper, I had no sense of the office politics, the divisions among people, floors, personalities. I knew only Ross. Hence when I was approached about organizing for more money, I didn't see how the issue was a "microcosm of the ironies, frustrations, and hopes" of the *Voice*. My attitude was strikingly naïve: if the paper could afford to pay more to the writers, it certainly should. The naïveté was in the "if": of course the paper could afford to pay more.

I had never considered what the classified ads brought in; I had no idea of how much anyone else on the paper made. I think I would have been stunned (as all the writers subsequently were) to know that Dan was taking a salary of $72,000 when I was paid $100 a week. But even without that knowledge, I felt that it was a good idea to check out the possibility of more pay. For me, it wasn't the principle as much as the reality. I was in my mid-thirties, had large medical expenses, no health coverage, no vacation, no sick leave, and occasionally wished I didn't have to write a long piece every single week to get paid. I worried a lot about what would happen if I became really ill.

Once when I thought I needed surgery, I rummaged about for old material that could be resurrected for articles. I found some sketches I had written six years previously of psychiatrists with whom I had worked. I gave them to Ross after changing the actual names. He never once questioned why I was giving him something so different in style and content from my previous work. Nor did I tell him. He loved them, and broke them into a five-part series.

The next week, much to my surprise, the first of the series was on the front page. The people who were interested in the politics of health thought something was indeed wrong with me; they wondered whether I was of sound mind to be writing such trivia. Others, particularly people in publishing, thought that I should stay away from politics and continue in the vein I had just started.

Since the surgery turned out to be unnecessary, I inadvertently had a few weeks' rest from writing. Only then did I tell Ross the real reason why my writing had so dramatically changed. He was very taken with what he saw as an act of courage—to keep a terrible fear a secret and go on as if nothing were wrong. (There was a real possibility that I had a rare form of cancer, and during the period the sketches were running, I had been having biopsies.)

Also, I think Ross really did prefer psychiatry to the politics of health and to health itself. Ross, who was squeamish about blood, was not interested in anything technical. The only time he ever insisted on my cutting something was when I did a piece on men who were having vasectomies; he did not want the procedure described. How like Ross to find the rejection of fatherhood more intriguing than how such a condition can be prevented.

But he pretended otherwise when it was to his advantage. It is now time to tell my part of the story and then to place it in the context of the other women's.

As I said, I knew little about *Voice* economics. I approached the whole subject with the blind faith that came after the paper published a piece that had been slipped under the door without changing a word, and after it continued to give me unlimited freedom. That was sufficient evidence for me that the *Voice* was a place of integrity. If writers were earning very little, I assumed it was because there was very little to give us. I was not then aware of the sale figures of the paper, which I learned only when the *Voice* writers banded together for the first time and someone pointed out that the paper had to be profitable to command a $3 million sale. The profits had to be going somewhere since they weren't going to the writers.

Accountability had been a *Voice* political cliché for a long time. Every institution in the city was excoriated for its lack of accountability to the people; so were individuals, whether they were landlords, bosses, politicians, publishers, or lovers. I had written a good deal criticizing medical institutions precisely because they were not accountable financially to the people who helped support them through taxes and other revenues. The first hospital series I did for the *Voice* concerned the issue of accountability: St. Vincent's Hospital was refusing to share financial information with an advisory board it was, by law, mandated to appoint. The issue of whether a hospital has to give out financial figures finally evolved into a lawsuit. So accountability was nothing new.

However, when we were gathered in Dan's office, accountability became a startling concept. Impatient with the Valentines being passed on to the *Voice* at a meeting arranged to discuss money, I found myself pressing Dan on the issue of accountability. Why not tell us, I suggested, exactly what the finances of the paper were? If it turned out that the *Voice* could not afford to pay anything more, then those of us who loved it so might continue to make the necessary sacrifices to go on writing for it. (There were, in fact, few writers who did not have other sources of income, and so the issue was partly a symbolic one.) I thought my suggestion reasonable. Dan did not.

With a movement unusual for a passive person, he whipped around in his swivel seat and said, "As far as you're concerned, Ellen, if it were up to me, I never would have had a health column in the first place." I was shocked. He said it as if every week, for a year or two, he opened the paper and, ah-ha, much to his surprise, a health column had been snuck into the *Voice* against his wishes by elves the evening before.

The mixture of hurt and anger was overwhelming. It is true that not once did Dan compliment me on my work or show any interest in it. I suspect that he didn't read it unless it was on the front page, which was infrequent. Except for a funny review of David Reuben's book on sex, the sketches of psychiatrists, and a story about gang warfare in the operating rooms of Lincoln Hospital—all of which appeared on the front page—Dan couldn't care less about what he assumed I wrote.

However, I had a different kind of encouragement. Every week I received between twenty-five and thirty responses to my work. Once when I wrote about a new clinic, the director told me that hundreds of patients had sought it out on the basis of the *Voice* piece. So, despite Dan, I knew the column was read. The number of reprints throughout the country, and even outside of the country, was proof alone. It seemed to me that the *Voice* should be proud to be the only paper covering profiteering in abortion and a host of other issues that had not yet gone public in the media. Dan himself might have no interest in women's health issues, but not to be aware of the thousands of women throughout the country who did was incredible to me.

David Gelber rose to my defense, pointing out that he had heard enthusiastic things about the column from many people and that it was one of the few new things in the *Voice*. For no matter how outstanding any single film or theatre critic might be, all the weeklies had film and theatre critics; few, however, had a column analyzing health from a political, economic, and sociological perspective .

Dan went on to say that if I was dissatisfied with what I was getting at the *Voice,* why didn't I see if I could get anything more elsewhere? Nat Hentoff pointed out that I had just had an offer for $2,000 for a piece the *Voice* was getting for the standard $100 I was paid. "Why don't you take it?" Dan replied, looking at me for the first time.

I had a hard time controlling the tears. Afterward I was determined to stop writing for the *Voice*. One might say I took Dan's advice; undoubtedly Dan would say it, eager as he was to take credit for whatever successes *Voice* writers had. After I stopped writing, a collection of my *Voice* pieces, which focused on women and health, was published in hardcover, and the paperback rights were sold for $100,000.

Of course, Dan helped establish me by giving me space in his paper. But I never thought it was as one-sided a thing as he did. I think it was impossible for Dan to believe that anyone who wrote for the *Voice* was not secretly using it and, by easy extension, him. However, when was I writing, I had no idea of a book coming out of the pieces. I was quite surprised when I was approached by several publishing houses (including the one the *Voice* was trying to establish) since I was not interested in doing another book. What I wanted to do was exactly what I had been doing; only I needed some more money. A salary of $10,000 rather than $5,000 might have kept me at the *Voice* forever if it had included health insurance.

It always struck me as ironic (as well as scary) that a health writer should be without health insurance. One of the issues we had planned to take up at the meeting with Dan was ways to provide coverage for those who were not technically on staff and yet were regular contributors. I was surprised at how easily the other writers were intimidated. But then I realized that for few was the money or the benefits a real issue. Dan was right. They needed the *Voice* more than the increase, and he could count on them not to do anything that would force him to become more accountable or less stingy.

Paul Cowan commented after the meeting that when he thought about it, what bothered him the most was that he didn't stand up for me. It seemed like a typical reaction—a retrospective decency, a regret that one could not be as brave as one would have wished. Very *"Voicy"* indeed.

But it was Ross, not Dan, and certainly not the other writers, whose weakness I could not abide. It was Ross, after all, who, along with Mary, had proposed the column, had met with me each week to discuss it. And it was Ross who should have spoken up when Dan said he never would have had it at all were it up to him. But instead what did Ross—the man who had been calling each night before the meeting to find out what the other writers thought of him, whether they still respected him—do? Blurt out, "Yes, Ellen, I would have liked more science reporting in the column." Ross, who could not bear to print that a vas deferens is cut during a vasectomy! Ross, who pushed me into the areas of sex and psychology whenever he could and out of the political area!

I knew as he spoke that none of his words had anything to do with what he thought: that all he could do at the moment was react to Dan; to show him that he was on his side; even to outdo him a bit by implying that he would have wanted more straight science reporting. I called Ross on it right after the meeting. All he could say was that he was out of control; of course, he didn't want more science; he didn't know why he had said that. He never even wanted the column "Science" written by Earl Ubell; he thought it boring.

It wasn't because Dan thought it so interesting that it had gone in. Science wasn't Dan's interest any more than were automobiles. But Danny List, the author of a column on that subject, called "Brakes," happened then to be the distributor of the *Voice*. And Earl Ubell happened to be a name, an acquisition, for the *Voice;* he had been Science Editor at the *Herald Tribune* before it folded and was a television personality.

It mattered little when Dan approached Ubell at a party and asked him to write a column for the *Voice* whether he, Dan, was interested in the subject or not. Nor did it impress Ross that the column—called "Science" in nice plain prose—was the first place where a description of the vacuum aspirator abortion appeared for a popular audience, an article that many a feminist clipped and Xeroxed in preparation for the upcoming struggle to change the abortion laws in New York.

Mary, who did not seem to have any great interest in science per se, was nevertheless sorry when she heard what had happened at the meeting. She genuinely believed that writers should be paid more, and she had always been supportive of my work. However, it was a private thing, not something she would risk taking a stand on with Dan. Yet it was Mary who was the first to tell Dan about the paperback sale; she enjoyed rubbing something about money in his face, particularly when it reflected a mistake in his judgment and a credit to hers.

Just as Mary enjoyed one-upmanship, she also enjoyed being generous. In her own style, I'll always suspect that Mary had a role in my paperback sale, although it was totally unplanned. One Sunday she spotted me sitting on a neighborhood pier that both of us used to bike over to. I was immersed in Ted Kennedy's book on health care and didn't see her as she pulled up on her bike behind me. As soon as she spied the book, she told me about the invitation she had received for his book party at "21" the following week. Would I like to go with her?

Ordinarily my answer would be an automatic no. I don't like to go to parties where I have not been invited and where I would not be comfortable even if I had. However, I had been told by the head of the hardcover publishing house that had brought out my book that it would be a good thing to be seen at as many midtown functions as possible during the period that bidding for the paperback sale was going on. One party with the Kennedys should count for several others, I figured, and there might even be a chance to talk to Kennedy about some of the issues his book had raised. Mary and I arranged a spot to meet ahead of time, since security was heavy and one had to have an invitation.

The affair was loaded with Kenendys, Galbraiths (his height makes him seem plural), Schlesingers, the horsey-looking wives, the in-laws (Stephen Smith pretended to be a reporter for *Women's Wear Daily,* which I believed), and a few publishing moguls. There was a receiving line for those who wished to congratulate Kennedy. When he appeared free of ceremonial efforts, I went over and asked him a couple of questions about health policy. I was particularly interested in knowing whether he had been influenced by a radical health research group in New York called Health-PAC.

As we chatted, I saw from the corner of my eye that a few of the publishing people were eyeing me from the corner of theirs. After the talk, one of them came over and congratulated me. "I see you handled yourself very well with the Senator. Whatever did you have to talk to him about?" I was amused by the comment. It didn't seem to occur to him that I had been talking about the one mutual concern Kennedy and I might share—the subject of both our books—health politics.

What did seem to occur to him, although he didn't say so, was the thought that, "Well, she's important enough to be invited to a Kennedy party [which was false], and if she handles herself with such ease with him, she'll do just fine with Cavett and the others [also false]." But the party, my presence, and my behavior made some impression on the publishing people. Shortly afterward, the paperback rights were sold to the highest bidder for $100,000.

I was still not writing for the *Voice* when Mary suggested an article. For the first time in six months, I considered returning. Undoubtedly, I was moved by her doing something for me that she did not have to do. But I think there were other reasons why the *Voice* became appealing again.

I liked the down-home quality of the place. So appealing was it to me that I never realized how little I felt at home. Years later, it was a shock to learn that Time, Inc.—the corporate media monster that assumed mythic proportions in the eyes of a true *Voice* writer, a place where every word was translated into *Time*ese and people had robot relations with one another—actually was the source of close friendships; people had lunch together, went to parties, got to know each other, as did people from *Sports Illustrated,* and the good old gray *Times* was absolutely raunchy compared to the *Voice.*

No one at the *Voice* wanted to believe any of it. It's amazing how glibly *Voice* people passed judgment on other places. They assumed that if you don't set out a chrome and glass table; don't have a receptionist in front of a semicircular table with good leather chairs nearby; but provide a place where the first impression is chaos and noise and nobody is apologizing for it or asking one to have a seat—then you are being granted spiritual freedom for life. The appearance of anarchy ought immediately to put on guard anyone who is in the midst of a moneymaking institution. It just means that the controls and powers and manipulations are beautifully and treacherously camouflaged. It seems unlikely that there exists a single corporation where the salary of the man heading it is a figure that nobody working with him could conceive. Only in a family can one keep secrets so well.

Yet the informality of the *Voice*—deceptive as it may have been—did go hand in hand with a freedom in terms of writing. However, that was no longer the sole appeal for me. I was returning in a very different state than the one I was in when I left: I was returning triumphantly. Dan had told me to go out into the big world and see how I would fare; it was as if he expected the nearest lion to come stalking out of the Central Park Zoo before I could earn a penny and that shortly I'd be groveling my way back, asking for refuge and begging to be given what I had relinquished.

Few people had ever left the *Voice* because they thought Dan exploitative. (In the early days, when the *Voice* paid nothing or almost nothing, many people left but realized that Dan could not afford to pay them. It's just that they couldn't afford to work for nothing.) Margot Hentoff stopped writing because of the exploitative conditions under Dan in the later years, and David Gelber left after the abortive organizing effort, spending some time as Program Director at WBAI before becoming the Editor of Boston's *Village Voice—the Real Paper*—until it was sold. (Even after only a year, he received a certain amount of money for his shares in the paper, as did all the staff.) He is now taking a crack at television reporting.

David was not someone in search of a father. He had never been able to relate to Dan; he was far too competitive a person to play child to Dan and too old to wish to be molded by him. Impatient and ambitious himself, he could not become another's lackey, even psychologically. Nor could he become one of Mary's boys. And he certainly could not relate to Ross.

There were women at the *Voice* who reacted the same way. They passed through briefly and went on to bigger and better-paying places, often with the encouragement of Mary, if she sensed they had confidence. In the earliest days, there was Jane Kramer, who became a staff writer for *The New Yorker;* then there was Stephanie Gervis, who became the wife of Michael Harrington and free-lances frequently for *The New York Times;* Susan Brownmiller left to go it alone as a free-lancer, and Mary Breasted became a staff reporter for *The New York Times.* Maureen Orth, now a Senior Editor at *Newsweek,* wrote a few pieces for the *Voice* when first she came East from California, using the paper as a showcase before moving on to more adult working conditions.

However, before the sale to *New York* magazine, there were few writers who left on principle only to return a while later. The mechanics, for those not familiar with a candy store atmosphere, are simple: my leaving was never official; nothing had to be done in the way of records when I left since I was never employed in the five years of writing for the *Voice.* Therefore, I did not have to be re-hired. I just returned.

Trouble was breaking out all over again at Lincoln Hospital; it did indeed seem like a "microcosm of the ironies, frustrations, and hopes of American society," and I was eager to write a long piece about it. I returned to the Emergency Room, where I hung out for an entire weekend to get a feeling for the place. I had researched out some of the facts to understand the structure, and I had thought about it all so I could combine the personal impressions—the "eye-witness" parts—with the more objective data and put it all into my own perspective. There are very few publications I know of where a writer has the freedom, let alone the space, to do that. The *Voice* was one.

Again I was impressed with the impact the paper had. Politicians read it; hospital officials read it; in fact, after the story, the acting administrator of the hospital begged me to put in a positive word about his performance and how well he was regarded by the house staff so that he could get a regular appointment. On the basis of the article, I was able to call the Health and Hospitals Corporation and ask them exactly why the man did not have a regular appointment. Was it because of his politics, as he maintained. Embarrassed at the implied threat of more adverse publicity, the Corporation finally issued a regular appointment.

From the time I wrote the Lincoln piece until my permanent departure, there was never any allusion to my absence. It was taken for granted that the bad blood had been washed away as much as it can be in a family. It was just one more secret to bury in the closet. I remained on, "doing my own thing"; however, having made a relatively large sum of money from the book had made me more aware of the writer's market. I now had free-lance possibilities, lecture engagements, and sundry offers for appearances.

I still did not like the life of a free-lancer, and elected to work where there was freedom from hustling and careerist concerns. What I did want was a steady base with some security about the future. I had earned enough money from the book so I could live without working for two or three years. However, it was just this freedom that enabled me to feel I could afford to demand the maximum security the *Voice* had to offer—a staff job.

The pay for a person on staff was then about $12,000 a year, which I could supplement by a few thousand free-lancing to give me the $15,000 that I now needed to live on. I had moved to a more expensive apartment and could no longer get by on $5,000, or even $10,000. Also, I wanted health insurance, and time for vacation and sick leave, and ironically, I wanted the recognition that comes with a staff job. I say "ironically" because I had more recognition at this point than ever before and logically should have had less need of it. But I was beginning to see how intertwined are recognitions and rewards with a sense of self-worth.

I was now more conscious of the woman writer's lot. For the first time, I started to monitor how frequently the male staff writers wrote. (There wasn't a single woman writer on staff; both Mary and Diane were editors.) I was shocked. Joe Flaherty could go for over a month before tossing off a piece, and he wasn't penalized by not being paid, as were regular writers such as Robin, who did not have staff jobs. It was the end of 1973, a time when the notion of equal pay for equal work would have been laughed at by the *Voice* editors, if you wanted to write about it, as a stale issue—*one that nobody disagreed with*.

And yet . . . not a single woman on staff. Only "de facto" staff jobs for women, to use Ross's phrase. I thought about it. When I mentioned to him that "de facto" writers made less than $5,000 a year at the *Voice*, Ross assured me that once he gained control of the paper things would be different. But he was vague as to when that utopian state would arrive, if ever. I wanted to know now if there were any staff openings, and if there were, who was going to get them. Ross squirmed, implying that he would always try to get me whatever I wanted but he wasn't quite in a position to do so yet.

His words were not convincing; they collided with images of Ross at the writers' meeting with Dan. I decided to talk things over with Mary. It was the end of the year, a neat time for breaks. A new year would be starting and, with it, a new job, if necessary. I had the feeling I would get a straight answer from Mary. I was right. She told me that there was no woman who could expect to be put on staff and that she saw little possibility for the situation to change in the near future. Although she didn't say it directly, she hinted that it might be a good time to move on, for my own sake, not that of the paper. I believe she was sincere.

Mary's visit happened to overlap with that of Robin Reisig, who was in the process of researching her story on *Ms.* magazine. What Mary said applied to her as well as to me, and she was in a less secure position professionally. I called to share the information and to discourage her from doing the *Ms.* piece. Knowing that the *Voice* could not offer her any job security, I thought it was an act of perfidy for Ross to have asked Robin to write it. Robin, however, saw it differently and continued to work on the story.

In the following year, five people were added to the staff: Howard Blum, Alexander Cockburn, Paul Cowan, Bob Kuttner, and Phil Tracy. All were men. In Bob Kuttner's case, it was Ross's decision entirely, although he had been writing for a much shorter time than many of the women who were not on staff. However, Bob wrote a column out of the nation's capital, and a Washington, D.C., dateline had appeal to someone who was already thinking in expansionist terms—like "going national." After a brief stint as a *Voice* staff writer (where many of his columns were rewrites of what had appeared in the Washington dailies, but one had to keep up with them to know it), he became an actual Washington reporter by landing a job on the *Post,* giving up the coveted *Voice* staff position.

It didn't matter to me who else was being put on staff, or who was not, for that matter. I felt I deserved it; there was no question in my mind about that. Aside from any psychological nicety a staff job provided, I also wanted to settle down. If the *Voice* could not offer me the modest financial security it offered others, then it was time for me to start looking elsewhere. Which I did. I regretted letting go of the one place that, for better or worse, had become mine, much like a mate. It wasn't until I began to listen to the voices of other women that I came to see the way we had all been blind to the issue of money.

Diane: "Everything that ever happened to me happened by Dan coming down and asking." Diane is not a passive person. She sails her own boat, does her own carpentry, fixes faulty electrical wiring, and can handle a plunger as well as a plumber. Yet everything that ever happened to her at work she sat back and waited for. Her firing was no different. Knowing it was about to take place, she waited for it—for Ross, that is, to gather the courage "to do it to her," her very phrase evoking some echo of a sexual assault.

And now what does she think of it all? She defends Dan totally, sees no connection between how the *Voice* was run—the lack of contracts, working conditions never being spelled out—and the fact that when Ross chose to get rid of her, partly for personal reasons, she was left without protection. He could "do it to her."

For Diane, that is freedom. Unions and contracts and talk of working conditions—do they not conjure up the brutality of the miners' lives on the other side of her mountain range in West Virginia? Are they not associated with the fierce cutthroat competition she saw on Madison Avenue when she first left home? Or is her loyalty to Dan loyalty to the father she never had, the new one who could do no wrong?

If people were organizing again at the *Voice,* she would still be on "the other side"—that of "management." "I would take that position again." When I heard her speak, I was sure it was the voice of her father, keeping a union out of the conservative paper, where he was the Sports Editor; or the Army officer suspecting people who made demands unless they were in positions of authority.

"It's a *Voice* thing, the money. Dan was once poor and had a lot of shames about money, and he never, for all his genius, could cut through them. He still seemed to have all the emotional reactions to money that he had when it was a genuinely risky thing to be head of the *Voice* and all he could be sure of was his own vision." (E.F.)

"But he was right. He had nothing."

"He had a paper that was worth three million dollars and

which he decided to sell even though he knew it would be giving up something he cared about."

"But he could still be living in a hovel. With no security for his family."

This is an incredibly moving testimony to blind loyalty. Dan lives in a large apartment on Fifth Avenue and is a millionaire. He has a family and all the comforts that go with a comfortable bourgeois life. Diane has no job. She still lives in the cheap cramped pad she took when she first arrived in the city. She has no family nearby, no financial security. What are her plans? She will never go back to publishing, for there was only one paper she ever wanted to work for "and that paper doesn't exist anymore."

She is totally apolitical; when pushed, she becomes the reactionary her father was, defending the boss, his need for money, at the expense of the workers' jobs, even her own. But what is one to make of her rage? An anger so strong that it is paralyzing; that if it were to be expressed, it would kill. All said calmly, except for an occasional cough, and the cigarettes being lit, one after the other. Is it masochism? Is it unresolved Oedipal feelings? A woman's need to fail? Fear of success? Is it the ladylike tradition of thinking money dirty, crass, crude? Diane still would not say what she was making when she was fired. "I feel that everyone feels they are making less than anyone else." Is it Diane's way of replying as Ross did when asked how much money he makes, "You can't ask a man that. It's like asking the size of his cock"?

"For myself, as long as it was the job I liked, I had job security. When it became something else, for myself, I didn't want job security anymore." A woman's purity. Can one imagine any man, including the ones she liked—Lucien, for example—saying this? Even Lucien, who also was once a reactionary, a West Point cadet, and who felt he owed his entire salvation to Dan, managed to wind up as a star reporter when Dan was offed.

"Even though the *Voice* is now a different place where you may choose not to work, it doesn't gall you in some way that something unfair happened?" (E.F.)

"Say I had been getting twenty thousand dollars a year in the end, which I wasn't. Say a hundred thousand. No amount of money . . . I don't think . . ."

"Suppose you couldn't support yourself a year from now. I don't know what your situation is."

"Nothing."

"Suppose a year from now the jobs you get would be even less desirable."

"I don't want to do anything I don't want to do. I saw an ad for a course in carpentry. I hope never to work in publishing again. I don't want to be an editor for a horrible publication."

Again, the woman's purity. And the hurt turned into proud defiance.

"There are certain things I'll never do. I'll never in my life write copy for an ad agency again."

"But there's a part of me that thinks that by the very independence you're expressing—that you just want to do the kind of work you want—it's going to make it impossible for others who follow you, particularly women, to ever get the ideal kind of work. Look, your job situation was very good; you knew what you wanted and you got it. That's not the situation for most people. It's almost always a combination of talent and luck and confidence and a variety of other things. I guess what I'm saying to you is if one cares or thinks of that, one can't help but feel that the *Voice* has something to account for. And I don't know exactly where but someplace so that Ross can't do what he did; so that the changes that make the paper a very different place could have been prevented."

"It's really difficult to think of the *Voice* in terms of women. It never became a question at the *Voice* until Ross was doing his thing. . . . No, Ellen, you're talking about the paper after Ross was there . . . If women had been able to stick it out, like Jane Kramer or Stephanie, they would have wound up making money."

"As I see it from the writer's point of view, when you really monitor the paper and go over it in some systematic way, it shapes up like this: when the paper was paying very little, it had women on staff. When the paper started paying more, it had no women writers on staff."

"The distinction I'm drawing is the presale paper, when it really was Dan's and Ed's as opposed to the postsale paper, when it was Bartle's and Ross's. I mean, Ross is enough to turn anyone into a crazy feminist."

"The owners of the paper at that time were Carter and Bartle. They say they doubled salaries. And that they were forced by the sale to sell it to *New York*. You know when Dan and Ed sold the paper it was a very peak time. I don't think they knew there was going to be this crazy combination of inflation and recession at the same time, with interest rates zooming up and all the rest. That would make them quite sinister if they had calculated all that out, because then you could have predicted some of the other things that followed. I don't think they did know. I think they sold it for very different kinds of reasons. They were tired, they sensed things were changing; it was too big once they moved from the old quarters. It's part of middle-aging."

"Yes, that's interesting. After we moved, that's when I stopped seeing Dan. Months could go by and I wouldn't see anyone. You say he saw the men, but only those who were there before. Anyone who came in after the move, like Phil Tracy, didn't get to know him. . . . In the early days, you were totally responsible for your job; you had total freedom; it was like having your own business. Nobody checked on anything. Someone could have flipped out and nobody would have noticed."

"Which is part of what made it a marvelous place to work at."

"Yes, it was. Except for the thing that it was alienating. Because of the kind of personality I have, I was scared of everyone."

Strange. A person who cherishes independence so feels at home in a place rife with secrets and conspiracies, and unspoken hatreds, and terrors and rivalries. Just one big unhappy family, as Dan said. And Diane, the supporter of hip capitalism, where one has the illusion that one is operating things on a small scale, on one's own, without any concern for the profits directly.

"One of the themes that runs through the stories of so many of the people I've spoken with is that people never felt certain they were doing the job. They really liked doing what they were doing, but there was always an insecurity on some level. Maybe that's what happens when you give people total freedom and you don't have some equivalent of a report card, although I wouldn't want to work at a place that did, either. But, you see, I don't think crummy working conditions are essential for running a paper. Nor do I think you have to have a corporate ambience if you pay people a decent amount. Things like that bothered me. It was at a time when it was a real hardship. The working conditions made a difference."

"That's capitalism for you," said Diane.

"Well, hip capitalism!"

"So if you don't like it, go somewhere else."

"But the whole thing is they weren't functioning like they

were part of a capitalist system. The *Voice* was always criticizing others for exploitation."

"When you say the *Voice* to me, the *Voice* is Dan and Ed. Dan and Ed never made any claims that the *Voice* was anything but a business."

"True. But I think they felt it wasn't like other businesses, and they were right, in some ways. It wasn't impersonal, and that was good. You didn't have the feeling of entering a building with gray faces. But, Diane, there really were hard times. Some writers were barely getting by, and they would have to go in and ask Dan for money. There was never any anger. That was Dan's genius. That he was able to exploit people and have them love him at the same time."

"I never signed a contract in my life."

"No contract, ever? So then it's never been worked out about vacation time or similar matters?"

"Well, about vacation. Ed used to come around with a sheet. I got this letter from Ross a few weeks ago. He writes, 'I understand that you're trying to get this vacation money, and Ely and Bartle and I have decided that the severance covers all that.' And you don't deserve anything."

"Didn't *that* make you mad?"

"I was beside myself. I was paralyzed with anger."

"I would be very upset about it in a larger sense. I would hope that things would change so that one day it couldn't happen. There has to be a way."

"This big radical, Bartle. Well. Ely said in conversation that his attitude was, Well, what has she done for us lately?"

"But the fact is no one had any of this spelled out. Many would say that if there's trust in a place there's no need for that. But I disagree."

"All that gets very sticky. If you decide that you're having a nervous breakdown for two weeks and you just can't come in because you've lost your mind, the *Voice* was pretty flexible. I've seen some pretty rough times, and there was never any question about anything."

Sad that so many *Voice* women were convinced that they were so near madness that should they actually get there, only a big Daddy would understand and forgive them and not kick them out. In fact, he might love them all the more for it. With such a conviction, it was hard to demand the kind of security that might have helped fend off mental collapse. Never mind the men who broke down, boozing out their brain cells with alcohol the way a sixties radical might have done it with dynamite.

"Did you have the kind of relationship where you went in to Dan and talked about your personal life with him?"

"I did in the beginning. I mean, I would like telegraph that something was wrong and he would pick up the message. But in the last few years, I didn't see him. I really believe in authoritarian newspapers. You ask me how I did what eleven editors are now doing. I don't believe in collectives."

As Diane prepared to go, she put on her parka, a big one, and her long brown hair fell behind her. She didn't look upset, or even angry, but her voice was shaky. "I was the only one who didn't get a raise when the brave new owners took over."

In all ways—time, dress, her office—Diane had escaped from corporate life. But as it was for Ross and almost everyone else at the *Voice,* the one thing that still remained a secret, an area of shame, was the one common denominator of corporate life in America— money. For Ross, it was like asking the size of his masculinity, and for Diane, too. For she had been one of the first women on the masthead, the first woman editor, and had silently fought it out with Ross, even using the power of her position for sexual conquest. But unlike Ross and the other men, she never thought about the future: her ambition was harnessed to the moment, and when the fighting got dirty, she retreated. A dozen years of a dream come true —and then all coming to nothing, like a small boat capsizing at sea.

It was a different story with Marlene. At least in one crucial respect: Marlene had always been politically concerned. Yet her sense of herself as an artist put her above workers' concerns too. They existed for other groups—poor blacks, poor Latin Americans, poor people everywhere except herself.

Marlene had a position about the differences in salaries at the *Voice;* she didn't defend Dan's making $72,000 when she was making less than $5,000. The evil, she thought, was that anyone should be allowed to make $72,000 rather than that she was making so little. "I don't think Dan should be getting seventy-two thousand any more than we should be getting bigger sums. No one is worth seventy-two thousand dollars."

That may be true in some utopian scheme where we all

barter with beads and paintings we have done, but the general urge toward everyone earning less rather than more reflected an attitude peculiar to the sixties, from which Marlene had not fully emerged. Were it not for the disdain of money affected by sixties radicals and the kinds of people attracted to the *Voice*, the exploitation practiced by Dan would have been difficult to sustain.

Marlene's revulsion for money was so extreme that she couldn't remember what she was paid at the *Voice*. "Five thousand dollars sounds like an enormous amount of money to me now. There's nothing I can do with money except pile it in a corner. I get freebees for the theatre, books from the *Voice*."

When I asked her if she always wanted to be in a dependent position for the things she wanted, she did not see the psychological relation between a woman's feelings of dependency and her sense of authenticity as a writer. Would Marlene see the woman in herself in opposition to the writer if she knew the writer could provide for her? We explored that for a while. And then I asked Marlene if she saw any relation between productivity and making money.

"To me, being assertive is a challenge in itself."

"Do you think there's any relation between money and confidence?" I continued, anxious to discover why four women, all of talent, had wound up without jobs and with less confidence than when they started out.

"If you accept their values," Marlene answered. "I chose to be *above* them."

Here was Diane in another form, but with the same results. Marlene would be true to her ideals, and if she couldn't get by with fidelity, then, and only then, might she compromise. In the sixties, it was easy to have pure politics; every radical did; nobody was going to compromise with corporate America except for the clichéd exception—a stereo set.

At the end of the decade, Marlene felt dislocated. There was no movement to transform alienation into an ideology and ideology, in turn, into a life-style. Power in America—whether it's Dan's $72,000 (actually, quite modest compared to real power) or some other source—might have been corrupting to free young spirits on the move. But women were learning that powerlessness was also corrupting; there was a relation between confidence and power. In this society, power was impossible to separate from money or the kind of recognition Marlene was seeking.

"People don't like to reward you, Marlene, if you constantly

sneer at them; it's rare to be recognized by a group toward whom
you display both contempt and need; the proud beggar rarely receives respect. You want to be published in good places. The *Voice*
was not a sufficient challenge partly because you could always count
on it."

"I want recognition, success. But without money."

"But money is tied into those other things you want. I don't
think you can divorce them entirely. It may be detached in your
psyche, and then I'm not sure. Or else why would the *Voice,* which
gave you everything *but* money, seem so unchallenging? Look, you
just said you don't need money, but when you came back you went
to Dan and asked him for more since your new rent is higher."

"My new rent *is* higher. Otherwise I wouldn't have asked
him."

"It's almost an aristocratic attitude you have, except you're
not an aristocrat. Hence, you have to make occasional token ac-
knowledgments of that world which is giving out the rewards you
seek or else you won't get them. For Dan, it was enough to need
him to insure an extra jelly bean."

Marlene said she didn't know what I meant. I tried to explain.

"Who's going to publish you? Publishing is part of a capitalist
society. All that hustling is there. Even more so. The packaging of
products. It's you they package, whether you approve or not."

But it wasn't just that Marlene would have to be seen at
parties, look a certain way, know certain people, and become a part
of a network in order to get recognition on her own. It was that
she would have to start to think differently in order to write effec-
tively—to reexamine her belief that all power is corrupting, all,
that is, except the power of the written word. She would have to
explore why she felt writing was so pure an act, the only one that
could in no way be compromised. Only by acknowledging the relation between success and money could Marlene understand this
society and, more important, understand herself and why she, like
Barbara, had been passed by.

I knew where she was coming from. First of all, she was coming from a family of no money; she had a gut reaction to class difference, which was easiest to spot with men because traditionally
they were the ones who had or did not have jobs. But through reading and traveling and life experiences, she had glimpsed other worlds
—ones where people acted with grace, responded to the nuances in

one another, and were generally free from the petty concerns of everyday life.

If one is not born to such a world—clearly a more attractive one than the one where money worries consume all energies and exhaust the imagination so as to eradicate the possibility of any vision—one way to transcend one's class roots is to adopt the attitude of the upper classes: a seeming indifference to money. This attitude —reinforced by a classy education—is the perfect coming together of class shame and female bias. The result? A confusion of sensibility and gentility. In other words, Wellesley all over again.

However, while it has always been considered unbecoming for a lady to go after money, it is equally unbecoming for a lady to have none. Only a tough man is enhanced by humble origins. (Or, at least, so it is in literature and with those who taught it in the Ivy League schools of the fifties.) Which is why it makes sense that Barbara, another poor woman who learned about the world outside her own through books, chose bullfighters and boxers—most of whom started out poor—with whom to identify. Both Marlene and Barbara, like a poor Jew who changes his nose and his name, had tried to assimilate; they were not to be associated with the concerns of the déclassé writer; they wanted to be part of the class of serious writers, ones who were "above" the concerns of the hack.

The holiness of the written word is an old tradition—aristocratic, ladylike, and even effete. The tradition was handed down to thousands of young women in the Seven Sisters schools who read literature in the Shakespeare gardens as they sipped May wine and then went into publishing houses at incredibly low salaries for the chance to touch up the words of a writer. To have suggested that they consider the business end of publishing, in the late fifties and early sixties, was so gross as to be unspeakable. Again—the confusion of sensibility and gentility—all those nineteenth-century heroines confusing the man with his manor. But Marlene and Barbara and Robin and Diane were not characters out of Jane Austen. (Although Austen would have understood that one way to rise above class origins, to be upwardly mobile, is to pretend to be above money. But she would also know that it was only an aristocrat who could afford to be!)

Marlene says: "I really believed what I heard in the sixties. I don't want to spend my life making money. I want to do something more meaningful."

Only lower-working-class people and upper-class people seem to think the two—making money and a meaningful life—are incompatible. One suspects that with the former, it is because society does not teach or allow them to combine both, and with the latter, there is no need—the money itself making the money.

It was the bourgeois class, the one of new money, against which all of Dan's "children" rebelled. Nobody thought it déclassé or grubby to inherit or marry into money; at worst, having money through family was considered an inequity of that ubiquitous social umbrella—"the system." Of course, a fair number of the radicals Marlene admired fell into that group, which was to get its come-uppance when Tom Wolfe donned a white suit and took to his pen.

The women who made the most money from writing in the early seventies were solidly bourgeois—they came from money and married it. Not family wealth but a lifetime's worth of comfort and security. Many wrote books about the frustrations of bourgeois institutions such as marriage—books which made money. The women never felt uncomfortable about it. For they had taken their fathers—successful business and professional men—and used them as models for their own careers. Their mothers became models for their husbands; hence, the phenomenon of the husband-manager (who often turns out to be a psychiatrist) guaranteeing (on the surface) Money, Marriage, and Mental Health and leaving the wife free to explore the limitation of the triple M corporation in writing!

The successful feminist authors who wrote in the mad-house-wife genre did not have the experiences of the sixties that the *Voice* women had had—being loners, pioneers, radicals roaming the continents, rootless wanderers in search of men, morality, and the distinction between the two. The "feminist mafia" was composed of women who married young and impulsively, divorced and remarried solidly. Their work experience had frequently been in the world of magazines, public relations, and other fields where to scorn money is to be a fool—worlds which have a profound respect for "making it" and marketing it, worlds where the exhausting ascent of the climber is not considered crass. At least if it is the ascent of man.

Women from these worlds came to perceive with greater clarity, although less vision, than the *Voice* quartet that making money was perfectly acceptable if a man did it and became grubby or suspect only when a woman was involved. For them, there was no confusion between gentility and sensibility; they were too involved in avoiding the lives of their genteel mothers, who, while "kept" by their fathers, missed out on adventure, excitement, and even the sleaziness that befalls "kept" women. In trying to overthrow a heritage that had damaged their mothers, the bourgeois feminist writers became pioneers in the pursuit of money.

Quite a contrast to the situation of the woman who has seen both a mother and father damaged by having no power. For her, it is hard to understand how it might be psychologically important for a woman to gain economic independence even if there is no economic basis for it. A woman whose parents were working class had to be a pioneer in all ways; the world was not a comfortable place. It was with the outlaw that she had the earliest identification —the black, the longshoreman, the teamster, the hard hat—as long as the man didn't come with an attaché case and tie.

Dan understood this identification. He, too, had shame about money, although as soon as his fears about not having enough were replaced by fears of losing it, he willingly surrendered his Bohemian post. But in the paper, Dan continued to push the populist hero, the dropout. However, Dan wasn't so different from the families of middle-class women. It was all right for a man to drop out. But a woman? Perhaps one reason Dan could never offer Barbara or Marlene staff jobs was because he really did not think a woman without independent means should take on the risk of being a writer. A perverse paternalism, it would seem, but I think he was trying to protect them. I think he believed they should get married, and get some security before giving themselves over completely to their work. Dan, like most men, would find it hard to accept the sacrifice of family, particularly for women he cared about. Nor did he seem to want poor people on his paper—people who came from undistinguished families. Richard Goldstein and Jack Newfield had to work harder than those more favorably born, although they were the more legitimate sons of Dan in a class sense.

The women who worked for Dan never appreciated the degree to which gender affected their careers. Unlike the middle-class women—good burghers that they be—they did not always have several eggs in one basket. Which left them without other sources of identity besides the *Voice*—home, family, the very things Dan approved of. Were Dan to write a book about the *Voice*, he might well conclude, as did Brendan Gill in his book about *The New Yorker* (a big unhappy upper-class family), "If we are lucky, we find ourselves with many fathers and perhaps, with still more luck, a few sons."

But I can hear Marlene thinking, "I don't want to be part

of any movement that wants to imitate men. If the aim is to make women presidents of banks and corporations, then count me out. I thought the women's movement questioned a society that produced competitive people. But instead, I'm told, we must learn how to survive like men."

Yes, one grants that that is theoretically true. One would think that the women's movement would have more in common with the counterculture and that feminists would act more like the flower children who rejected their parents' affluence and all that went with it.

Then why are these women writers acting like the sons of working-class fathers, upwardly mobile with a vengeance?

And again one gropes one's way toward an answer. How for the daughters of families where there was a class dissonance—one's parents having never been to school and oneself having gone to a classy college, albeit on scholarship—one way to overcome discomfort over class was to embrace the world inhabited by favorite characters from fiction, the gentler world of sensibility, where one was free from worry over material concerns, where only spiritual impoverishment was to be taken seriously.

True, feminist fiction writers who were making hundreds of thousands of dollars writing about the frustrations of marriage in the seventies seemed to reinforce in their real lives what they questioned in their work. But couldn't one grow to have compassion for that particular split? Those of us, myself included, who started out thinking it was arrogant for anyone of privilege (who hadn't renounced it) to write about oppression and whose politics came out of our activism, had come to see that the poor do not have a monopoly on oppression—tired and homeless and hungry though they may be. And if we cared to look, we were beginning to see that the radical men with good politics—those who cared about the have-nots of the world—often had little understanding of women.

The *Voice* is the best example I know of why women must rid themselves of the seductive but misleading notion whereby gentility and sensibility are so intertwined as to be the same and where the only way to escape is to be one of the boys. Had there been a single woman at the *Voice* with any power who could have offered support to the rest of us—strong and not strong, lonely, and looking for love in our work—we might have wound up in different situations.

Diane and Barbara and Robin and Marlene. Different voices and yet the same. Marlene, whom I've come to know the best through these talks, strikes me as the one most receptive to change. She senses that her politics are stale, yet she can't give them up entirely; that is like asking someone to commit philosophical suicide (her phrase). But she does want to feel engaged again; she does not dream of going off and becoming a carpenter, and at last word, she was taking a course at a woman's school on how to have more confidence.

Some Shift Alliances

Abner Symons

"All of us who are square or straight wish we weren't. An enormous number of people of all ages—not hippies or Westchester types—like the honest, probing, obsessional note of the *Voice*. You don't have to have love for a mutually beneficial relation. There are a number of people who find home at the *Voice*."

John Leo

John Leo doesn't look like the Louella Parsons of the press. He's clean-cut, and his striped shirt and tie hint at the affliction of propriety one develops at a strict Jesuit prep school. Nevertheless, John has an interest in the nonestablishment world; he, unlike other *Voice* writers, had had experience with the best of the establishment press, having been a reporter on the *Times*. Yes, *The New York Times*. While it is a shared opinion among some at the *Voice* (given expression by Mary Nichols) that *Voice* writers are unemployables, the corollary is that anyone who leaves the *Times* to come to the *Voice* is a suspect character, one whose mental health is tottering on the verge of collapse.

John looked perfectly normal when he came to the *Voice* in 1973. Having been inspired by the excitement generated by the annual *(More)* convention—an event that has similarities to the Oscar awards—John conceived of the idea of a press column for the *Voice*. The paper reminded him of a community bulletin board, which was appealing to someone trying to escape the rigidity he had known for so much of his life.

At first, John thought it remarkable how open everything appeared. People hung about on the fourth floor "bullshitting." (John had been brought into the *Voice* by Lucien Truscott, with whom he was sharing a summer house.) "Maybe it's important for people to have some dead time. Bullshitting is often creative." To someone who was not allowed to talk in school, bullshitting may have taken on imaginative aspects that would surprise any kid who spends time on street corners.

But along with the friendliness, John noticed right away

that no one was in charge. He had, at the suggestion of Lucien, spoken to Dan Wolf about a press column. Dan agreed to have one on a trial basis for six months. John was to be paid $150 a column, having made it clear that he wouldn't write for less—a hint to Dan that dissident though he might be, in search of community, bulletin boards, and even bullshitting, he was not an obsequious child. Dan assigned him to Ross.

"He struck me as a very intense, perhaps troubled, fellow" (it was the "fellow" part that made him so endearingly un*Voice*ish in speech) "who seems to have difficulty in answering his phone." However, John was pleased that Ross never messed with his copy, and in May, his first column appeared in accordance with the idea, format, and name he had suggested—"Press Clips." It was to run alternate weeks, which it did until John picked up a paper in September and there was "Press Clips," but with a different by-line —that of Robin Reisig.

Earlier Ross had asked John whether he minded if other *Voice* people wrote about the press and John had told him that he was a writer, Ross was the Editor, and therefore it was his responsibility to decide who wrote what, in accordance again with the fine Jesuit training he had known, where roles were always clearly defined and hierarchy was never questioned.

John was not claiming he owned any one topic; nevertheless, he had thought up the name and format for "Press Clips" and was dismayed to see another name attached. Again he paid a visit to Ross, since reaching him on the phone had become impossible. John told him he felt strongly about the use of "Press Clips" by others. Ross agreed that it was wrong, and the next week, when John did not have a column in the paper, "Press World" made its debut, along with the outstanding debutante of the year—Alexander Cockburn.

John, still a stranger to the mores of the *Voice,* did not even consider that a column which had been receiving good notice would be handed over to someone else without his being informed ahead of time. Nor did it ever occur to him that chiseled features, a clipped Oxford accent, and the ability to drop the name of Jane Austen as gracefully as that of "the Continental press" would be the basis for a transfer of power at the *Voice.* No, community bulletin boards are known for their democratic, even populist feel, not for snobbishness.

But there it was. After a paltry attempt to disguise the snatching away of John's column by sandwiching it in with a different name, no such disguise was attempted: "Press Clips" appeared openly, and the by-line was Alexander's, not John's. John was perplexed because Rosss had said flatly that it would never happen again. By now John knew that Ross was a telephone dodger. But an out-and-out liar, too?

John called Ross on Monday, Tuesday, and when by Wednesday he hadn't returned any calls, John went to see him, only to be told that Ross was busy. John said he could wait. But Ross insisted that he couldn't possibly talk; that he was just too busy. By now John was beginning to sense that "the man was a coward. He can go back on his word, he just can't face up to it."

John decided to write Ross a letter explaining his position: he would like to write the "Press Clips" column. If Ross wants it, fine. If not, he'll stop. Two weeks later, he received a one-line note from Ross which said that it was clear from John's attitude that he didn't like the *Voice* and therefore he was stopping the column.

John then decided to stop all dealings with Ross and to appeal to someone more responsible. He wrote a letter to Dan, who had, after all, hired him. But he received no response. Thinking that the letter hadn't reached Dan, he personally delivered a second note in which he asked if Dan approved of what was going on.

"I got a civilized genial brush-off from Dan with an apology that things hadn't worked out. I was surprised. I considered Dan a unique personality. He doesn't seem a threat to anyone. He's an educated and sensitive man. He's a thinker; he knows what's going on. He and Ed, partially through luck and whatever deals they made, struck a note of journalism that had to be struck right at the time, and they continued for ten years. I was a little dismayed but I didn't want to portray myself as a victim."

All those martyr–victims with blood from the crosses he had had to say penance to, kneel to, pray to, confess to!

John had wanted something less byzantine; something more childish, more amateurish; it was the amateurishness of the paper that had initially appealed to him—the way the mistakes were worked out right there in print; the way the paper allowed its writers to grow and exhibit their growing pains at the same time. The *Voice* had some wonderful stuff and some terrible stuff, and you took your chances when you bought a copy, like a child putting his hand into a grab bag and not knowing whether he would wind up with some silly old toy nobody wanted or something wonderful that a fool happened to discard. There was still a wholesomeness to the *Voice* when John went to work there in 1973.

"Yet it was not appealing to be fucked over by a bunch of amateurs." Particularly by one such as Ross, where amateurishness became something else. For an entire summer, John and Lucien fought over the question of whether Ross should be or had been lobotomized. By the fall, it was becoming apparent that Ross was far from lobotomized; he executed his deeds with the cunning of one whose brain cells are acutely intact.

When Ross made up his mind to replace Leo with Cockburn but could not tell John of his decision, he offered to run a piece John had written months before about dog shit. "I guess he's going to do something for you when he's about to fuck you," John said in retrospect. "Like Napoleon. Whenever in trouble, give someone a medal."

But John wasn't interested in medals or ego messages; nor was he looking for the love of a father. He, like Diane, was trying to escape a conservative heritage.

"All of us who are square or straight wish we weren't. An enormous number of people of all ages—not hippies or Westchester types—like the honest, probing, obsessional note of the *Voice*. You don't have to have love for a mutually beneficial relation. There are a number of people who find home at the *Voice*. Lucien credits it with changing his life; it kept him from becoming a West Point martinet."

Perhaps somewhere there was a hope of salvation buried within John—a spiritual quest rather than a quest for an individual idol. But John came to see the *Voice* as a halfway house, a place with "institutionalized neurosis," even if it was on a community scale. He also came to see that it wasn't merit alone that counted, a revelation that those who have been to good schools, where they were rewarded for being bright, and who then go on to good jobs, where they are again rewarded for performance, have a hard time understanding, no matter how bright they are. And there are probably few brighter and more articulate people who passed through the *Voice* than John.

In no way, however, was John self-advertising; quite the contrary—he acted as if he took orders. Expecting order was his sin: it made him seem square to Dan; Ross didn't know how to break through the psyche of someone who expected him to play a part that didn't hinge on Ross's knowing how the other felt about him. John had a dignity that was uncommon at the *Voice,* and that, too, was confused with squareness. Although Dan may have found John lacking charisma and chic, he was unfortunate in not recognizing that along with the superficial plainness went a loyalty that would not be found in the man who replaced John.

After John was no longer writing the press column, he looked around for other jobs. He was still interested in small community-oriented publications. He considered an editorial position on an upcoming one—*The SoHo Weekly News,* which was trying to become the old *Village Voice.* When he could not get fair terms financially—he wanted an exact 50-50 split with Richard Goldstein, who had offered him a couple of thousand dollars and 30 percent of the shares—he went on to become the editor of a new section at *Time* magazine called "The Sexes."

It may at first appear as if John was doing exactly what he had been destined to do—work for Time, Inc. But it was, on closer inspection, an unconventional choice for him to wind up in "The Sexes"—perhaps a solution to working out the personal and emotional, "the honest, almost obsessional" tone that had attracted him to the *Voice* initially.

It was clear, too, from his choice that John was not so vulnerable to *Voice* judgment: *he* did not consider himself a psychic cripple who could function only at the *Voice,* as so many of his colleagues feared themselves to be. When he was shunted aside, he went on to something else without blaming himself or the *Voice.*

However, when Jack asked him whether he would like to write a piece for the *Voice* once he had left, he said he'd be happy to do so on one condition—that Ross apologize. John had been sucked in ever so slightly in the *Voice* psychic whirlpool; but when he was hurt, he reacted differently from the others; he was too mature, too proud, too alien to be beggarly, and too Catholic not to think of penance. Ross must apologize and he would forgive. But it never happened and John never wrote for the *Voice* again.

Abner Symons

"For a sycophant such as myself there is something dizzying yet exhilarating at the thought of so many new asses to kiss."

Alexander Cockburn

It isn't easy to become a media star overnight in New York, no matter how talented you are. However, if that is the aim, there are certain obvious career choices. First, it is wise to insure yourself of an audience, and there are few safer ways of accomplishing this than by reviewing other writers. Hence, the acquisition of a press column. But not one to be printed anywhere; it would hardly serve careerist aims to have it in *Today's Health* or *Family Circle*. No, be choosy about where the column is to appear.

The Village Voice has always had a shaggy respectability: literate folks read it and write for it. The *New York Review of Books* is mandatory at some point, although rather limited by itself as well as risky, if you wish to avoid the automatic accusation of elitism and cliquishness. Besides, if you want a discriminating audience with a populist tinge—lest anyone come around accusing you of being a West Side intellectual—you cannot limit your writings to the *New York Review*.

(More), of course, is another good choice. Although (or because) it is the gossip rag of the media stars, it is devoured by those whose occupation is to criticize the press for overlooking the working man of middle America. What once transpired between a shopgirl and her *Silver Screen* magazine has now been given a respectability by the TV talk shows—the forum for stars of Harvard, Hollywood, Shea Stadium, and Random House.

One need only switch on the tube to get a worldly sense of gossip—be it Gore Vidal or the Happy Hooker. Even uncharismatic people who glitter far less visually and radiate less irreverence are as much a part of the who's who of fame in America, the pursuit of celebrityhood having become respectable. Even an academic who writes a scholarly treatise aspires to be profiled in *People* and interviewed on "Today."

But it takes somebody familiar with royalty of the real sort—either you're born into it or you're not—to understand how mobile a society America is; how easily one can substitute stardom and have the populace live a vicarious life. It helps to have a British schooling, for there you grasp that royalty is—oh, my dear—a bit of a burden, and if you have pretensions to royalty, you have to present your fame as a bit of a burden—something you disdain but allow out of largesse.

Now, in order to accomplish this in New York, it helps to have a real British accent, gained at Oxford, as well as the face of a choirboy. But even that is not sufficient to guarantee a meteoric rise in the field of journalism, although British accent and blazered features go far even on an imbecile.

When you add to this mounting list of credentials an in-law who owns the paper for which you want to write, a partner who is a real Rothschild as well as a very talented writer, a father who is famous as a radical journalist back home, a fancy apartment seems superfluous; there is already enough for instant journalistic success in New York.

But, of course, there is more. The politics must be as correct as the publication, the pad, the parties at which one is seen in the perpetual ascent of media social climbing. Unlike a pimp, who can get away with a silver Cadillac and multicolored high-heeled shoes, a journalist on the make must constantly be more subtle.

In the selection of topics, two work well: radical politics, particularly if there is an international slant and oil can be woven in, thereby touching all at once on economics, exotic countries, and pedestrian domestic concerns such as fuel for one's car; and gossip about the polite sadism of people in high position in British life, as if a snicker about the banality of upper-class morality can excuse it.

What besides family, education, in-laws, social circles—the obvious credentials—enabled Alexander Cockburn to become a media star overnight without anyone ever suspecting him of careerist intent? Surely not his talent alone, for there are far too many writers of talent floating in the great sea of anonymity. It's worth looking into the kinds of things that are not spelled out on book jackets, on TV panels, on mastheads, to find out what gives a person the confidence to go after what he wants in so calculated a way. Particularly at the *Voice,* where even those few who knew exactly what they wanted had a hard time asking for it. And those who asked had a hard time getting it.

Alexander Cockburn is the only person at the *Voice* who has a "special" salary arrangement, according to Ross Wetzsteon, who mentioned this quite incidentally (seemingly unaware of its importance). It is likely that Alexander would understand more readily than Ross the relation between confidence and special money arrangements. Cockburn is the only one who is paid both a regular salary and an additional amount for each article he does other than than the "Press Clips" column that he so deftly inherited from Leo. Although this arrangement is not widely known at the *Voice* and amounts to very little actual difference (it is done primarily for tax purposes, since Alexander is a British subject), the importance lies with its singularity. Given the psychology of the *Voice,* it would not matter if it were half a pence more. To be singled out in the one area that the *Voice* traditionally has been withholding does not hurt one's confidence.

Cockburn was brought into the *Voice* to head the publishing line the paper was trying to launch after a previous director had left. Immediately, he was given his own office (which not even Jack Newfield has) and an expense account with which to woo authors at lunch. It's hard to say how much serious courting actually went on since the only person Alex seduced into publishing a book was himself. There is something of monumentual splendor in the annals of self-promotion to get a coveted job, use it to publish your own book (based on articles you had already written), and have everyone think the success is due entirely to your genius.

To insure friends on all fronts, Alexander carefully mapped out the critical territory ahead of time, writing favorable reviews for others, such as the adulatory one of Pete Hamill's Christmas memoir; Alex knew better than to cultivate only one camp, and like any good chess master, planned several steps in advance. Dan, blinded by the accent, seemed to overlook that the end goal of chess, as interpreted by Alexander in his own book, is patricide. Only Jack Newfield and Richard Goldstein—immigrant sons with

New York accents who do not masquerade in maroon velvet dinner jackets—were viewed as opportunists by Dan.

Alex, however, was no fool; he saw that Dan was on his way out. (Of course, it was easier for him not to be a fool when he was related to an owner of the *Voice*—Bartle Bull.) He could use the *Voice* books to get what he wanted, since Dan was not much interested in the project anyway. He saw the new people had more power, and even if he personally had little use for *New York* magazine, Clay Felker had far more power than Dan. And in accordance with the rules of chess, with which Alex was so familiar, the goal of the game was as natural a move as that in any game played in an English sitting room with card tables and tea. And perhaps as amusing as wanting to spank young girls if you were a member of Parliament.

But no one in the New York publishing world would notice an act of patricide, no matter how symbolic, any more than one would detect a careerist if he got himself up in aristocratic drag. It would take Alexander to expose himself. "For a sycophant such as myself there is something dizzying yet exhilarating at the thought of so many new asses to kiss." (Part of his column about the sale of *The Village Voice* to *New York* magazine printed in "Press Clips" on June 13, 1974.)

There is a final footnote to the story of the rise of Alexander Cockburn: the fall of Judy Coburn, a name pronounced as it is spelled and less suggestive of bad-tasting puns. Judy had been doing the kind of writing that Alexander admires; she wrote a column from Washington that had a radical perspective before going off to Vietnam, from where she sent the *Voice* its only reportage from that area to balance the continual coverage of "combat in the erogenous zone."

However, as in the case of Marlene, when the time came to round up staff reporters for the new *Voice,* Judy was overlooked. It was Cockburn who was offered the special deals; not Judy, who perhaps had less relish for new asses to kiss.

And when the *Voice* made a decision to send someone to Israel to cover that war front, it was not Judy, although she had requested it since she had spent time there. Instead, Lucien was assigned to go. Lucien, the former West Point cadet who never seemed to recover from the loss of a uniform, explaining that his initial unease as a foreign correspondent was because he did not have a trench coat.

He, like Alexander, had the right training in switching loyalties—be they from the Army to the *Voice,* from Diane to other women, from Dan to Clay. Perhaps it is not by chance; both Cockburn and Truscott were sons of successful fathers (Claude Cockburn is a well-known British left journalist, and Lucien's father, the third Truscott, was a career Army officer), and both came from prestigious schools where authority and uniforms are as much a part of everyday life as bread and butter. How easy it was to switch to buttering up.

But Lucien had a hard time with the new *Voice* regime, and a little over a year after Felker took over he (and Clark Whelton and Ron Rosenbaum) quit.

Alexander, after a brief stint as a movie critic on "Roundtable," a TV talk show hosted by Harold Hayes, former Editor of *Esquire,* acquired a column in that publication called, with classic simplicity, "Crime." In the October 1975 issue, his column was devoted to "Mom and Pop Murders."

Fred W. McDarrah

"By now I felt I was in the hands of a sorcerer. Dan had a malevolent hatred and a primitive competitiveness."

Richard Goldstein

"I hate the upper East Side mentality—power and money. But Felker is no worse than any other owner. Anyone who owns things is likely to be a prick. That's how you get to own something."

Robert Christgau

Fred W. McDarrah

It must have been a surprise to Dan that a boy from the lower East Side, son of a postal clerk, could do it. Actually be the first rock critic in the country. As much of a surprise as the rise of rock; rock was loud, and Dan was losing his hearing. Still, he had his fingertips, and the blood in them told him not to dismiss rock even if he couldn't respond to it.

Richard Goldstein, like Jack, was a graduate of Hunter College and, like Jack, looked Jewish. However, unlike Jack, he had gone on to the Columbia School of Journalism, and it was there that he had his first success—a story called "One in Seven: Drugs on Campus." He was paid $700 to have it splashed on the cover of the *Saturday Evening Post* (an amount he would later earn at the *Voice* only by writing thirty-five stories). His success at the "J" School (as he came to call it) did not stop there; it was followed by a chapter on psychedelic music in the *Velvet Underground*.

Richie had grasped two things: pop art is a natural place for lower-middle-class children to gain upward mobility, and as a son of a civil servant, he could afford to take the risk of becoming a critic in a new field, countering the safety of a civil servant's job— the very word "servant" somewhat distasteful. (It seems an odd coincidence that two other New York rock critics have similar backgrounds: Robert Christgau, the other *Voice* rock critic, is the son of a fireman, and Ellen Willis, *The New Yorker*'s rock critic, is the daughter of a policeman.)

Richie had his share of ambition, but he was not like the other students at the "J" School. The mannerisms of elite institutions had little appeal for the short, robust lower East Side boy,

180

who looked as if, with a few years and a few pounds, he could become the ceremonial master at circumcisions—there was something in the slant of his dark brows that had a hint of the exotic, the far Russian.

Nevertheless, the "J" School was nice to throw into one's bag of credentials in case anyone came snooping for background. It certainly impressed editors. But Richie wanted to write for only one publication—the *Voice,* the place that had spoken to him when he was getting used to the "J," making the transition from the lower East Side to the world beyond. Only at the *Voice* could he be himself and not be looked upon as a freak. "I was too self-involved to be part of the anonymity of straight journalism."

Richie asked Jack to serve as his point of entry into the *Voice.* Jack spoke to Dan, who was impressed with the "J." But when Richie told him that he wanted to be a rock and roll critic, Dan asked, "What's that?" (Only a year prior had the Beatles stormed America, and although Dan knew that they did not represent an entomological species, he very likely dismissed them as a passing fad, knowing that anything British can win the heart of America momentarily.)

Dan could respond to Joan Baez singing softly about eternal themes; rock and roll, however, lacked the gentleness of folk. Yet Richie had accomplishments that were irresistible, if incomprehensible. In June of 1966, Dan sent him to cover an event—the Sound Blast concert. Fred McDarrah was there with a camera, and in the next issue there was a banner, "Goldstein—Pop Eye see p. 66." Dan's cunning again proved correct, and the *Voice* had another first, a precedent for the entire nation.

Richie was thrilled when he was given a weekly column. That he was paid only $20 a week for the four years he wrote the column did not bother him. He hardly had time to notice it amidst the glitter of the rock world where he now hung out, meeting the famous stars of the day. "I got exactly what I wanted." Richie's experience with money had been his father's small but secure paychecks at home, so the small but secure paychecks Dan now wrote out seemed natural. Only his parents thought he was a maniac to have chosen such a career.

Eight months after he had been writing for the *Voice,* Richie got a call from Clay Felker, who was then with the magazine of the *Herald Tribune.* Clay asked him to lunch at the Actors' Club.

Richie thought Felker a strange and arrogant man, so different from Dan, who was shy and retiring and did all his business in his office, never over lunch. Richie was aware of Felker's ambition; as a Midwesterner, he seemed to need fewer cover-ups than his Eastern counterparts, as if he had been formed by the flat and open prairies, where there were few aliens, few others, few differing from oneself. He seemed freer of the poses that were endemic defenses to those from New York.

Felker offered Richie $150 for a column—exactly seven and one-half times the amount he was getting at the *Voice*. Richie accepted. "You're doing very well," Dan commented. By now, magazines from all over the country were eager to interview Goldstein, and when *Newsweek* ran a profile which mentioned that "adventure has its limits. Goldstein is making only a hundred and seventy a week [$150 from the *Trib* magazine and $20 from the *Voice*]," the writer had no idea that the sum was larger than what Dan, Richie's family, and Richie himself ever dreamed he would earn by being a rock critic.

An established success, Richie married in 1967. The ascent into middle-class life was accelerating, but to Richie it felt more like a fall. "I had lived in projects all my life. And the *Voice* was my one way out. But into Bohemia, not the bourgeoisie." Yet there he was. It began to erode his psyche, niche by niche—success. The *Voice* had been the right scale, the place where he felt at home.

Perhaps the time was ripe for a change—away from music, back to the world of social events. When the Columbia riots came— with the blown-up threat of Harlem storming the gates of the classic campus—the *Voice* came of age journalistically: its writers were issued police cards, giving them official access to the drama of the sixties.

Richie had something other than a traditional reporter's eye, and the scene at Columbia—youth rebelling against the authority—was more compelling than rock. He went to Dan and told him he wanted to do reporting; in exchange for a staff job at $200, he would give up writing for Felker. Dan refused. Richie was stunned; his first impulse was to sacrifice his writing career. He thought of becoming a veterinarian, but instead developed a massive writing block.

"I never articulated my resentment or realized it was over money. I just never made the connection at the time between Dan saying no to the money and my inability to write. I felt desperate psychologically. I loved Dan and the paper too. I asked Dan if I could go cover an Angela Davis hearing and he said, 'I know you don't have money now and you're only asking to do it to get out of New York.' "

It was now 1971, and Richie was undergoing a full-blown identity crisis; his marriage was breaking up, he was involved in a complicated love triangle, and even though he felt bitter toward Dan, he went to confide in him.

"Well, you've had an interesting year," Dan told him. "Don't be so panic-stricken. You should write more for the paper."

"By now I felt I was in the hands of a sorcerer. Dan had a malevolent hatred and a primitive competitiveness. 'What you do you do just like Craig Karpel,' he would tell me, or there would be heavy philosophical statements like, 'most people escape from reality. You escape into it.' Only afterwards did I realize that they meant nothing."

For Dan, however, they seemed to work as ways to keep his odd process of invisible domination working; the sorcerer's apprentice spinning, the witchcrafter's ways working. And then came a halt —the writers gathering together to organize.

Richie traveled in from Connecticut for the meeting in New York. He was looking for a way to destroy his need for a father figure and wanted to do what Jack had done—exorcise Dan from his soul. Out of hurt and the sense of betrayal that he had been shunned as a son, Richie decided to write for Felker once again. "He couldn't control me. It wasn't necessary to have blind loyalties to him."

Felker responded by offering Goldstein an editorship at *New York* magazine for $5,000 and $750 to $1,000 for each article he wrote for the magazine. "I no longer cloistered myself in the safety of the *Voice*. I was getting about twelve to thirteen thousand from *New York,* and when the merger came Clay asked if I wanted to be senior editor for the *Voice* at twenty."

Richie accepted. But it wasn't the money as much as returning to a first love.

Back came another *Voice* writer—rock and roll critic Robert Christgau. He was returning for different reasons. He had never had the love-hate relationship with Dan; he had never felt betrayed by him, nor had he turned to Clay for revenge—an eerie rehearsal of the final scene, when all the writers would go along with Clay. Bob, like Richie, had always thought highly of the *Voice*. It, along with *Esquire,* is the only publication he could see himself writing for.

Bob had written for a "real" newspaper—*Newsday*—after he left the *Voice.* He had wanted to reach a large audience, and *Newsday* had a circulation of 420,000. Loyal son of a fireman who got his B.A. late in life at night school, Christgau had an affinity for middle-America, popular culture, and AM radio. His own life-style was closer to that of the counterculture, in contrast to both his father and most of the others at the *Voice,* who sneered at conventionality and lived solidly conventional lives.

"Editorial freedom—the kind I knew at the *Voice*—wasn't a problem at *Newsday;* I was granted it right away. But somehow I hated it. I never related to Long Island people despite the notion that I could. I didn't get much mail and my friends didn't read me." In short, Bob came to see what attracted most writers to the *Voice* —their readership. "You were read by people like yourself. You were engaged in some sort of dialogue, not just cranking out lines when you wrote for the *Voice.*"

As Christgau came to appreciate Manhattan, he, too, responded when Felker offered him a job as Music Editor at $15,000. It wasn't that he wished to live chicly, as one *Newsday* person predicted, "You'll have a co-op on West End Avenue in no time." Bob was intent on preserving his own life-style; he didn't know how long he would ever be at one particular place, didn't want to get bogged down with a life of possessions. But he was planning to get married shortly and wanted a family.

After living in Colorado and taking a six-month leave from *Newsday* to travel around the country, Bob no longer felt like returning to Long Island. "I never fit in at *Newsday.* I was an ornament, and although they were reluctant to lose me, it wouldn't kill them, they knew." When Clay offered him the job, he was happy to return to the *Voice.* Illusionless about its earlier mystique, he had few conflicts over the ouster of Dan.

"Dan sold the *Voice* down the river five years ago and has been milking it dry ever since. This is a unique publication—the only place I feel at home."

While Christgau credits Dan for creating the place, he is not upset that it now belongs to Felker. "I hate the upper East Side mentality—money and power. But Felker is no worse than any other owner. Anyone who owns things is likely to be a prick. That's how you get to own something."

Fred W. McDarrah

"It was my dream job. Sometimes I felt it was so good that I thought I was exploiting the paper."

Ron Rosenbaum

No one seems sure how he got the name "the Dostoevski of the *Voice*," but everyone seems in agreement that Ron Rosenbaum is "in a class of his own, maybe even a Tolstoy," as Robin Reisig put it, varying slightly the generally accepted comparison. With a wild beard, Ron looks more like a religious fanatic—a rabbi who goes around burning flags of Israel because he believes in waiting for the Messiah rather than a state born of human planning. Something all too rational about that. And besides, there are always Hadassah ladies lurking behind Zionism, and one suspects that behind the prophetlike beard there is an acute social observer.

Before Ron started writing for the *Voice*, his biography was suprisingly straight. He grew up in Bay Shore, a Long Island suburb known to New Yorkers as the town en route to the Fire Island ferry. It was mainly a town you got out of in a hurry. Ron left when he took off for Yale to study English literature. Upon graduation, he received a teaching fellowship. Suddenly, in the middle of the term, he took off, as if the ferry were about to pull out. The only Yalie remnant he grabbed with him is the six-foot scarf, and then, one suspects because the royal blue is a perfect match for his orange beard—both colors suitably unsubtle and flashy.

In the summer of 1968 Ron had covered the Chicago convention for the *Suffolk Sun*. Back at Yale, poring over umlauts and ablauts in the Harkness Tower, replaying the streets . . . he leapt from Middle English right back to the sun—the *Suffolk Sun*.

As the summer approached, Ron saw an ad in *The Village Voice* for an Assistant Editor on the *Fire Island News*—a summer

186

weekly that specialized in who was the guest of whom and ads. Ron took the boat over, and by the end of the season he was the Editor. The paper had one crucial reader—Rhoda Wolf, who mentioned Ron's name to her husband. When Ron wrote to the paper asking for a job, he was not a total stranger.

Dan sensed Ron was special; he was straight and he was not straight; he had Yale but he had Fire Island; he knew literature (one can only surmise what the reaction of Dan, who never graduated from college, must have been to someone leaving a Yale teaching fellowship for a job as a journalist). Ron had other habits: he turned on, he seemed familiar with what was happening—a Yale hipster. Better than Harvard, which any genius—even a Jew—could impress. Yale was less of a cliché, something new for Dan; it was a bit intriguing, the place where all the corporate businessmen and bankers came from—the ones who became more conservative after college rather than more liberal—the Tafts rather than the Kennedys.

It was the sunset of the sixties—September, 1969—and Dan was already sensing the need for something new, the Kennedys and Don McNeil now all vivid victims of the decade. Ron looked as if he could survive. Dan hired him on the spot. Ron was probably the only person in *Voice* history to get a staff position without ever having written a single word for the paper. However, someone had to go, and Joe Pilati was the one. Joe had been covering the hip beat to some extent, working as a reporter under the tutelage of Mary Nichols. Joe was liked by everyone and is now a reporter for the Boston *Globe*.

Ron didn't worry much about Joe; he didn't know him. Nor did Dan, who was more interested in the new talent. Dan had a precise ability to spot flaws, and Ron found that coming in and talking about a story was valuable. Only one or two remarks by Dan and a story would click, take on a shape. "It was his passive directness." On the other hand, Ron considered Ross passively indirect, manipulating writers all the time with a quiet troubled air. "He had to say 'terrific' before he could criticize, and he had to tell you the eight other writers who could never do the story you did before he managed to get out what he didn't like." While Ron granted Ross his brightness, he preferred to work with Dan. "He never condescended to you. He would just cock his head a little and know you're stirring over something."

Ron enjoyed the office squabbles as well as his sessions with Dan; it all seemed part of family life. He hung about listening to Mary and Jark argue: "They like hating each other; Mary likes making trouble, finding out where people are misbehaving." And Ron liked watching. He was one of the few *Voice* people considered a creative writer (as opposed to a reporter) who hung around the premises. Of course, he didn't do his writing when others were around. According to mythology, he wrote late at night, after "running"—"I never jog"—several miles around a gym and then returning to his home, located across the street from the *Voice*. His own rooms were eye level with those of the paper. At night, he might turn on and then decide where to work—at home or at the *Voice,* to which he had his own key. People treated Ron's working habits with much the same awe they reserve for the dying; the mystery of genius invokes its own fear.

About once every three weeks, Ron produced a story for the *Voice;* every week, however, he picked up a paycheck. Because of the relaxed schedule, he was able to write regularly for *Esquire,* whose editors spotted his talents early on. The *Voice* was a dream job; like Diane, Ron had found the kind of thing he had wanted to do all his life before he actually got to doing it. But unlike Diane, he felt totally at home.

As with Cockburn (and in contrast to Richie and Jack), Ron was given total security from the start; he was never told he had to prove himself, was never kept dangling, which may be why he enjoyed his work. "It was my dream job. Sometimes I felt it was so good that I thought I was exploiting the paper." For the few people as fortunate as Ron, the question of talent is not as simple as the other *Voice* writers believed. That is, if you are told you are the Dostoievsky of the *Voice,* if you are paid to write whatever you want as frequently as you choose, if you are given preferred treatment—the treatment of a genius—it is a lot easier to develop whatever talent you have, small or large.

There is, of course, nothing criminal about being talented; it isn't Ron's fault that he was born "the Dostoevski or perhaps Tolstoy of the *Voice.*" Except . . . people who are labeled geniuses tend to think they should get preferred treatment; that there is no need for them to concern themselves with the plight of the others who have either less talent or less opportunity to develop it but who are nevertheless equally essential for the existence of a publication like the *Voice.* Not all readers read Ron; there are an equal number who bought the paper only for Jill Johnston or Jack New-field or Nat Hentoff and didn't want anything as oblique as Ron's writing. Many readers want something more pedestrian, more to the point.

The trouble with having a dream job is that dreaming is so solitary; it doesn't include others. Both Ron and Diane made their adolescent fantasies into dream jobs—as if a magician taught vocational guidance. For both Diane and Ron, Dan was the real magician who had made the fantasy, the dream, come true; it was Dan who had made the *Voice* home instead of West Virginia, an advertising agency, or Yale.

Yet there was always a suspect character lurking about, one without backbone, one who lacked the heroic qualities Diane and Ron admired. Loyalty was the core of their faith; both doubted if Ross were capable of it.

Ron and Diane had chosen wisely, and they were loyal to the person who had enabled them to feel free, to do what they wanted; they appreciated the privilege of a dream job. It was all because of Dan, Ron believed—a strangely myopic vision for a visionary. Although several years separated the points at which Diane and Ron started working for the *Voice,* Ross was no threat to either at the time each started; he still had no power. It was only when Bartle and Carter came in in 1970 that Ron and Diane sensed change was in the air. Still, life went on as usual from day to day—Dan was still there, and that was the main thing.

Ron considered Bartle and Carter "ineffectual and cheap, getting in on funky reality for good dinner conversation." That pissed Ron. Funk was serious. Not camp. But funk. Never saying you jogged (as he knew all his Yale classmates did), but "ran" instead. In fact, Ron didn't "do" anything any more than he was "into" things; run and leave it oblique; don't spell out the refer-ences; treat life as if there were narcs nearby; things are clipped, not quite to the point; sign your pieces "R"—close but not spelled out. Funk is a world to half live in—a world of the borderline—that's what funk is all about—lots of style all messed up with great irreverence—American icons, genuine shabbiness and warmth thrown together. You couldn't use "funk"; you couldn't go slum-ming in it or make it into a plaything because the straight world bored you. Funk was closed to Bartle Bull and Carter Burden.

To Ron, Bartle was a "spoiled rich brat. He couldn't get the

Voice book line going and he resented self-made people like Dan. He had never made anything on his own, but at least Ed was around to bail him out with the business end. But it galled Bartle and Carter that they couldn't show results. They had to bring in a heavy like Felker. Felker was intrigued with Dan. Felker had offered people jobs who had turned them down to write for the *Voice*."

More powerful than the power Felker represented to the "two rich kids" was that he was someone who lived the way they did, traveled in their world. It was uncomfortable for Bartle to be down at the *Voice* alone, where nobody trusted him and in defense immediately stereotyped him as a spoiled rich brat. He might as well be out on a safari, so alive with mistrust were the creatures around him. It didn't really matter that he had been involved with radical politics and worked for Bobby Kennedy and Carter. What counted at the *Voice* was knowing something about Village life from the inside out. Bartle was the first at the *Voice* who was real upper class and did not come to the *Voice* in search of downward mobility.

Few others at the *Voice* lived a counterculture life-style; Don and Ron came the closest, but even they were only ambassadors to that world, and Dan and Ed had become millionaires, living an affluent life-style. Nevertheless, they understood the Village; in their souls, they were Bohemians. And Dan had once been poor. He, above everyone else, understood upward strivings; they were the key to the whole psychology of the *Voice* family, even when they went in the reverse direction. This was the one thing Bull would never understand no matter how much Marx he might read; it was too abstract, too disconnected from his life. He really believed that everyone wanted to go to parties in the Hamptons; and while it was true that almost everyone at the *Voice* would have liked a house in the dunes, there was a genuine revulsion for what the Hamptons represent. Bartle was too literal about the East Side mentality; it was easier to make the Village into a metaphor than to do it with his own turf.

It required a Dan or a Ross to understand that strivings contain conflict and contradiction, an urge, a pull toward the familiar, that which is closer to home, whether it be funk or Fifth Avenue; and a countertug toward the unfamiliar, the exotic, the alien, the other, that which one never knew.

Ross wanted it more than he didn't—the power, the glory,

which he could convert into sexual currency. Ron became convinced that Ross had started to enter secret negotiations with the "enemy" almost a year before Dan was actually ousted. There was a long graffiti poster on the fourth floor, where *Voice* people recorded running dialogues with each other; one week it might contain many little jabs at Mary about the mafia, which she took in the spirit it was intended—a whimsical bit of affectation. Ross, however, started to take the criticisms seriously and tore down the poster. Ron believes he did not want people to know that he was working with Bartle. Ross had to act quickly and decisively, as one would when one made up one's mind to do a dastardly act. Get it over as efficiently as possible. Ross suffered; he did not like to have to think in terms of efficiency; it was antithetical to his nature. But once rid of Dan, he no longer would have to.

There was a dinner with Bartle at Lutece. (It was another burden to Ross that he was not free to brag about all the fancy places the new people were taking him to.) "He just went tiptoeing down the corridor of the fifth floor to Bartle's office, which did not remain Bartle's for long," Ron recalls. When Clay came by one day, he ordered Bartle down to the floor that had remained unused and unrented (except for its momentary function one year as the place for *The Village Voice* Christmas party). Now it was virtually boarded up. "When Bartle was ordered to 'the third,' it was like ordering somebody into exile. Jack and Paul offered to leave the room, but Felker replied that there was no need. 'We'll take care of it now.' "

To Ron, it may have been the executioner who was now taking over, but to Ross, who had suffered countless humiliations with Dan, it was a savior. For years, Ross was in search of an authority figure; he thought he had found one in Dan only to realize he had been deceived. How happy he now seemed to see the new father act with directness; Clay didn't appear cruel; he was what Ross wanted so badly to be—a man who could do things without feeling tormented, a person who was not a slave to his psyche. But Ross wasn't quite up to Clay. And so he continued to get into trouble.

Marilyn Webb had asked to go to Houston to cover the Maharishi Ji event. Ross agreed to send her and gave her $150 in advance. When she presented him with $880 worth of expenses for her story, Ross said he couldn't reimburse her but that he would get the money for her in the form of advances for other stories. Marilyn pointed out that that was not the agreement; Ross argued it was. But Marilyn had proof that Ross had offered to cover all expenses and presented the paper in which he had written it to Dan. When Dan saw it, he agreed to pay, even though he disapproved of such extravagance. Ross was humiliated once again.

Dan began to hear more talk about Ross—stories about money and women. Rumors followed Dan around at parties, like shadows, about what was going on in the front office. Dan spoke to Ross, who was, at the time, feeling depressed and self-destructive. But he couldn't bear to leave his daughter without a father. Such statements were part of the compulsory sensitivity that Ron couldn't tolerate. As soon as he saw it hinged to the desire to undo Dan, Ron started to fight back.

Meetings were planned; there were to be secret calls to decide what to do about things. It was becoming essential to know where everyone stood, to make each person spell out his loyalties. The rites of tribes and secret societies were not lost on Ron—Skull and Bones at the Szechuan, located on MacDougal and Bleecker, right in the heart of the Village.

Ron planned to interrogate Ross amidst the tea and red wallpaper. Initially, it was thought that Ross should not be invited at all; the meeting should be devoted to planning what to do about Ross; to spelling out for once how Ron felt about Ross—how he suspected him of collaborating with the new owners to get rid of Dan and Ed. But there were others who refused to exclude Ross; he had been a member of the family (no matter how lapsed) for too long; if he were erring, he should be criticized.

Ron wanted Ross to commit himself publicly to saving the jobs of Dan and Ed. There was still almost half a year left until their contracts expired; plenty of time for negotiations. "We are all unanimous about retaining Dan and Ed," Ron said aloud in the Chinese restaurant, focusing on Ross as he asked for a show of hands. Everybody turned toward Ross. Ross raised his hand with the others. One week later Dan and Ed were fired.

A call from Felker's house in the Hamptons went out to Ross, who now had himself a house in the Hamptons too. (Goodbye to mosquitoes and family on a run-down farm in Vermont.) Felker grilled Ross about what went on at the restaurant and subsequent meetings. Ross gave a "laundered Mark Antony account, telling Clay that Dan was a passive genius; it might seem as if he is doing nothing, might look as if he is doing nothing, but actually . . ."

Ron couldn't bear it any longer; he had to confront Ross on a one-to-one basis—the kind Ross understood. Ron accused him of being a collaborator. Ross admitted he had mixed feelings about Dan. But Ron wasn't talking about feelings; Ron was talking about actions—Ross's acting in concert with Bartle. Ross was upset that others could hear. Like a civilized spouse in the midst of a fight closing the door so that the maid doesn't overhear, Ross requested they move. Ron continued to scream at him that he had been telling lies for a long time, one after another, and because he was weak he had to lie about his lying.

Ross felt the sting of the accusations. Had he killed off his father (making it a homicide this time around instead of a suicide)? Didn't Ron understand that such implications were driving him crazy; that he, Ross, was suffering a great torment, and that Ron was not the only one with feelings of regret? It was not as if he were enjoying it all—this killing off of old friends, family figures, fathers. It had made him . . . well, let's just be polite and say "hors de combat."

A little less than a year after this conversation, Ron walked up to Clay Felker, told him he was destroying the *Voice,* and tore up his paycheck in front of him. He was the first writer to leave the *Voice*—a dream job—since the take-over.

Shortly afterward, Ron's work was featured in *New Times,* which is run by George A. Hirsch, originally co-publisher of *New York* magazine, but whose only present connection is that of a stockholder.

Abner Symons

"In the spring of '72, I had a very intense relationship with someone who for about six weeks got an occasional piece into the *Voice* because of my relationship. I went with her for about a year, but for about six weeks my editorial judgment was confused by the fact we were going out together."

Ross Wetzsteon

Ironic that the man who winds up "hors de combat" started his career as a free-lance writer for *Playboy, Cavalier,* and other men's magazines. After six or seven years of free-lancing, Ross came to *The Village Voice.* In the beginning, he did proofreading one day a week for $50. It was a lowly job, requiring patience and a sense of the meticulous. Ross did it well, but his talents exceeded it.

After a few months, he was given a writing assignment by Dan. Ross's first piece was an antipoverty story "because Dan liked such stories." After six months of writing to please Dan, Ross felt he could assert his own interests, which were more literary, closer to books. The time was 1967, and the *Voice* was starting to expand. So was Ross's family, which now included a daughter as well as a wife, making income more imperative.

Having moved from proofreading to writing, Ross was able to slide into editing without much fuss. By 1970, he was one of the two most powerful editors of the paper. Of course, there was Diane for the Back of the Book. But she didn't really count as an editor. Reviews were either good or bad, accepted or rejected; little editorial talent was involved. Her main job, as Ross saw it, was the layout of the paper. Along with the barely discernible upward movement came increases in Ross's salary, as quietly granted as were the changes in position.

When Ross first came to the *Voice,* his annual income was $2,500; by 1970, it had reached $10,000; raises went in hopscotch jumps from $25 to $30 to $35 to $65 for the drama reviews he was writing regularly; in addition he was paid a modest salary as an editor. "I believed naïvely that the raises were based on a fair portion of the profits and that Dan and Ed were fair and generous people."

Ross shared with Dan a myopic view about money; both having experienced financial struggle, they found it difficult to see anything but struggle in the lives of others. What is peculiar about a personal sense of deprivation (shared in varying degrees by most *Voice* writers) is the extent to which it blinds one to recognizing change. So strong is the desire, the need, to see oneself reflected in another in order *not* to feel alien—to make a collection of aliens a family—it became impossible to perceive that someone had finally made it and was no longer in a down-and-out position.

When Dan and Ed, the once penniless fathers of the paper, sold it for $3 million, people remembered only the years of struggle. Even Dan and Ed seemed to function as if everything were shaky. The move from the old rickety building on Sheridan Square to the solid new quarters on University Place unsettled Dan. At Sheridan Square, people were on top of one another and Dan could hear everything. Unaccustomed to separations cemented by walls rather than by himself, Dan started to lose his hearing.

Ross saw that Dan was also losing his interest in editing; Ross was now reading 95 percent of all the manuscripts that came in. Dan as Editor in Chief was a charade; it was Ross who was making all the editorial decisions as well as doing the reading. Dan had said he was the "glue" of the *Voice;* that he had no discernible function; if he were on vacation, there was nobody who could duplicate his job. The only concrete things he now did were signing the pay sheet, opening and distributing the mail, and talking about the front page with Ross and Fred McDarrah or Abner Symons, the *Voice* photographers.

Dan's psychological presence defied job description, yet people believed the paper could not have survived without him. Dan was the conversational guru for a generation of writers. Such characterizations required translation into the specific when Dan presented himself to the new owners—Carter Burden and Bartle Bull. They were told that Dan was the only person in New York who could get people to write for so little—people of talent and originality. To the two young millionaires, that was a talent far removed from a guru's; it was the genius every financial wizard wished to possess. Any man who can exploit people and have them think he is wonderful is no mere conversation guru. He is a very shrewd businessman.

Genius that Dan was, he didn't seem aware that his magical powers depended on his being in control—on owning the paper. According to the conditions of the sale, Dan and Ed had a five-year contract that might or might not be renewed. The decision was no longer theirs, however. Dan started to think about it. It seemed odd to be employed by somebody else on the paper he had created from scratch. Suppose the new owners were as arbitrary about hiring and firing as Dan had sometimes been. There was a challenge to security that no amount of money could overcome. Dan was still a victim, having exchanged the money insecurity—which had made the $3 million sale irresistible—for a new and even bigger one—uncertainty about the future. Would he be kept on, renewed by two young rich kids who had never built anything by themselves?

"I'll never stay here that long," Ross recalls Dan saying after the sale, as if he already envisioned his own undoing and planned to avoid the humiliation by leaving voluntarily. "I hate this place so much. I can't come in another day." But even Ross, the sole person to recall such speeches by Dan, thinks they were the words of a frightened man and were not to be taken seriously. Often such sentiments were uttered right after a particularly intimate talk with a writer whose sense of himself had just been restored. Dan *knew* he still had an important function. But suppose in five years . . . ? There was always that question to contend with now.

Meanwhile Bartle was wondering how he could get into a position of real power, not the phony one which would exist as long as Dan was there. And Ross was beginning to wonder about a change which would relieve him of doing all the work while someone else got the credit. It was in his interest to line up with Bartle; they had a mutual goal. But just as Dan could not foresee his own mortality in selling the paper to Burden and Bull, Ross couldn't see that even if he succeeded in getting rid of Dan, he might not inherit Dan's job, or keep it. Now there was another person who was out for power; another person who had lost a father when he was young—Bartle Bull. Yet neither Ross nor Bartle alone could get rid of Dan; there was too much guilt. And Ross understood Dan much better, partly because they were of similar sensibility.

Carter and Bartle felt the paper was becoming stale; it needed change. Dan could not abide that. "It was," said Ross, "like a father of a young girl telling her you can't date—you're only twenty-six." (An interesting observation coming from Ross, who would later write about the mixed feelings he would have when his own daughter lost her virginity; how he would, of course, want her to grow up a woman but how simultaneously he would want to kill the bastard who made her into a woman, feelings evoked when he saw his daughter read on her own for the first time.) Bartle was being put into the position of a twenty-six-year-old woman forced to be a virgin; he still had, despite his ownership, little control over the paper. Dan and Ed remained the couple in charge.

"Some sentences I'm not going to let you quote unless you quote them entirely. When you ask me what I think of Dan, I'm going to insist that the sentence begin, 'Dan was one of the wisest and kindest people I ever knew.' There was a combination of deep skepticism and kindness and apparent openness that led people to really feel they wanted to do their best, to really strain because approval meant so much and was really so slow in coming. This combination of someone you admire very much and at the same time is very withdrawing elicits enormous amounts of self-propelling motivation to fulfill what you think will satisfy him. Over and over people knock themselves out.

"What happened historically is people would come to the *Voice,* do extraordinary work for a period of time, and then suddenly disintegrate. To sustain this kind of relationship over a long period of time is just too emotionally draining. If you think of yourself as a daddy or a shrink—as a support—you can elicit good work over a short period of time. But as in any supportive therapy, you manipulate and exploit people and they have to rebel.

"I really think at the root of Dan's personality is the absence of any human feeling for people. I think this is masked—that's a terribly unfair thing I've just said. When he sold the *Voice,* he didn't realize the extent to which the sale involved a loss of control, that he was no longer a free agent. At first, Dan and Ed thought they'd retire. About a year and a half before the five-year period, they heard they might not be renewed. They withdrew without letting anyone else take over. Bartle and I felt frustrated. Ostensibly we were editor and publisher on a day-to-day basis. But we weren't allowed to make the changes that we considered would make the paper grow. I was not given authority to change those parameters.

"Everything was so psychological, so familial, so political, so manipulative. None of this was ever aired, but I'm convinced in my heart that most of the bad things that came out about me were planted and orchestrated by Dan and Ed because, for whatever reason, Dan didn't want me to replace him and he knew Carter was thinking that way about him. I saw very explicitly how Dan went about trying to discredit Bartle. He had such an abiding self-hatred that his basic enjoyment out of life was manipulating people. He enjoyed turning people on, turning them off; some people like to mold clay. The thing that would most astonish his most reverend disciples is that X would leave the room and tell you Dan is the greatest person and Dan talks about X right after. It's that detachment and manipulating me because what he's telling me is, 'Ross, I'm closer to you. I'm confiding in you as X confides in me.' That feeling of being the special favored one. He was very good on that."

Ross—a fraternity boy at Cornell, fresh from Montana, studying engineering, working hard for straight A's. Finally he drove himself to a nervous breakdown, which allowed for a shedding of the old self. Once re-created, Ross turned to literature and writing, and started to make friends with the other "literati"—Eastern boys like Ron Sukenick and Marty Washburn and Dick Schaap.

Now, years later, there was another self to shed—the overworked Ross from the old *Village Voice.* After Felker took over and Dan was gone, Ross moved into newly renovated quarters—a large office which he lined with cork. On one wall hung a map of the Hamptons; it had two circles—Clay's house and his. On another were the covers of the new *Voice,* one next to another, with the large cover "theme" staring out into office space. Outside his room was his secretary; Ross had never had his own secretary, but now there was a woman to spare him the bother of telling callers he was in a meeting when in fact he was discussing his private life with an old writer friend.

Ross started to dress differently. He cut his prophetlike beard —allowing Ron the distinction of looking like the house religious fanatic. His hair was now trimmed, as was his neatly tailored suit, nipped slightly at the waist. Gone were the old loose corduroy pants and the T-shirt. It was strange to see Ross in a seventies version of the man in the gray flannel suit (the attaché case the giveaway detail). He would be the first to recognize costume and how easily we can be fooled by snatching an image from popular culture and mistaking it for substance.

And yet there he was—running out of his office with a file card in hand, holding it up and asking, "Guess whom I had lunch with. Gloria Steinem. Gloria Steinem." Ross gaining a feeling of authenticity through an attaché case and Gloria's telephone number. There was other VIP paraphernalia: editorial cover meetings, conferences, lunch dates, expense accounts. He was on the brink of the major leagues, along with Dick Schaap; soon he would be able to call anyone and get them on the phone; never again would he be rejected. The whole world has to love you when it needs you and you have the power to do things for people. Doesn't it?

A period of rehearsing had preceded this new Ross. The metamorphosis had not taken place overnight; only an attaché case can be acquired so quickly. For a long time, Ross had been preparing for power—slowly, quietly, accelerating with small increments. After the sale to Burden and Bull, Ross expanded his friendships with women writers along with his editiorial duties. His own marriage was going through a difficult transition, and he needed friends. He and his wife, whom he had known since his college days, had purchased a Park Slope brownstone, had a farm in Vermont, an adorable baby daughter—everything an up-and-coming editor should have. And yet the closer he came to the ideal image—the "shoulds" of life—the more restless he felt. Part of him understood that as the human condition—all the existential feelings that were too clichéd to even utter.

But there was another part less prone to philosophizing—the part that had always fantasized about something different, choices, freedom, experimentation. Ross proposed that he and his wife enter an "open marriage." She agreed; it seemed better than none. And then, as often happens with open marriage imposed upon one partner, Ross left, having used the open-marriage period to make a transition.

For a long time, Ross was lonely. He lived in various sublets, taking his child for half of the week while struggling with the gaucheries of dating the other half. Ross was emotionally monogamous and sexually curious; he wanted a constant at the end of the day—the same face, the same furniture, the nest, the hearth, the home. It didn't matter what name you gave it.

"In the spring of '72, I had a very intense relationship with someone who for about six weeks got an occasional piece into the *Voice* because of my relationship. I went with her for about a year, but for about six weeks my editorial judgment was confused by the fact we were going out together."

"I take that to mean you published her."

"Yeah. I realized I made a mistake. People told me. I finally came to my senses. I admit it openly. It was a horrible mistake."

"Was it horrible because her stuff wasn't good and wouldn't have gotten in otherwise?"

"Toward the end, I gave it to Diane. I realized I shouldn't edit it. It was marginal. Looking back, some of it was awful, some of it was pretty good. The question was I lost . . . Since that time, I've nothing to do romantically, sexually, with anyone who has had an article in *The Village Voice* except the lady I'm now living with. And I accepted that article before I met her. I dated several people."

Ross then mentioned four New York writers, adding, "I feel so humiliated having to go through a list of my dates. I was in a period of extreme loneliness."

Ross had maneuvered things so that he was the victim, not only of loneliness but of interrogation. Yet it was Ross who had brought up the entire subject.

"One of the things I'd like you to do, one of the things I'd like to talk about, are some of the things being said about me. Some of the things enrage me. Do you want to ask me what they are?"

I said I'd listen to whatever he wished to discuss. "The rumor that bothers me the most I'll bring up myself," he began, revealing as much about the pathology of insecurity as about loneliness. So convinced was Ross that what people were saying about him was far worse than the actual facts, he then proceeded to talk into a tape recorder about how he had published a writer because he was sleeping with her. This is hardly without precedent in the publishing world, but it is the sort of information that few editors would want to get down on the record, However, if the imagination is cruel enough to create a world of harsh judges, then the truth may always seem tamer than what one assumes is being whispered behind one's back.

At first, there was something moving about Ross's confession. The sheer self-destructiveness of it—recalling the murderer in "The Tell-Tale Heart"—followed by the note of atonement. But all I had to do *not* to be moved was to think of Robin and the other women who had been writing away rather than nurturing Ross, who had *not* been given a nest at the *Voice*. When Ross chose Bob Kuttner above Judy Coburn for a staff job because he liked the idea of a Washington correspondent (which Judy had once been for the *Voice*), giving him a sense of a wider base, that was not Ross the compulsive confessor; it was Ross the power broker.

I thought of the five people who had been put on staff during the time Ross was so lonely and how they were all men. I wondered what became of the woman who was published during the brief period when he "lost all judgment." What became of her emotionally as well as professionally when he lost sexual interest? Was she discarded for the next? There were reasons the casting couch was an evil system. It would not suffice to say that it took two to tango, two for tea, that no woman *had* to bed down with a man if she did not choose to. For it was men who had the power to print them, and as long as that was so, women would be "fucked over" in more ways than one. And sadly, they would often defend the men who did it. That was part of the "fucking over."

Ross was convinced that it was Dan who was spreading all the rumors about him. But Dan did not gossip. He was a private man; nobody ever learned about the personal lives of others (or even his own) from Dan, although one learned about the private lives of everybody (including his own) from Ross.

There must have been mixed feelings when Ross remembered how he had gone to Dan and how Dan had listened—especially now that he had betrayed Dan. He must have feared that Dan would do the same. But Dan never did; it was a projection of guilt. Patricide was more than a theme for a Greek tragedy; it had become a theme in Ross's life, starting with the first betrayal to himself, when he stopped writing theatre criticism and started assigning pieces imbued with a different sort of drama, the coming apart of couples. A far drearier drama than any he ever had reviewed in print but one that was central to his own life.

Dan didn't think in such terms. He may have withheld the kind of explicit approval Ross needed; he may have been indifferent to the more conventional manifestations of ambition. But Dan protected you if he considered you part of his brood. And Ross had been a part of it for a long time. It was Ross who had acted in a calloused way, getting rid of Dan, and then Diane, who had actually been there before him; it was Ross who was now taking women's movement stars out to lunch and simultaneously printing anti-women pieces.

And now came feminist therapy. It had been a haunting topic for several years. Initially Ross had given it to Vivian Gornick, the *Voice*'s first official feminist writer (the real first was Jill Johnston, but she remained unacknowledged as such at the *Voice*). Ross wanted a cover story—the feature of the week, like Pineapple Punch ice cream. He was once again in familiar waters—the treacherous erogenous combat zone. The article—a rather long and tedious one —referred to the analyst as "she" while the writer discussed theory. It was a nice nod to the etiquette of the movement, but an awkward one since the therapist in the writer's experience turned out to be a man. Hence, a gauche shift to "he" as soon as the writer started to tell her own story. However, Ross didn't want anybody accusing him of being antifeminist; not after all those nasty rumors about the casting couch, which had, thank God, been put to rest as he cleared the record of "Dan's distortions."

No one can say how much a part Ross had in assigning Clark Whelton a piece on Jane Alpert's dogs when Jane Alpert surfaced from the underground and handed herself over to federal officials. But there were ironies in the story that Ross would appreciate. Clark had been the writer responsible for first raising the public consciousness on the dog shit issue and Ross had been the editor who decided not to run Jane Alpert's piece on her conversion to feminism because it spoke about a dead man's sex life. How could he defend his reputation and give all the real facts into a tape recorder, as Ross had done? Something was going on: the paper ran a loving memoir about Jane's dogs by the chief foe of dog shit and not a word about Jane herself.

It is equally hard to know how much direct influence Ross had in approving the Margot Hentoff piece on abortion—a defense of the friend-of-the-fetus position as the *Voice*'s sole commentary on the controversial Edelin conviction. But when the *Voice* denounces abortion—the one issue it had early and consistently supported—as murder, things are pretty mixed up. Again, the paper seemed to be frantically deciding which direction it should take. It was as if there no longer were any principles left, even liberal ones. Selling papers was all that mattered, and if outraging feminists did that, so what?

But nowhere did Ross's views find better expression than in an article called "Husband Dumping," written by Jane Jaffe Young. In the beginning, there is a description of a phenomenon—youngish couples move to Park Slope (as did Ross), buy old brownstones (as did Ross), renovate them (as did Ross), feel part of the renaissance of Brooklyn (as did Ross), and then the woman becomes involved with feminism (as did Ross) and dumps the mate (as did Ross).

Nancy leaves "bed and bored" (the inability to resist coyness even in a seemingly serious piece is evident); Karen "simply packs her bags one day, leaving her children, husband, and elegant house"; another woman, an unnamed friend of the author's, discards her husband when a young man, "cool as a cucumber," bluntly says, "I want to go to bed with you." Her husband feared the young guy was "a sexual acrobat, and I couldn't live up to five rounds a night."

What emerges from this inventory of dumpings is a picture of woman as cruel, sex-starved, ready to discard a loyal albeit insecure man as soon as the opportunity presents itself. One need not wade through the prose to get the point; a look at the "graphics" will do—a cover featuring the severed head of a man about to be crushed by a high-heeled foot of a woman posed above it. So pleased were the editors with the picture of man as victim—discarded, dumped, stomped over, and crushed by crazy, voracious, insatiable (except by young studs) ingrates of wives—that they repeated it as an insert within the piece.

Ross, however, doesn't lose all sight of sensibility. He manages as its editor to see that the story never loses its bittersweet quality. At first, there's "a rekindling of energies, an intellectual, emotional, and sexual renaissance courageously and even joyfully undertaken." But not for long. "An underlying ambivalence" begins to fester. "Seeing a still-united Park Slope family on a Sunday romp in Prospect Park, many of us feel wistful; a dream has died . . ."

Further into the story, there is even an allusion to a "long-lost father," one of many traumas a women's group goes through together. As one reads how "anxiety about going over the hill induced a feeling of urgency that would have been unthinkable a few years earlier," it becomes hard to believe that the writer's name is not a nom de plume for Ross, so close are the descriptions to his own life, right down to the way "we were used to compulsively unburdening ourselves."

Nearing the end at last, where all the women have gone off, all the husbands have been dumped, there is a need—an aesthetic need—for balance. The piece has to be resolved; the dissonant note struck must be softened; something not quite as wonderful as was hoped for and yet not too horrid must be achieved—a wistful, slightly regretful feeling, reminiscent of all the Family of Man pictures, those Park Slope brownstoners sitting on their stoops, still together, having just come from a romp with the family dog and kids.

"We recoil at the mere *thought* of binding contracts. However, the options of the seventies represent only a partial solution to our problems. Still haunted by the sharply etched tintype of a nuclear family, we sooner or later shun the emotional void of one-night stands and seek a fulfilling relationship that will evolve into some sort of ongoing commitment."

Sentimentality lurks as perilously close as a husband dumper. But Ross seems intent on having an ending that makes it clear life is a cycle; soon one will re-create the old form, settle down with high hopes, only to realize later on that they are less than one dreamed. Vintage Ross—the ambivalence, the attempt at resolution, the interest with marriage and mates, the happy ending, sort of (with a touch of "ironies, disappointments, and hopes that represent a microcosm of the world" perfectly inserted):

Upon close inspection, the description is neither detached nor resigned. A wife "dumping" her husband as if he were garbage —irresponsible to children, home, and mate with fervent equality— displays an anger that is hard to understand if one assumes it has something to do with Ross's own life. It was not Ross's wife who "dumped" him; it was Ross who "dumped" her while she stayed home, scared and undeveloped and with a young baby to care for, believing that Ross could have his choice of any woman writer in New York as he sought "a rekindling of energies."

Why then is it the woman who is the villain, the guilty one? Is it she with whom Ross identified? Ross the feminist, Ross the sister, Ross the fellow sufferer. Ross seems to subscribe to the notion that it is man who is the victim in this society. But he has a strange concept of women: at times they are strong, unpredictable, and capable of destruction. Yet women can make men guilty by becoming sick, depressed, suicidal. Is that better than becoming angry? Who knows?

What does begin to emerge, however, is how one man's insecurities were not only responsible for introducing the "casting couch" to *The Village Voice* (ironically, one of the first papers to discuss sexism in society) but also played an important part in determining what kinds of stories are featured in the *Voice* and with what point of view. And now the last link—the one which connects sexual insecurity with money.

At the time the writers were trying to organize for more pay and Ross was asked what he earned, he responded with his rather unsubtle equation between masculinity and money. When Ross achieved more status and a hefty increase in salary after the sale of the paper to Felker, the same question was posed. Again he couldn't say, but this time the reason had a more ladylike tinge. "It's a matter of decorum." He was, however, curious about how much people thought he was making, whether the world still assumed it was a puny amount or whether it now had a greater respect for his manhood.

Ross himself had not the vaguest idea of how much Dan had been making before the sale of the paper. Dan's salary of $72,000 came as a shock to just about everyone. Until the sale to Carter in 1970, Ross could not recall any talk about money. It was only after the sale that people began to realize that the *Voice* was profitable. Yet Ross did not want to question Dan's share.

"I felt they went through it, you know, the old capitalist ethic. They put their money, their faith, their time, they went through it. But they should have taken a hundred thousand dollars of their profits and divided it into thirty ways. Why couldn't they send Andy Sarris, Feiffer, and Hentoff two thousand dollars wrapped up in a bottle of champagne?"

The suggestion reeked of a slightly more bubbly paternalism. How easy it was, how much more gracious, to think of a ceremonial gesture rather than to figure out what share they were entitled to on the basis of their years of working for nothing. How about taking the paper under the new ownership and working out a plan to insure that workers have a share of the profits, a share of the shares?

But nothing like that occurred to Ross (or Bartle, who boasted of his radical politics). Both seemed content to continue to run the *Voice* like a plantation with a slightly more generous owner, one who might remember small occasions, forgetting that Dan had too: subletting Marlene's apartment when she was away; going to the bank when Barbara was robbed; and Ed coming through with the most magnanimous offer of all, handing over his posh penthouse to Barbara for a few weeks while keeping her pay at $20 an article.

It was not as if Ross dismissed security; as soon as his child was born, he "needed a basement to carry me through," something that would not fall out, that could not be taken away; what is usually known as a salary. But there was the "decorum" matter. It was a nice word—"decorum"—used to explain why Alexander Cockburn got a special salary arrangement and why it was not discussed. Used to explain why Robin Reisig didn't get a special salary arrangement or, in fact, any salary at all. And why Ross couldn't say what he was paying her as a "de facto" staff member—in other words, doing all the work of a staff member but receiving none of the financial or psychological rewards of a salary. No basement, so to speak.

And this decorum thing might come in handy later were writers to ask for more money.

"Dan felt himself the guardian of Carter's profits. He was the only person who could get writers to write for so little. He presented this image to Carter very explicitly. I heard it. He said the newspaper business is very volatile. I may use those arguments myself."

But why was his current salary so private a matter? "It's a very perverse idea. Outdated. I'm very outdated. I don't think it's anyone's business." When it was pointed out that lack of accountability, for which Ross had criticized Dan, was now being practiced by Ross himself, Ross launched into a new argument, getting away from the etiquette of it all. "Let me say this. I'm in a position to know I'm accounted for. I was named the editor on a Tuesday night. By Thursday afternoon I had to make an important decision. There had been an intolerable situation, with staff people getting different amounts of money. I had to decide whether to give everyone a hundred dollars more or raise everyone to three hundred, which meant some would be getting bigger raises than others."

Ross went ahead and made what struck him as the fair decision—to bring everyone to the same salary, thereby avoiding the charge some had against Dan of favoritism.

Fair though it may be for all staff writers to receive $300 as a salary, even though some received only a $50 increase while others received a $75 one, it was still one man who was part of management deciding what was right. Suppose his judgment had been wrong. Suppose that despite the best of heart, the best of intentions, he had thought everyone should receive the same increase. One could easily make out an argument for equal increases. In fact, one suspects it was primarily wanting to avoid Dan's ways that influenced Ross.

But it was no different from Dan's way; it was now Ross who was making the decisions. There were no contracts, no union, no guild, no security: if Ross decided one day he didn't like you, he could let you go; there was no grievance procedure, none of the grubby mechanisms that labor had worked out to protect the worker. There was no need because there was Ross and his heart, and he was determined to be fair, to be different from Dan.

"I make the decision on money. I proportion out what I have available, which I don't decide. Let me explain my attitudes. I'm in a situation where everyone who wants more money comes to me. I just have so much to give out. I get a budget based on Clay's fairness and I'll make a budget based on what I know is best. The only thing I can do is see that X gets paid comparably to Y."

Sounds fine. But suppose Ross thinks it is "fair" to pay Robin one-third of what staffers receive for the same amount of work. Or suppose Ross thinks it is "fair" to pay Alexander in a special way to help him out with his taxes.

"If I have a secretary who has a child and gets no child support while Judy Daniels [Managing Editor of the *Voice*] has a secretary who gets ten thousand dollars a year elsewhere, I decide to give mine a ten-dollar-a-week raise. I think this is fair."

And indeed it would be were all the paper subject to socialistic principles. But then it would be hard to explain why Clay Felker receives $120,000 in contrast to Robin's $4,500 and why Bartle receives any money at all (let alone a salary of over $70,000).

But Ross was not proposing any socialistic running of the paper. Of course, he would encourage writers to express their approval of socialism along with their concern for the plight of the workingman. And how strange that the writers who most often did this were those who were demanding the most capitalistic, least socialistic treatment, right down to special financial arrangements (made possible, in part, by other sources of money) worked out in total secrecy.

Ross admits that Cockburn, for example, had an unlimited opportunity at an early stage, but "that's because Dan was enamored of him." When pressed about the "fairness" of Cockburn's special salary arrangement (which Ross had been so lacking in "decorum" to reveal), he was uncomfortable. "Alexander made a very strong pitch for it. He's that kind of person. There are other writers who would find it intolerable to be paid an incentive to write."

I asked if he knew which writers would find it intolerable to get both a salary and an incentive in a unique have-your-cake-and-eat-it-too way. Ross was evasive. And when I asked why there was not a single woman writer on the staff, Ross replied, "You're not going to let me get away with my basic answer that we have women editors."

No, I said, I'm not going to let you get away with anything.

Scenes

Norman Mailer Gives Birth
(Along with Dan and Ed)
to The Village Voice,
and Then Abandons the Baby

In a period of roughly one generation—nineteen years—the *Voice* changed ownership, going from Dan, Ed, and Norm to Bartle, Carter, and Clay. Dan, Ed, Norm. Bartle, Carter, Clay. The names say a lot. But not enough. Here, then, is a slightly fuller account of the history of *The Village Voice*.

On October 11, 1955, the following notice (not very well edited or proofread) was sent out for immediate press release:

A lively new weekly newspaper, *THE VILLAGE VOICE*, appears for the first time on Greenwich Village newsstands (and some others) on Wednesday, October 26. Serving the Village area (estimated population: 100,000) as well as neighboring communities, it will be a paper appealing strongly to people everywhere interested in the arts and the special entertainment and shopping facilities that are unique to the internationally famed district.

Both the publisher, Edwin Fancher, 31, and the editor, Daniel Wolf, 33, of *THE VILLAGE VOICE*, have lived in the Village for at least a decade and believe it to be the most unique and interesting community in America, a vital creative center and an exciting place to live in and visit.

THE VILLAGE VOICE has been in the planning stage for months. Its first issue will be 12 pages and have a 20,000 circulation delivered by mail, carrier and newsstand. Guaranteed circulation for advertisers will be 10,000 copies weekly. (Single issue, $.05; five months' subscription $1; one year $2.

This release was printed on stationery that bore as its heading: The Village Voice—a weekly newspaper. Below was its original

214

address: 22 Greenwich Avenue, New York 11, New York. A telephone was listed as WAtkins 4-4669-70-71. (The number remained unchanged for almost twenty years, despite two additional changes in address, the replacement of letters by all numerical telephone listings, and the expansion from two-digit postal zones to the "zippier" five-digit number.)

Attached to the first page was a second sheet of plain paper with the heading, ADDITIONAL BACKGROUND:

> Publisher Fancher, a practicing psychologist whose varied career has included doing research for Cornell Medical College and the Institute of World Affairs, taught psychology at high school, also studied at the University of Alaska (where he contributed a column to a local newspaper), has worked, at times, as a trucker in the Village.
>
> Editor Wolf, formerly with the Turkish Information Office, has the unusual distinction of having written the Greek, Roman, Arabic, philosophy and psychology sections of the *Columbia Encyclopedia*.
>
> The newspaper's "back of the book" section—movies, theater, books, music, painting—will be under the direction of Jerry Talmer, associate editor. Mr. Talmer, 34, is a free-lance editor-writer and a regular contributor of articles and reviews to such magazines as *Architectural Forum* and the *Saturday Review*. He too is a Greenwich Villager of ten years standing. Among the contributors to his departments will be Margaret Marshall, Gilbert Seldes, Norman Mailer, Ernest Jones, William Murray, Nancy Hallinan, George Wright, William S. Poster, Philip Booth and Dustin Rice.
>
> News Editor for the VILLAGE VOICE is John Wilcock, 28. Starting as a cub reporter in his native England at the age of 16½, Mr. Wilcock later joined the *London Daily Mail* and the *London Daily Mirror*, largest-selling daily on earth. A UP night city editor and assistant editor of Canada's *Liberty* magazine, he came to New York in 1954 and until recently was an assistant editor of *Pageant*.
>
> In charge of production is Nell Blaine, a former art director of the UJA, a book jacket designer and the subject of one-man shows as [a typo, no doubt] such places as the Virginia Museum of Fine Arts, the Jane Street Gallery and the Tibor de Nagy Gallery. Business manager Joel Slocum, 24, besides being a fourth-generation advertising man is a Greek and Latin scholar who speaks four languages.
>
> Numerous Villagers drop in at all hours and contribute their

services. A housewife comes in after her baby's asleep; an actor spends spare time doing gold-lettering; others help type, do research.

In addition to news of all Village activities, THE VILLAGE VOICE will contain pictures, features, complete off-Broadway theater reviews and listings as well as book, art, music, dance and other reviews. Column will deal with off-the-beaten track in shopping, fashions, food and photography. An Arctic explorer will be among travel contributors and The Village Idiot—besides reflecting some of the nuttier aspects of the local scene—will [unreadable] such novelties as a long-running chess game with his readers and a poll of Villagers who don't work for a living.

The same year the press release was issued to announce the new paper, Dan married Rhoda, a childhood friend of Norman Mailer's sister, Barbara. Known professionally as Barbara Olson, she later put together an anthology called *The Bold New Women*. Not surprisingly, exactly one-third of the fifteen contributors were staff writers for *The Village Voice*. It was 1966, eleven years after her brother had put in $15,000—$5,000 at the start, another $10,000 toward the end of the first year—to get *The Village Voice* going.

For the next twenty years, Mailer continued to have some relationship with the paper he helped to found. In the beginning, he contributed not only money but also his own voice. His column was called "Quickly, a column for slow readers." It contained what was to become a *Voice* trademark—an easy put-down of the reader:

> Greenwich Village is one of the bitter provinces—it abounds in snobs and critics. That many of you are frustrated in your ambitions, and undernourished in your pleasures, only makes you more venomous. Quite rightly. If I found myself in your position, I would not be charitable either.

From the start, Mailer had a grasp of the liberal's need for a whipping (as long as it was delivered in words and he/she could sit comfortably in a chair while it was administered). Mailer was the first to articulate the underlying conservatism of this off-beat publication.

> . . . Indeed, even the *Village Voice*, which is remarkably conservative for so young a paper, and deeply patriotic about all community affairs, etc., etc., would not want me either if they were not so financially eager for free writing, and a successful name to go along with it . . .

Mailer had also grasped Dan's attraction for "names." Not only was Mailer sought; here is a list of some of the writers Dan Wolf included in an anthology of early pieces from the paper, which was published as *The Village Voice Reader* by Doubleday in 1962: Katherine Anne Porter, Steve Allen, Allen Ginsberg, Gregory Corso, Niccolo Tucci, Lorraine Hansberry, Jean Shepherd, Gilbert Seldes, Alexander King, John Cage, Max Eastman, Charles Abrams, Kenneth Tynan. (Not all are still "known," but at the time, they were all "names.")

The book appeared seven years after the publishing venture was started, when the *Voice* was just beginning to break even financially. Dan, however, still had a feel for the insecure, if one is to "interpret" the piece he chose among his own very infrequent *Voice* writings to go into the book. Called "What Did She Have to Be Secure About?", the piece is about a young child who wishes to visit his mother in jail and is taken there by a down-and-out friend (presumably the mother's boyfriend) who cannot yet break the news that Mother is no longer in the jail. She is dead. Here is an excerpt:

> A psychologist had once told her she needed security. But what did she have to be secure about, he [her boyfriend] wanted to know. Her mother had said good-bye to her when she was 14 . . .

In just one page, the themes of *Voice* history are touched: obsession with security, the sadness of those who lose a parent at a young age.

Mailer rebelled. He didn't want to write stuff guaranteed to make a liberal heart bleed. Was there anything but salty tears that would come out if you stabbed a liberal in the heart? Aren't they all a bunch of cowards who turn away from the sight of the bright red gushing forth? Aren't they really less "hip" and more "square"? Mailer hinted in one of the earliest examples of hip machismo:

> . . . this country could stand a man for President, since for all too many years our lives have been guided by men who were essentially women, which indeed is good for neither men nor women. So, to me, Ernest Hemingway looks like the best practical possibility in sight, because with all his sad and silly vanities, and some of his intellectual cowardices, I suspect that he's still more real than most, you know?

By the time Mailer was ready to exit from the *Voice*, his column had undergone a change in name. "The Hip and the

Square" is what he had come to call it. His last column was his thirteenth, a number modern edifices would not even acknowledge, and thus Mailer remained on good terms with the demonic. In it he wrote: "They [Dan and Ed] wish this newspaper to be more conservative, more Square—I wish it to be more Hip." Column Number 13—the Farewell—had started out as a review of *Waiting for Godot*. Mailer hadn't seen it, but he already sensed he wouldn't like it— that it was some sort of endorsement of impotence: ". . . What I smell in all of this is that 'Waiting for Godot' is a poem to impotence. . . . So I doubt if I will like it, because not everyone is impotent, nor is our final fate, our human condition, necessarily doomed to impotence . . ."

And then as if he were writing a follow-up thought to his earlier endorsement of Ernest Hemingway for President—a real man, not one who is really a woman—Mailer meditates on the meaning of the word "Godot." He thinks it's too obvious to connect it with God. Unless you mean ". . . God-O, God as the female principle, just as Daddy-O in Hip means the father who has failed, the man who has become an O, a vagina."

What a legacy "Norm" left as he made his way out—God-O, Daddy-O, fathers who fail, men who become O's, men with women's sensibilities. Perhaps they should not rule the country. But how about a paper?

The first *Voice* office,
Greenwich Avenue

Fred W. McDarrah

Sheridan Square office;
people waiting for latest issue

Fred W. McDarrah

Fred W. McDarra

Norman Mailer and Dan Wolf in Sheridan Square office

Fred W. McDarrah

Ed Fancher, Dan Wolf, and Bartle Bull outside University Place Office

Fred W. McDarrah

Maurice

Sarris: Taking Sex Straight—p. 5

thevillage **VOICE**

20c

20c New York City; 25c U.S.
Copyright © 1971, The Village Voice Inc.   THE WEEKLY NEWSPAPER OF NEW YORK   ● Vol. XVI, No. 5 ● New York, N. Y. ● Thursday, February 4, 1971

CENTRAL PARK AS ARCTIC NEW YORK   Voice: Fred W. McDarrah

Three prison proposals

New ideas for old jails

by Jack Newfield

It has been another average week in New York City's jails. A white correction officer at Rikers Island beat up Panther 13 defendant Robert Collier. Charles Desmond, the 74-year-old former Chief Judge of the Court of Appeals, went through the Tombs for the first time in his life, and said he was "speechless. The first impression is shattering." A state study of the municipal prisons was released, warning that continued "lack of recreation facilities, depressive living conditions, and overcrowding" were a "threat to public safety." Despite the solemn vows "no reprisals" last October, eight more inmates were indicted in the aftermath of the autumn rebellions, bringing the total to 42. The official city report on brutality by guards at the Long Island City jail was delayed once again. And Mayor Lindsay published an article in a new magazine—Juris Doctor—for activist lawyers. The piece was called "The Credibility of the Law," and in it the Mayor wrote: "We must bring new ideas to old jails through sensitive imaginative humane prison administration by people who know sociology, criminology, and the law. Our prison systems must be rehabilitated before they can rehabilitate. Young men and women can help to do that."

*   *   *

My purpose here is to propose, with a minimum of rhetoric, three simple ideas to help improve the city's six detention prisons.

1. The most basic fact about the city jails is that most of the 11,000 men and women who are there should not be in prison at all. More than half are in jail only because they are awaiting a trial, are poor, and can't make $500 or $1000 bail. For someone who is jobless and without a family, $ 500 bail might just as well be $5 million—he can't raise it. But the fact the judge set such low bail suggests the inmate is probably charged with a misdemeanor and is not the second Mad Dog Coll. Moreover, sta-

Continued on page 46

I witnessed the beatings

by James O'Loughlin

I was an eyewitness to the events at the Long Island City Jail, to the beatings and the climate prevailing and leading up to the injustices which happened. This is my story.

7.10 a. m., Monday, October 5, 1970—It was just about all over—the Mayor was inside the jail conferring with the Inmate Grievance Committee and the last of the hostages had been released from the Long Island City Branch of the Queens Jail, the scene of the original jail takeover by inmates on the preceding Thursday, an event which precipitated riot and revolt in three other city jails.

Suddenly, one of the inmate leaders, Victor Martinez, appeared in a third-floor window and shouted through a bullhorn that the guards were beating up inmates in the prison yard. "The pigs are beating us up. The Mayor went on the radio to say there would be no reprisals but

Continued on page 46

SoHo Saved

The city Board of Estimate gave its unanimous approval last week to a zoning plan which will permit up to 1300 artists to live in their working lofts in the SoHo manufacturing district. A certification committee consisting of 10 artists from SoHo and other areas of the city, and 10 representatives of artists' housing groups, art dealers, art schools, and Local Planning Board 2, is being formed to insure that only full-time artists—rather than wealthy dilettantes and hangers-on—will occupy the newly legalized lofts.

The politics of rape— a selective history

by Roslyn Lacks

"Ultraje!", Spanish for "outrage," describes more accurately than "rape" the feelings expressed by dozens of women who recently spoke out on rape at two blocks west of Eighth Avenue's Porno Strip—a proliferation of shabby erotica promising "Pure Pleasure for Adults," "Sexual Freedom in Denmark," and "Rubber Anniversaries" (whatever *that* means).

Whatever it means, the ladies two blocks away weren't having it. Vulnerability, fear, humiliation, shame, and anger were the feelings that prevailed at the speak-out in the theatre of St. Clement's Episcopal Church. Rape—metaphorical and real—was examined in detail and proved brutal and shattering, adolescent fantasies notwithstanding.

I arrived at the meeting swathed in ambivalence, uncomfortably embracing both skepticism ("It's your dream, lady") and sympathy. During the after-noon, feelings shifted and new polarities emerged.

According to New York's Radical Feminists, who sponsored the speak-out, rape in big cities has increased 46 per cent in the past year, "the logical result of women being told to be submissive to the dominant male." In reviewing the afternoon's testimony, I attempted to trace sexual patterns from the baboon to modern man.

The strongest male baboon, I am told, banishes weaker males and takes all females for himself—establishing, perhaps, the prototype for viewing woman as the property of man. It

Continued on page 44

Abner Symons

Voice cover, February 4, 1971

Tarantula Meets Mustang:
Bob Dylan Gives His Blessing to Patti Smith
By Jim Wolcott (P. 99)

50¢

the village VOICE

Patti Smith and Dylan after her concert

"Copyright 1975"
The Village Voice Inc.   VOL. XX No. 27   THE WEEKLY NEWSPAPER OF NEW YORK   MON. JULY 7, 1975

Timetable for the Fall Fiscal Crunch

KEN AULETTA (P.6)

S&M: Flirting With Terminal Sex

RICHARD GOLDSTEIN (P. 10)

Bikers & Hot Mamas: Why Exploitation Movies Get to Us

MICHAEL GOODWIN (P.65)

Playing Tennis in the Shade: Billie Jean's Partner, Mona Schallau.
Fred Misurella
(p. 18)

The U. S. Post Office: First Class Mess.
Phil Tracy
(P. 8)

What's New From Venus? Women in Sci-Fi
Barbara Damrosch
(P. 39)

Abner Symons

Voice cover, July 7, 1975

VOICE

PUBLISHED WEEKLY (THURSDAY) BY THE VILLAGE VOICE, INC.
Daniel Wolf, president, Edwin Fancher, secretary-treasurer
80 UNIVERSITY PLACE, NEW YORK, NEW YORK 10003
Editorial WA 4-4669
Display advertising WA 4-7880
Classified advertising WA 4-7130

Edwin Fancher	Publisher
Daniel Wolf	Editor
Diane Fisher	Associate Editors
Ross Wetzsteon	
Mary Perot Nichols	City Editor
Howard Smith	Assistant Publisher
Jack Newfield	Assistant Editor
Michael Zwerin	European Editor
Joe Flaherty	News Features
Vivian Gornick	
Ron Rosenbaum	
Lucian K. Truscott IV	
Fred W. McDarrah	Staff Photographer

Member: Audit Bureau of Circulations

Subscription price $6 a year in the United States and its possessions
foreign $7.
Second-class postage paid at New York, New York, and at additional mailing offices

Abner Symons

Voice masthead, October 22, 1970

the village VOICE

Published weekly (Monday) by The Village Voice, Inc. 80 University Place, N.Y. N.Y. 10003

| Clay S. Felker | Editor-in-Chief |
| Milton Glaser | Design Director |

Thomas B. Morgan	Editor
Judith Daniels	Managing Editor
Gil Eisner	Art Director

Senior Editors
Karen Durbin Eliot Fremont-Smith
Richard Goldstein Jack Newfield
Ross Wetzsteon

Associate Editors
Audrey Berman, Helena Hacker, Diane Straus

Staff Writers
Ken Auletta, Howard Blum, Alexander Cockburn, Paul Cowan, Joe Flaherty, Vivian Gornick,
Blair Sabol (West Coast Correspondent), Howard Smith, Phil Tracy,
Brian Van der Horst, James Wolcott

Department Editors
Alexandra Anderson	Art
Jon Carroll	West Coast
Robert Christgau	Music
Andrew Sarris	Film
Burt Supree	Listings

Assistant Editors
Rosemary Cira (Centerfold), Roderick Faber,
Susan Klebanoff

Editorial Staff
Mary Margaret Goodrich, Mary Ann Lacy, Sonia Jaffe Robbins, Charles Whitin

Art Department
Robert Eisner	Associate Director
John MacLeod	Assistant Director
Fred McDarrah	Picture Editor
Sylvia Brody	Picture Research

Production
| Jack Berkowitz | Manager |
| John Jay | Traffic Manager |
Staff: Paul Bresnick, Pegi Goodman, Steven Levi, Hal Muchnick, Ronald Plotkin

Advertising
Stephen M. Blacker	Associate Publisher, Marketing
Bernard Stolar	Advertising Director
Jack Kliger	Classified Advertising Director
Alberta Harbutt	Classified Advertising Manager
Rose Ryan	Classified Consultant
Eckart Guethe	Research Director

National Account Managers: Bob Crozier, Carol Smith.
Local Account Managers: Stock Doughty, Jackie Rudin.
Mark Finkelstein, West Coast: 6290 Sunset Blvd. L.A., Ca. 90028 (213) 466-3488
Sales Representatives: Leo Adelsohn, Joel Berger, Mrs. Carol, Dan Horowitz, Phyllis Miller

Supervisors: John Belknap, Pat Joyce, Delphine Oravetz, Ellen Owens
Staff: Sylvia Angel, Gina Barnett, Maria Berkowitz, Toby Bellin, Lucille Bellobrow, Richard
Bender, Sally Benjamin, Bill Cabeche, Louis Colca, Paul Coughlin, Janna Davis, Elizabeth
Faiella, Linda Fitzgerald, Danielle Fox, Vicki Francis, Robin Freed, Lea Fuhrman, Beth
Glick, Keith King, Wendy Kortrey, Colette Lageoles, Arthur Lindsay, Mona Lourie, Steve
Nelson, Bruce Novack, Deborah Paley, Louis Papaperpou, Mellios Papaperpou, Lynn
Peterson, Jim Poett, Craig Purpura, Katie Risch, John Rommel, John Ryan, Virginia
Sandelli, Bonnie Scheibman, Barbara Springer, Ron Traeger, Esther Travers, Joe Turner,
Regina Wachter, Deborah Weiner

Finance
| William J. Ryan | Vice-President Finance |
| William Dwyer | Controller |
Supervisors: Sabina Roseman, Theresa West
Credit Managers: Steve Ettkins, Carmela Matarazzo
Staff: Jean Finley, May Jean Lee, Philip Levine, Esther Ridgely, Valerie Storer,
Gail Straus, Kristine Ziek

Circulation
David Shanks	Director
Ken Tapper	Manager
Karen Salerno	Promotion Manager
Gayle Weinberg	Promotion Assistant
Eileen Tracy	Circulation Assistant
Evelyn Anderson	Subscription

Administration
| Jane Maxwell | General Manager |
| Jon Sosa | Office Manager |
Staff: Narong Anomasiri, Keshavan Maslak, Ramona Negron, Glenn Prine.

Member Audit Bureau of Circulations

Subscription price $15 a year in the United States and its possessions — foreign $20
Second-class postage paid at New York, New York, and at additional mailing offices
Postmaster: Send Form 3579 to Village Voice, Box 2975,
Boulder, Colorado 80302
Other mail: The Village Voice, Inc., 80 University Place, New York, New York 10003

Clay S. Felker, Chairman and Publisher/Milton Glaser, Vice-Chairman
Bartle Bull, President
Stephen M. Blacker, Vice President/Ruth Bower, Vice President
William J. Ryan, Vice-President, Finance
Editorial/Business 741-0030/Display-advertising 741-0020/Classified advertising 741-0010

Abner Symons

Voice masthead, November 10, 1975

The Voice *Speaks for Itself*

ATTICA

". . . In assessing the blame for the sordid murders at Attica, no person or group will bear a heavier burden of guilt than the contemptible '60s radicals . . . Armed with the ideas of '60s radicalism, they [the prisoners of Attica] put some of them into practice. Among their first decisions was a death threat against their hostages. . . ." That was Clark Whelton writing in *The Village Voice:* "Attica: the death of '60s radicalism. (For the entire article, see *The Village Voice,* September 16, 1971. Author would not give permission to reprint article.)

It was not sheer paranoia that lent credibility to the story that the inmates were killing the guards at Attica. On Tuesday, September 14—the day the *Voice* was to go to press—page one of *The New York Times* read ". . . In this worst of recent American prison revolts, several of the hostages—prison guards and civilian workers— died when convicts slashed their throats with knives." As Hentoff (who summarized the New York press coverage quoted here) was to point out the following week, "Not even an 'it was reported' or 'officials said.' "

Those who determine editorial comment also accepted reports from prison officials as the truth. In its lead editorial, the *Times* said, "Prisoners slashed the throats of utterly helpless, unarmed guards . . ."

The *Daily News* made it sound as if its reporter actually witnessed the violence against guards. "I Saw Seven Throats Cut," screamed the headline. "Eight of the dead hostages died of slashed throats. The ninth was stabbed to death," read the "news."

While the New York *Post* was a bit more sober in tone, it, too, saw no reason to question the "facts" or to report that what was being printed was based solely on official prison reports.

So Dan was not alone. Most of the New York press, or at least those who run it, were willing to accept the story of white guards being mutilated by black inmates.

However, the other papers did not have to worry about losing radical readers; they could correct themselves a day later, when official autopsies showed that it was bullets that killed the guards. And by Wednesday, the dailies did. But Wednesday was the day that the *Voice* hit the newsstands and there was no taking back the Whelton story that day.

The following week, September 23, *Voice* readers received a different view. On the front page were four photographs: one showed a policeman clubbing a black man, stripped to his waist and curled up with pain (a scene Fred McDarrah shot at a Harlem demonstration against Attica). Another showed a black woman holding a poster with the words "Murder In Attica" scribbled over an intense and suffering face of a bearded black man. The other two were of Rockefeller and Kunstler.

Two of the three front-page stories were about Attica: "An Epic of Failure," by Mary Breasted, on the efforts of the Attica Negotiating Committee, and a more impassioned and partisan story by Jack Newfield called "Attica: The animals were outside." Included on the front page was a directive which read like an alert: "For other articles on Attica, see pages 18 and 19." There one could read a continuation of Newfield's piece, a story about how the inmates inside the prison were denied medical attention by a group of doctors who had come to Attica to help out, and part of a state report on prison conditions released less than two weeks before Attica, detailing the conditions which, "if allowed to continue, will make the disturbances at the Auburn Correctional Facility (November, 1970) only a prelude to a nightmare." Not a single ad appeared; only a picture of two protesters, one a young black girl, another a white man, holding a poster which read "Avenge Ponce, My Lai, Attica."

On the opposite side—page 19—a box contained part of a letter from an Attica inmate that Jack Newfield had received during the week. The headline was " 'Death awaits us because we will not submit,' " the last line of the printed portion. Below it were three other Attica stories: a piece by one of the rare black contributors to the *Voice,* Dalton James, called "Hitcher's Attica: 'We are ready, Bro.' " It related a conversation James had with a black brother whom he picked up in Florida, who spoke with pride about the courage the Attica inmates showed in their willigness to die. Dick Brukenfield, who ordinarily reviews plays, wrote about field trips to Harlem for guards at Green Haven Prison to acquaint them with the reality of life for ghetto dwellers.

But the real stroke of genuis was to include amidst the reportage a Clark Whelton piece that was totally sympathetic to the inmates. For a moment, it must have seemed to a reader of the previous issue as if he were hallucinating. For the same man who could state that there was nothing else for the police to do but attack rebellious inmates, acknowledging that it was "ugly, and bloody" but concluding that there was no other course, as a prelude to blaming Attica on the sixties radicals, was now saying the following week: ". . . Nelson Rockefeller's responsibility for the slaughter at Attica is clear and unmistakable. Rockefeller chose gunfire instead of words and the consequences of his decision will remain forever attached to his name." Again, another photo, showing marchers holding up posters and banners protesting Attica. And again, another small alert in the midst of the Whelton piece to "see Hentoff, p. 32, for another view." On page 32, Nat outlined the distorted press coverage in the major New York dailies, tactfully omitting the Whelton piece of the previous week.

But not everyone at the *Voice* cared to erase it from his memory. Paul Cowan, Jack Newfield, and David Gelber wrote a letter to the *Voice* which was printed. It started out: "Dear Sir: Clark Whelton's article blaming ' '60s radicals' for the Attica Massacre was disgraceful" and ended on an equally strong note: "The principal blame for the Attica Massacre rests with Nelson Rockefeller. He is responsible for the murders—guards and inmates. In a just society he'd be impeached, tried in criminal courts, and given a life sentence in a real rehabilitation center."

Jeanne Goldschmidt wrote a letter saying: "I was going to say 'Clark Whelton exemplifies everything that's wrong with ' '60s liberalism.' But shit, he's no liberal. Liberals have hearts . . . But Whelton is pure spleen. Blaming the Attica massacre on 'outside agitators' puts him on the level of Bull Conner. . . . There has to be a place on Rockefeller's staff for a mind like that." And there had to be some embarrassment for the *Voice* with a letter like that. For Jeanne Goldschmidt was not only a talented young writer but also the wife of Mike Kempton, son of Murray. (Tragically, Jeanne and Mike were both killed shortly afterward when their car overturned.)

And there were others, enough to warrant a separate boxed section of letters called "Aftermath of a Massacre." Were it not for the clever about-face the next week, in which Whelton himself substituted Rockefeller for sixties radicals in placing the blame for what happened at Attica, the piece might have been entitled "The Death of Voice Liberalism" instead of " '60s radicalism." But Dan knew exactly how to recoup. Even after the issue on Attica *from a radical point of view,* the *Voice* continued to run pieces on Attica. On the front page of the September 30 issue, now removed by a two-week space from the first Whelton piece, one of the two front-page stories was " 'Rocky ain't nothing but a re-nigger!': Attica memorial in Bed-Sty," written by a black man. Above the piece was a picture of an Attica prisoner's coffin being carried down the church steps of the Cornerstone Baptist Church in Bedford Stuyvesant, and inserted in the article was a small photo Fred shot of blacks in prison. Under the picture: "see page 5."

There Jack had a story on "The men in the middle: Black correction officers." On the next page, although not advertised on the front, was a piece in the column "The Press of Freedom" (reserved for nonregular contributors) called "Alfred Leonard Williams: A man of reason died at Attica." Williams was a black man trying to understand what had made him a criminal—thoughts he was in the process of recording when he was killed at Attica.

Two pages later was a story written by a man signed, "Your friend." He turned out to be a white Attica inmate who had witnessed the recapture of the prison and recorded the activities of the troopers in a letter he sent to the Fortune Society which was forwarded to the *Voice.*

Two pages later appeared "Letter from Dannemora: 'These pits of hell,' " which Jack received and printed, including in his introduction the facts that "while inmates are without toilet paper and underwear, Dannemora warden LaVallee lives in a new ranch house that cost the state $110,000."

Several pages later Nat Hentoff continued to take the press to task for its Attica coverage, again ignoring Clark Whelton.

For a long time, not a single word appeared about the "contemptible radicals of the sixties."

JANE ALPERT

In an introduction to Jane Alpert's "Mother Right: A New Feminist Theory," Gloria Steinem wrote in the August, 1973, issue of *Ms.,* ". . . We publish this document in its entirety to share with all of you who read it the personal voyage of one woman through and out of the patriarchal left. And to let you know, Jane, wherever you are, that we hear you. Women are listening to each other a little better now. The dialogue of exploration can begin."

Then began the article Ross had turned down. Alpert had sent it, along with her fingerprints (to prove its authenticity) and three requests: 1) that it be published uncut; 2) that no photograph of her accompany it (she was still in hiding underground); 3) that as much reader response as possible be printed. *Ms.* had no difficulty honoring all three requests. Ross did. The first one bothered him. Ross did not want to print anything damaging about the potency of a man unable to defend himself. Yet in an article that took up ten full pages in *Ms.* magazine, there was only one sentence concerning the potency of Sam Melville, Alpert's former lover, who was subsequently killed at Attica:

"He [Melville] was sexually impotent unless he could fantasize the woman he was with as a prostitute and she went along with the fantasy."

Alpert had requested that there be no cuts. So Ross cut the whole piece. It did not matter that this was an historic document, a letter from a woman who had been an activist and who was now renouncing the sixties activism for feminism. Although there was that one sentence that Ross could not bring himself to print, there was also an analysis of what her experiences as a Weatherwoman had done to her, with references to Mark Rudd, H. Rap Brown, and other sixties activists the *Voice* had spent a lot of space covering. So intense was Alpert's reaction to the male-dominated left that she even went so far as to state:

"And so, my sisters in Weatherman, *you* fast and organize and demonstrate for Attica. Don't send me news clippings about it, don't tell me how much those deaths moved you.

I will mourn the loss of 42 male supremacists no longer."

When a little more than a year later Alpert came out of hiding and handed herself over to federal officials, the *Voice* printed a piece called "Jane Alpert's Lost Dogs: A Decade Gone Sour." This time Clark focused on John Keats and Bernadette Devlin, Jane Alpert's "two fat, tan puppies." He told what good care Alpert took of them as "they gradually grew large and sleek," before going on to describe how one night he heard a woman calling, "John Keats! Bernadette! And before I could see her face I knew it was Jane Alpert and that something had happened to her dogs."

When she finally "walked up the courthouse steps" some four years later and all the reporters were asking her about Patty Hearst and Mark Rudd, Clark had another concern.

> I waited outside the office and rode down on the elevator with her. A couple of other reporters had questions, then I asked her about John Keats and Bernadette. Tears briefly blurred her eyes.
>
> "I never found them," she said. The door opened and she went outside, through the press cameras, and down into the subway. For the past few days I've caught myself looking for her dogs again. David Hughey served two years in prison, Sam Melville is dead, shot down during the uprising at Attica, but the dogs would only be six years old. They were very beautiful, and it's possible that someone has them and they're somewhere near by.

Superficially the piece seems harmless enough, even if it does seem absurd to use Jane Alpert's surrender as an excuse to tell a My Friend Flicka story. (Particularly when Whelton had previously written about the hazards of dog shit and the pathology of people who own dogs.)

But there is one paragraph that suggests the piece is not simply an ode to two lost dogs.

> I had felt very uncomfortable talking to her, a mixture of guilt and something else I couldn't classify. The guilt part was easy. For three years I had hatched plots in my head to bring down the government that was responsible for war in Vietnam. I blew up banks, derailed trains, and sabotaged factories. In my head. Actually, I did nothing except march in protest demonstrations. . . . violence fantasies had just been a kind of cathartic exercise in counterterror. But, according to the charges to which she pleaded guilty, Jane Alpert had really done something. She had acted out my daydreams, and for that reason I felt partly responsible for her fate . . .

Strange talk for the man who held the "contemptible '60s radicals" responsible for Attica before he underwent a quick conversion in print. And now, four years after Attica, what was one to make of this? Was Whelton *still* proving that he was not as inhuman as those letter writers accused him of being? Was it Whelton, the reactionary, who could now respond tenderly to a woman (through her two lost dogs) who had, in effect, *also* rejected sixties radicals as contemptible and gone on to develop her own reactionary theory?

Whatever was going on in Whelton's mind is beside the point. What is revealing about *Voice* writing is how one man's obsessions can become the basis for an entire political analysis. This gave *Voice* coverage its distinctive tone. But both the Attica and Alpert incidents and the weird way in which they turn out to be related (it was Alpert's statement that she could not mourn the dead men at Attica that caused a rift among feminists) indicated that the *Voice* was moving away from its liberal-Bohemian position, drifting toward a tighter, security-oriented, middle-class readership long before any new graphic design made the change visible.

(The Whelton piece on Jane Alpert's dogs appeared in the November 21, 1974, issue of the *Voice*.)

THE NEWFIELD-NICHOLS FEUD

On November 25, 1971, Jack Newfield wrote in *The Village Voice:*

> There seems to be a trend in local journalism subordinating ideas and issues to gossip and rumor. The trouble with this trivia tendency is not just that it demeans the quality of political debate and neglects economic interests behind personalities, but that the gossip is often untrue.

Newfield then goes on to cite what he considers an illustration: Allen Wolper wrote up an exchange between Ted Kennedy and Mayor Lindsay for the New York *Post* as if it "were the rematch between Muhammad Ali and Joe Frazier," when according to Jack, who was at the cocktail party where the two politicians met, "nothing happened."

The next week, December 2, 1971, Mary Nichols wrote a *Voice* column entitled "Private Opinion: Issue Journalism or Co-opted Journalism?"

"Jack Newfield's attack on New York *Post* political reporter Allan Wolper was a scurrilous piece of journalism. I am ashamed that this newspaper published it." Which was enough for *The New York Times* to put a man on the Nichols-Newfield "beat." And in the Sunday *Times,* December 19, 1971, a Frank Prial piece had the headline: Columnist and City Editor Are Leading Figures In Village Voice Factionalism."

> The Village Voice, the prosperous and proudly contentious Greenwich Village weekly newspaper, has been beset recently by a rash of internal factionalism, according to staff members.
>
> The central figures in the reported divisions at the Voice are Jack Newfield, a columnist, and Mrs. Mary Perot Nichols, the city editor.
>
> Mrs. Nichols has accused Mr. Newfield of attempting to turn the paper into an organ of the New Left. Mr. Newfield denies this and, in turn, has charged that Mrs. Nichols is trying to use the paper to promote the interest of Representative Edward I. Koch, Democrat of Manhattan's 17th Congressional District.

While Prial goes on to talk about the efforts of writers to organize for more money, it is incidental to the Newfield-Nichols feud.

> Mrs. Nichols said yesterday that "I am ashamed this paper printed the Newfield column." Mrs. Nichols added that Mr. Newfield and his friends at the Voice, whom she called "liberal groupies," had attempted to influence editorial policy, to kill columns by other contributors and to give the newspaper an open commitment to the political left.

Jack, on the other side, was quoted as saying he thought Mary " 'an illiterate Lee Mortimer' and a 'mental case' if she thinks I am for John Lindsay." (Jack, as Prial notes, had written about thirty anti-Lindsay articles at the time Mary accused him of trying to ingratiate himself with the Lindsay organization.)

When Dan was asked for his views, he told Prial, " 'That's what happens when you're a writers' paper rather than an editors' paper. I wouldn't use the language Newfield uses, nor, for that matter would I use the language Mary uses." (It's an interesting aside to note that Mary, but not Jack, is referred to by Dan on a first-name basis, which at the *Voice* was an indication of being "family.")

About the attempts for more money? Dan chose to tell the *Times* that "some staff members had come to him and asked to talk 'about the direction the paper is going.' " (Nobody had even had a chance to bring up the paper's direction, so put off was Dan by the issue of money, which *was* what the staff members had come to talk to him about.)

Prial quotes him as saying, " 'That disturbs me. If you're going to develop an ideology and cease to be an open paper, then you're going to have to question the political credentials of everyone who writes for you.' "

It was, Prial reported, Hentoff who told the *Times,* " 'There was a big meeting over pay about three weeks ago and this ideological thing never came up. In fact, Jack resolved to remain off a committee of nine who went to negotiate with Dan Wolf, just to keep ideology out of the money problem.' "

Back at the *Voice,* Mary was far less restrained. In the December 2 piece for public consumption entitled "Private Opinion," she states:

> I myself date the new Newfield politics to about the time he was one of two New York City reporters who attended the New Hampshire wedding of Lindsay's assistant, Jay Kriegel (which happened to be the weekend of the Attica riot). While Jack may have thought he was invited only because of his charm and good looks, I think he was invited because the Lindsay crowd thought they could use him.

And once again Attica raises itself as an issue alongside the sly innuendo about Jack's good looks. (For the record, Jay Kriegel's wedding took place September 18, 1971, the weekend *after* Attica.)

Mary could sound so self-righteous about the need to keep journalism separate from personal bias; yet Mary consented to review Jack's latest book for the *West Side Literary Review.* With wonderful irony, the front page of the April 25, 1974, issue headlined "Who judges the judges' judges?" and then devoted the entire front page to Mary's review of Jack's book, *Cruel and Unusual Justice.*

Even Mary must have been embarrassed; she begins her review on an uncharacteristically self-revelatory note:

"Let me state my bias at the outset. For any reader who does not know, Jack Newfield and I have enjoyed (endured?) a journalistic feud for some years. Sometimes our feuding has been carried on in the pages of *The Village Voice* and once it even broke into *The New York Times.*" After distinguishing herself from Jack by saying she believes in telling the truth while Jack believes in printing his personal views, she then goes on to include in her "review" the following:

> Lying, and the contracts he performs for politicians in his writing are something I deplore. Since we work on the same newspaper, there are times when I feel I need to separate myself from him.
>
> Then there is the soft way Newfield treats Mayor Lindsay, though his prison system was in many respects as bad or worse than Rockefeller's, as compared to how he treats Rocky. Rocky plots his moves against the poor "with four or five other rich Republicans . . . over wine and steaks . . ." We never hear what Lindsay eats or drinks. [A strange criticism for someone who purports to be an objective reporter interested in the larger issues.]
>
> ". . . forty-two men died at Attica because Nelson Rockefeller would not go to the prison and join in the negotiations." But Lindsay did go to the prisons during riots and he turned his back on the beatings described above, and broke his promise of no reprisals. True, he didn't arm his police with dum-dum bullets as Rocky did. [Mary writes as if this were a small difference.]
>
> But Lindsay's prisons in some ways, at least according to Newfield's own stories, were worse than Attica. For example, in Attica we learn that prisoners only get a change of underwear once a week. But when Newfield and Congressman Edward I. Koch visited one of Lindsay's prisons, they found a man who hadn't had a change of underwear in 6 months. . . . Attica sounds like paradise compared to Lindsay's prisons! [Attica sounds like paradise? Mary may believe in objective reporting, but she certainly is not put off by exaggeration.]

"Who influences Jack Newfield?" she asked at the end of her review (which read more like an inventory of Newfield's "unevenhandedness"). And Mary supplied an "objective" answer:

> Is it late night sessions in Jimmy's with Richard Aurelio, Mattie Troy, Jimmy Breslin, or Pete Hamill (the self-appointed ethnic and folk heroes of New York politics)? I wonder what makes Jackie run.

Unfortunately, Mary never seemed to wonder beyond the worlds from which she felt excluded and which she tried so hard to enter.

On Monday, October 27, 1975—Veterans' Day—Mary was fired after seventeen years at *The Village Voice*. Perhaps, a "veteran" of one war too many.

The Voice *Grows,*
Makes Money, Moves,
and Fred McDarrah Takes Note

Within the fifteen years after the first copy of the *Voice* appeared in October, 1955, the following things happened:

Dan and Ed moved the paper from Greenwich Avenue to a small triangular two-story building on the corner of Sheridan Square. Dan could hear everything that was going on anywhere in the building.

Circulation increased from the 2,500 of the first issue to 10,000 shortly after.

On Pearl Harbor Day, 1962, the New York Typographical Union Local No. 6 called the longest newspaper strike in the history of New York. Readership jumped from 17,000 to 135,000. Mostly from newsstand sales.

The paper increased from twelve pages to seventy and advertising expanded from 20 percent to 65.

For the first time in seven years, the *Voice* started to show a profit. Dan and Ed were able to recover their investments of $60,000.

Ed married a former schoolteacher. She became pregnant.

Ed bought a penthouse co-op in a building at Fifth Avenue and Eleventh Street.

Dan bought a co-op in the same building and moved in with his wife and children.

Each continued to remain listed in the New York Telephone Directory.

In April, 1968, *New York* magazine emerged from the ashes of the *Herald Tribune*. Shortly, it had a circulation of 355,000.

On August 10, 1968, Don McNeil walked into a pond near Woodstock, New York, and never came out alive.

In 1970—the beginning of the year and the start of a new decade—Dan and Ed sold the paper for $3 million. The new owners were a young City Councilman, Carter Burden, and his campaign manager, a young Wall Street lawyer (and former Harvard classmate), Bartle Bull. Carter was then married to Amanda Paley, stepdaughter of William Paley, Chairman of the Board of CBS, and Bartle to *her* college friend, Belinda Brite Bull. Each had children. Each lived on the upper East Side. Together they formed a company called Taurus Communications. Carter owned 71 percent of the stock and Bartle 29. For $3 million, the partners of Taurus Communications acquired 80 percent of the *Voice* stock.

Dan and Ed stayed on as minority stockholders. Each signed a contract with the new owners which was renewable at the end of five years. Dan remained as Editor. He received $72,000 a year— $60,000 in salary and $12,000 in bonuses. Ed, who was now co-publisher with Bartle, received two-thirds of that amount since he worked two-thirds at the *Voice*. The other third he was a psychotherapist in private practice. Nobody at the *Voice* (except Ely Kushel, the accountant) knew these figures.

The paper continued to prosper under the new owners. Bartle installed himself at the *Voice*. Carter rarely appeared except at the *Voice* Christmas party with *Voice* writer Mary Breasted. Carter and Amanda separated. Bartle remained married.

Bartle moved the *Voice* from Sheridan Square to a large five-story building on University Street and Eleventh, a few blocks from Washington Square. Formerly the *Evergreen Review* had been located there. But *Evergreen Review* had gone under. So had the *East Village Other* and *Rat*. The new building had elevators and sturdy walls. It was hard to hear what was happening from floor to floor.

Dan began to lose his hearing.

The price of the paper rose to twenty-five cents. Advertising grabbed 71 percent. The paper now contained 120 pages.

Circulation reached a peak of 150,000.

Voice writers received an average of $100 a week. Over 90 percent of the articles were by free-lance writers. They did not receive any benefits such as vacation, sick leave, or health coverage.

234

Some started to wonder where all the money was going. Not to them, a few had figured out.

A group of writers met. They decided to elect a committee to discuss the question with Dan.

Dan did not like to meet with committees. Dan did not like to discuss money.

One *Voice* person decided to deal with Dan individually. He had known him a long time, going back to the days when Dan lived alone with his mother. He had come to work at the *Voice* almost from its start. Here are the letters he sent to Dan.

May 15, 1974

Dan: Today is an historic day. The Voice went to 136 pages. Fifteen years ago on May 20, 1959 the paper was 12 pages. Today's paper has 36 pages of classified ads alone.

In 1959 when I first started publishing pictures and selling one inch ads for The Voice we got post dated checks of 25 dollars. I didn't complain because the paper was barely surviving. But those little ads I sweated to get for you helped keep the paper going.

Now that the Voice is doing well, I think you should go over my note of March 20th and come to grips with the reality of what I have contributed these past 15 years in relation to my current take home pay of 185 dollars and the Voices' profit picture.

Here is my income tax return to dispell your fears that I am growing rich from my Voice check. My expenses run into the thousands and deducting these from my taxes leaves nothing for saving, nothing for my old age, nothing for private schools for my kids too. Should my kids be condemned to IS 70 because their father can't make a decent living from a job he's held for 15 years. Must I punish my wife by making her work forever because I can't bring home enough to support my family.

It is self evident in the paper that I do twice as much work now than I did 2 years ago. For a 47 year old grey haired photographer I think a *take-home* pay of 250 or 300 is not unreasonable nor unrealistic because the Voice can in fact afford to pay more. Right now I need *nearly two* paychecks to cover the rent.

Is it asking too much for you Dan to now show your appreciation for good work, loyalty and longevity by now paying me a salary that I can live on.

Fred W. McDarrah

Mar. 20, 1974

Progress Report—Fred W. McDarrah

Dan: It is very easy to say no to just about anything without knowing the reason or without making an honest judgment based on an accurate evaluation of the situation. When you say no to a 10 year old it's "no because" and that's final. Usually the answer is arbitrary. This note then is to give you sufficient information based on facts to show that I am requesting more paycheck because the time has come and I deserve more. I have earned it. I work hard and am entitled to make a decent living from The Voice.

Economics of the Paper—First of all it is clear to me that The Voice can afford to give me more money because it is the largest paid weekly in the country and there is no two ways about it, it is profitable to somebody. I am not a stockholder, nor do I have any equity except my paycheck. The longevity I have accumulated is worthless from the standpoint of a pension or annuity or income in any way after I leave or after you leave. In other words the paper grows in circulation, advertising, income and future profits but I as an individual employee do not benefit by this. This is one of those things we don't talk about and that is understandable. After all, I wasn't here in 1955 with money to invest nor was I here the first day. However, I was here in the 50's and did my share by selling ads to meet the payroll. I chose this as my career and I have no regrets and although I am not the direct beneficiary of the profits the Voice now makes, I do feel that my contribution is worth more than $185 take home pay. It is a poor excuse and a deception to say the Voice can't pay me more, and if the old "wage freeze" chestnut is pulled out, then I suggest naming me a phoney associate publisher or phoney Vice President so that I can legitimately get a decent raise.

Salary 1958-1974—Let's take a brief look at various paychecks made to me over the years to show exactly what we are talking about:

	Take Home Pay
1973	$185.60
1972	169.65
1971	162.25
1970	153.21
1969	124.37
1968	107.52
1967	60.97

In 1966 I was paid by the picture and my average pay was $55 with a take home of $47.55. In 1965 my Voice pay was $30 a week with a take home of $28.59. The years before that I got $25.00 a week as the photographer, the same as Gin Briggs before me. I am putting all this down on paper for you to see because it is so easy to forget that some of us here have put in a lot of time and effort and dedication to make the Voice the success that it is today. You and Ed likewise, but you are owners. In my thinking there comes a time when our longevity chips would be worth something and maybe now is the time.

Salary Adjustment—I'm not asking for stock in the company. All I'm simply asking is that I get paid a respectable salary. I would be ashamed to tell anyone that the Voice take home pay is only $185 in 1974. It is ludicrous. I will never get paid what I think I am worth or what other comparable papers pay for a picture editor, but certainly I should be getting at least $350 to $400 as a picture editor. I am no longer just the photographer but someone who is directly responsible for what goes into the paper each week, and I should be making just as much or more that some other Voice editors, some of whom may do less than I do and make more. The problem is that you have locked me and yourself into a 1955 time and pay zone and it is impossible to break with it. Kids right out of college today start jobs at 15 grand a year as messengers. And some hack picture editors get 20 for doing nothing.

Picture Editor—I admit that I forced you to name me picture editor and that I have labored each time to convince you that I should get more money. Nothing comes easy and only once did the Voice without asking increase my salary. That was in 1972 when everybody got 11 dollars when the Voice writers went on strike. They have done very well and now even get a kill fee. But let me go over exactly what I do as picture editor because I guess it is a job I created for myself. In the past year, as always, I have been responsible for taking all the photos, assigning them or obtaining them in one way or another. Recently I have had Abner Symons doing theatre pictures because this work is valuable asset to that section of the paper. I am also with great strain, trying to get both Janie Newfield and Rachel Cowan to improve their work because I think that at some future time they will be helpful to the picture section. I have resolved to accept these two and will make every effort to improve what they do for us. There are a number of other photographers I want to cultivate because it is essential for the growth of the paper to have these photographic resources on tap to give the pages new life with each issue. The Voice can no longer be a one photographer paper even if, painfully, it cost more to deal with outside pictures. It is unrealistic to revert to a 1955 concept of using what we get as an economical compromise. If I have never made this clear before it is not my intention to have a staff of photographers. But I do want to have qualified free lance contributors who can be depended on to produce. We need a network of photographers in places like Washington, Chicago, San Francisco because it is essential to the growth of the paper. For a newspaper the size of The Voice is it unrealistic to depend entirely on the work of one photographer. Calculating last year, I alone was directly responsible for at least 35 front pages. All the photos having been taken by me. In addition, I have worked on the front page make-up, a self-assumed task I started last year. I also started marking and sending out the pictures, often checking the makeup on Tue. More than three quarters of the picture spreads were devised by me. It will come as no surprise to you, but look at all the front pages going back a dozen years and you will see hundreds of pages of picture stories that I conceived and executed. No other paper in the United States has so consistently had high quality work week in week out. You are usually not very generous with your praise and for some reason you think that if you say something nice about my work that I will immediately ask for more dough. Well after all these years I am convinced that I am one of the best photojournalists in New York regardless of whether you will admit it or not. But the real issue here is not your compliments, but my Voice paycheck. And you can only convince me that I am right by paying me a salary comparable to what I am worth to the paper and the caliber of work I do in comparison to other photographers and other picture editors. If I am overstepping my role by calling myself a picture editor when I am in reality a simple, glorified photographer then perhaps I should relinquish this fake title and work on cue and assignment under the direct supervision of the editor or perhaps the Voice should hire a picture editor and I will gladly and with great difficulty follow orders like they do on the other papers. I may have to swallow my pride to stoop that low but then, am I really a picture editor or is this just a bunch of bullshit like Howard Smith's title of assistant publisher. If I am a picture editor, I should be paid like one.

Prizes—I know you don't think much of prizes but I am the only one on the Voice who has won 11 awards for work directly related to the paper. This may seem like a trivial matter to you but I think there is a good reason why I have won these awards. Aside from the fact that it may have been my turn to win a Guggenheim you can rest assured that I won because my work was better than the other applicants.

Centerfold—It's not that I expect an award or prize for everything I do but I think it's time you knew that I did an enormous amount of work on Centerfold for 1973. I never expected you to mention it, nor did I even expect you to read what I wrote. But I contributed countless pictures on my own and wrote over 135 reviews of films, art shows, photo shows, book reviews and on numerous other events. I helped on Centerfold when everyone else on The Voice rejected it as a source for their coverage. I never asked for extra money, nor did I expect it. It's easy to say well who the hell asked you to do it in the first place. The answer is nobody asked me I just did it. I just felt and still do that it is a part of the paper where I can make an unselfish, worthwhile contribution. I also remind you that I did a definitive park fence survey last year that was an unequaled massive research project that was done on my own without a profit motive. I just felt it had to be done by me. Many Voice people will not spit unless they get paid in advance for it or unless the spitoon is put on their expense report. Others just want free Florida trips for frivolous boxing matches or to cover spring training ball games.

Expenses—Perhaps it is not clear to The Voice but I pay all my own expenses. I pay for all my film, all my cameras, all my auto expenses, for all the gas I use on Voice business. I pay for all my phone calls dealing with Voice work. I pay all my own postage. And occasionally the Voice pays for a free-bee hotel. But by and large these everyday expenses are what add up to thousands of dollars. There is absolutely no Village Voice overhead involved in what I do. I have no Voice office, no phone, no desk, no cubicle, only a mail drop. Although I deduct a large part of my expenses, my deductions are now greater than my income. Again, I am not whining about this, just stating a fact that further justifies more money.

Cost of Living—You certainly are aware that last year coffee was 94¢ a pound and today it's $1.34. The cost of living has skyrocketed. My expenses have skyrocketed. My rent has been increased by $75 a month since January, gas for my car used to be 43¢ a gallon; it's now 60 to 65¢. Expenses on the Voice likewise have increased, paper, labor, printing etc. But in a corporation the higher expenses can be more easily absorbed over a larger area and the burden is less. In my case I have no where to go except pay the higher costs.

Outside Compensation—Although I make additional money on book royalties and picture sales the extra income has no bearing on my

Voice salary as a full time salaried employee. It's what I do for the Voice that should determine my salary. For your information I sell very few pictures to outside sources. Last year I think I had two pictures published in Newsweek and maybe one in Time. Many outside publications will not use my work because of my strong association as the Voice photographer. They say I didn't realize that you could sell us a picture. When did you ever see my pictures in the Arts & Leisure section of the Times. But Voice free lancers do publish there. It is unfair for you to think that outside sales make up for what the Voice doesn't pay me. I should be paid for what I do for the Voice and additional sales should be an incentive and not a penalty. Even if my wife works or if my kids shine shoes for extra money it has no bearing on what I am paid. The fact that I MIGHT own a cottage in East Hampton has as little to do with your owning a co-op on 5th avenue or Ed Fancher owning an $8000 Mercedes or Bartell Bull owning blue chip stocks. If Andrew Sarris buys a co-op on East 88 Street does that mean we reduce his paycheck as a penalty for having a rich wife. It is very flattering and an honor to be asked to teach at The New School and this directly as a result of my connection with The Voice. But the fact that I rejected it simply means that I felt that devoting 8 or 10 weeks to teaching would mean that I would not be able to concentrate on my job at the Voice, and perhaps there are other projects I want to work on. It's as simple as that. I also turned it down because $650 is not enough for my time. Beside it would be counter productive to penalize someone salary-wise just because he enjoys a certain success. If I take a teaching job for $650 should my salary be reduced. Or should I have taken it because the Voice feels that I should make up my income deficiency elsewhere. I should think that success would be rewarded rather than penalized.

How Much am I Worth—I feel that now is the time to be paid a higher salary, as though I were brand new. I've served my time as an apprentice and now should be paid a man's wages which The Voice can surely afford. What may seem astronomical to you is actually a modest living wage for a family of four based on today's economy. On a gross salary of $400 the take home pay is only $276 and on $350 salary the take home is only $248 or $102 going to taxes. The taxes consume 1/3 of the paycheck. Picture editors on the national weeklys get up to $50,000 a year. I'm not asking you to pay me more money because you owe it to me. But because I have earned it and have proved I am entitled to it. Besides this, I certainly think that if you expect professional standards in our writing and in our photography, then we should pay respectable and professional wages. In fact we are better than the mass media and should actually be paid premium wages and not underground payscale. After all these years I have earned the right to work in the style I created, that is best suited to me. In actuality it is the Voice style. We do not work on Madison Avenue nor do we conform to their style of operation. But to penalize us or to punish us for finding our place in the working world is unfair and wrong. On the contrary, I am fortunate that there is a Village Voice because without it all of us, including you, would fit nowhere else. But to have this held over my head and to penalize me financially forever is only self-serving to you because you then have a built-in excess to never give me what I should get.

The Future—There is no way of knowing what will happen if you and Ed decide not to renew your option next year. Perhaps this is something that is on my mind more than on yours. But the question is what happens to all of us who have put in so much of our creative lives into the Voice. As I said before I am not a stockholder, all I have is a job. I am not expecting a guarantee from anybody. We have no pension plan, no annuity, no stock option, no fringe benefits, no bonus, nothing. Again I accepted this situation as it came and have made the best of it. But I put this to you now because maybe you have thought about this and wondered what will happen to all of us who have so faithfully and loyally stuck here all these years because we thought we were doing the right thing. Maybe we are all misfits thrown together with a common goal and a shared cause. But along the way we parted financially. The realities of today, unfortunately, are too related to dollars and cents, security and where do we go from here.

Fred W. McDarrah
March 20, 1974

HERE IS A LISTING OF FRED McDARRAH'S AWARDS:

Fellowship in Photography
  John Simon Guggenheim Memorial Foundation 1972
Best Spot News Photo Page One Award Honorable Mention
  The New York Newspaper Guild 1971 (Welfare Hotel)
1st Place Spot News Photography
  National Newspaper Association 1971 (Welfare Hotel)
3rd Place Picture Story
  The New York Press Association 1970 (Bed-Sty Slum)
2nd Place Spot News Photography
  The New York Press Association 1970 (Handcuffed School Door)

1st Place Picture Story
>The New York Press Association 1969 (Robert F. Kennedy)

1st Place Spot News Photography
>The New York Press Association 1968 (Newark Riots)

2nd Place Spot News Photography
>The New York Press Association 1967 (Allan Ginsberg)

1st Place Feature Photography
>The New York Press Association 1967 (Flag Burning)

1st Place Best Pictorial Series
>National Newspaper Association 1966 (N. Y. World's Fair)

3rd Place Feature Photography
>The New York Press Association 1965 (Mobilization for Youth)

3rd Place Spot News Photography
>The New York Press Association 1965 (Jeff Poland Sex League)

1st Place Spot News Photography
>The New York Press Association 1964 (Ed Koch and American Flag)

In June of 1974, half a year before the five-year contract of Dan and Ed ran out, Carter and Bartle sold *The Village Voice* to New York Magazine Company. It was a good sale. They had bought the paper for $3 million and sold it for $5 million. That left them with $2 million in profit. Taurus Communications exchanged its shares in *The Village Voice* for 34 percent of New York Magazine stock and $800,000 in cash. New York Magazine Company took on the debt of $2.5 million, which Taurus owed the bank.

For the first time, the *Voice* became the responsibility of a publicly owned company. Carter Burden holds 24 percent of the stock in this company and Bull 10.

Voice writers forgot their anger at Dan's greed. They remembered the freedom he had given them to express themselves. They remembered how he had supported them when they couldn't express themselves. And they worried about the new people who weren't from the Village. Carter promised to use his weight to see that things would not change, some said. Others doubted whether he said it and if he did, whether he meant it. A few said, "Let's wait and see."

New York Magazine Company has assets of $11 million with nearly one-fourth in cash and marketable securities. New York Magazine had sales of $9.7 million dollars and profits of $401,000 in 1973. The previous year their sales were $7.4 million and profits

$246,000. The *Voice,* in contrast, was not growing. Circulation hovered between 140,000 and 150,000. Clay Felker, President, Chief Executive Officer, and second-largest stockholder (10 percent) of New York Magazine Company could not be a fool.

Yet people felt fearful. Or at least apprehensive. They wanted continuity. When they learned that Dan and Ed were *not* going to remain on after the sale, there was a sense of sadness. This is how they expressed it in an editorial printed in the *Voice,* July 18, 1974:

> Dan Wolf and Ed Fancher did something very few people do in a lifetime—they created a new idea. That idea is the Village Voice.
>
> The year 1955 was the time of McCarthy, the Cold War, the Silent Generation. As Wolf himself once wrote, "the best minds in America were repeating themselves." In the middle of the wasteland, and with only $15,000, Dan and Ed started the Voice.
>
> In time, Wolf fashioned a new concept in journalism. He let writers write. He edited sensibilities, not copy. He shared with writers his remarkable psychological perceptions. He tempered their enthusiasm with skepticism and a sense of history. And he printed articles he personally disagreed with.
>
> Most importantly, Dan and Ed cherished individuality. They recognized and understood that people produce at different tempos and in different ways. They created an environment of total freedom. Over the years other publications emulated The Voice. None succeeded in capturing the essence of this newspaper. Because for 19 years its soul was Dan Wolf and Ed Fancher. We are their children.
>
> As Don McNeil wrote in the dedication to the collection of his Voice pieces, "I always knew in my heart that I'd find a newspaper to love, and I've found one."
>
> —the writers and editors
> of the Village Voice

Following the editorial, there was a perfunctory statement about the two people in charge as of that issue—Ross Wetzsteon, who became Executive Editor, and Bartle Bull, who became the paper's Publisher.

Within a year, neither was at the same post. Although Ross's name remained on the masthead as Executive Editor, it was Judy Daniels, formerly of *New York,* who managed the paper editorially. Hence, her title: Managing Editor. Subsequently Ross's title was made more consistent with his job, and he was demoted to Senior

Editor. Bartle's name disappeared from the masthead as Publisher when he was let go.

Other changes took place. The paper went up from a quarter to thirty-five cents and shortly afterward to fifty. Eliot Fremont-Smith, who had been the book critic at *New York* (and once was a *Times* daily reviewer before becoming head of Little, Brown publishing and then going on to work on the newly revised and now defunct *Saturday Review* under Nicolas Charney and John Veronis), came down to head the *Voice* book section.

Ross, who had one time written reviews, went back to his first love and was once again turning out perceptive works.

The inside of the *Voice* headquarters was redesigned, and eighteen editors and managers were added.

In March of 1975, a new name appeared on top of the *Voice* masthead: Clay Felker, Executive Editor in Chief.

A New Father Takes Over:
Clay Felker

Fred W. McDarrah

Clay Felker

This interview was recorded on July 22, 1975, in the offices of New York Magazine. Except for a few phrases that were not clear on the tape, Clay Felker's words remain unedited.

On September 4, 1975, Thomas B. Morgan was appointed to a newly created post of Editor of *The Village Voice*. Previously, Tom Morgan was a press secretary to former Mayor John V. Lindsay. After he left City Hall in 1973, he went to work for New York Magazine, where he was a Vice-President and Assistant to the President. He has extensive writing and editing experience.

Tom Morgan is currently married to Mary Strawbridge, a daughter of Vice-President Nelson Rockefeller.

Thomas B. Morgan

Fred W. McDarrah

248

* * *

Tell me a little bit about how you got into the whole business. I know that both of your parents were in the business.

I never wanted to do anything else.

Where were you born?

St. Louis, Missouri. I grew up in Webster Groves, Missouri. It was the quintessential American suburb. It was right in the middle of the country. As soon as I knew I was going into journalism—my parents were both University of Missouri journalism graduates and felt that I should not do that. They felt I should learn something rather than a technique. So I went to Duke to study political science, and at school I was the editor of the school paper, which I changed from a weekly to a twice-weekly. And I liked it. After that—I really got my journalism training in the Navy, where I was trained as a photographer. Prior to that, I was a—I worked on a Navy newspaper for a couple of years.

What was it called?

Blue Jacket. Then I was trained as a photographer. I spent a year and a half as a photographer. Then I got out of the Navy. After the Navy, I came to work in New York and I worked briefly for an advertising agency. Well . . . my first job was with my father's newspaper here in New York.

Which was the . . . ?

The *Sporting News* and the *Sporting Goods Dealer*. It was the St. Louis *Sporting News*. He was the Managing Editor. Not only was he the Managing Editor, he was also the Editor of the monthly *Sporting Goods Dealer,* which was a trade publication. I was both a correspondent and sold advertising in the New York office. It's dreadful being on the other end of the teletype from your father. Checking in and checking out on how many sales calls I made that day . . . It was murder.

Do you have siblings?

I have a sister.

Younger or older?

Younger, and she's married to a contractor in St. Louis. Her son has worked for me a couple of times in the summertime and spring work breaks. I don't know what he wants to do—

One last question about your background: How would you describe what class you come from?

Well, I've always described myself to myself as middle-class, and I once discovered that that's unusual. Because I was making a statement to a bunch of people and said this kind of positively and discovered that nobody likes to describe themselves as middle-class. They either are proud of being the working class, kind of defiantly, or else they claim they're upper-middle-class. In my opinion, there is no such thing as aristocracy in America in a true sense.

There is the media-created aristocracy, that's what we have. The celebrity as aristocrat. That's why there's such an interest in personalities. It is in lieu of an aristocracy that is defined by inheritance.

That's right. To me, in America, there's either working class or middle class. We have inherited a certain kind of tie to the land. I think this is one of the things that baffle people. Let me put it this way—I am a journalist. That's all I am. This stance if you take it to a logical conclusion is extremely baffling to people. One can't be pinned down to a class or even necessarily to a point of view.

There's also something else that I find very curious. When all these stories appear and nobody ever focuses (to me) on what I'm about. Never.

I know your background from the Herald Tribune Magazine, *but not before that.*

I came to New York. I had summer jobs and then worked at the *Sporting News.* When I finally came to New York, I went to work as a sportswriter on a paper. I worked on the last two or three issues of a paper called *PM* which changed into the New York *Star.* I was a sportswriter and I got a job in the summertime as a sportswriter. This was, again, one of those summertime jobs. From that, I went to work on the New York Giants baseball broadcast in this advertising agency. They sponsored the New York Giants baseball broadcast, and I traveled with the team and did the statistics and also was the agency's liaison with the team. I traveled around for three years, and I began writing some sports stories for the *Sporting News* and other publications. In 1951, I was getting kind of tired of the baseball nonsense. Sports was never particularly interesting to me. But because of my father's connections, this is how I got into journalism. I had a helluva time getting out. The next job I got was a sports reporter for *Life* magazine. I was very much stuck with it. But finally I got out of that and I became a general assignment reporter in what they call "news front"—the general assignment-type part of *Life* magazine. Then they decided to start *Sports Illustrated*. They asked me, Don Scanche, and one other fellow to set up a developing unit to help develop *Sports Illustrated*. Which we did, and then that unit began to grow.

What year was that?

I can't remember. Whatever year it was that *Sports Illustrated* began. And that was the turning point in my life in a way. In that unit—which was isolated in that vast Time, Inc., building— we also had financial people, promotion people, advertising people. We were all working together as a unit in a compartmentalized corporate style. Before, nobody ever got to work with anybody in a business way. So that for the first time I saw all the elements of the publication being put together.

I learned a great deal about publishing there, but I was not interested in sports whatsoever. I was terribly bored by it. I was really interested in working up visual styles and learning about promotion and how you started a publication. However, as a reward for this we got *Sports Illustrated,* and they were always testing our magazine and almost none of them ever got off the ground. But this one got off the ground. As a reward, I was finally sent to Washington as a political reporter, which is what I wanted to do. I was there during the Eisenhower Administration. I spent a couple of years there. I loved that. Then my friend, Peter Maas, whom I went to college with—he was the Editor of the *College Humor* magazine and a columnist for me. We were best friends. He had been offered a job to be an editor at *Esquire*. He turned it down but instead recommended that I get the job, and they offered me the job. I came into another fascinating publishing moment, which was the remaking of *Esquire*. Of course, my experience with *Sports Illustrated* is what qualified me for the job in their eyes. So we changed *Esquire* from a girly magazine. There we began to develop a concept of the new journalism. And I worked very much with Tom Morgan on that, who was a contract writer. He had been an editor there and had left in order to devote his full time to writing. And a lot of other people, but Tom was very important to me, showing me the style. From there I met Mailer and assigned him to the convention. He didn't know much about politics, so I had to accompany him to the Los Angeles convention. I was his political guide there. I remember when we drove in from the airport Mailer saying that the only political writing he had done was in the style of Marx but it wouldn't work here so he didn't know what he'd say here. But I just acted as his guide. I didn't tell him what to write nor purposely we didn't discuss it. We never wanted to discuss it. But I was his editor. So I stayed with *Esquire* for five years, and again, it was a small company and I became intimately involved in other aspects of the business, as all the editors of *Esquire* did—circulation, promotion, and it's a marvelous training ground. Arnold Gingrich was one of the great teachers because he had the strength to allow young men to make mistakes, give them their head, and gently guide them. At the end of five years, I went on to the *Herald Tribune*. I got married at that time, but I wanted to strike out on my own. Frankly, I'd been kind of a difficult person in a corporate situation. I have my own ideas on how things should look and how they should sound and what should be done with publications. And I become impatient and frustrated when those publications don't reflect my ideas. So I recognized a long time ago the only way I was ever going to be happy was if I had my own publication. So I left *Esquire* and spent six months researching and working on a project for a business newsletter for International Business, promoting international corporations. This was in 1962. It taught me a great deal about business, though. The project didn't work out because what I had in mind was too expensive to do to provide the proper kind of services. Well, I wanted to set up a network . . . have academics around the world who would spot trends, and I did work with a number of these people.

So this was in between Esquire *and the* Tribune?

Yes. I also had just gotten married then, and I figured I'd better try something before I had to take on too many family responsibilities.

Did you have independent means?

No, but I had saved some money. It cost me all that money. It cost me about fifteen thousand dollars. My wife, who was an actress, had taken off a year so we could be together for the first year of our marriage, so at the end of the year neither one of us had any money. This was compounded by a problem. She had never had her tonsils out and she had infected lungs that continually gave me strep, but she didn't get it. She was a carrier. So I was sick for the first two or three years of our marriage with these recurring bouts of strep. She finally had to go back to work because we were more or less out of money. And that's how I found out that she was a carrier. She could go away and I'd get well, and she'd come back and I'd get sick again. But it still took me a couple of years to get her to submit to an operation. But in the meantime, because of my experience, I had a number of consulting jobs. I've always had the ability to think up story ideas quite rapidly, which is a function of a point of view. And it's also one of the things that I prize—I put a value on journalistic endeavors. And so I got a lot of jobs as a consultant. I worked for Viking Press. I worked for Curtis Publishing Company. I worked both for the *Ladies' Home Journal* and later on *Holiday,* thinking up story ideas for them. I was hired by the *Herald Tribune* to help redesign their Sunday newspaper because Milton Glaser and I had worked on some redesigns of a Southern newspaper when I was at *Esquire.* So we did these designs in the late fifties or early sixties. Then I tried a television show. All this went on at once. When Shelly Zelaznick, who was the magazine Editor, stepped up to become Sunday Editor, I was offered the job as the magazine Editor, although I had been on the magazine right from the very beginning as a consultant. I think I stuck with them for about five years. Up until the time the *Herald Tribune* was killed by the final strike and then—

Did you enjoy the job?

I loved the job. The *Herald Tribune* was making terrific progress, journalistically speaking, and a lot of new young talent. Jim Bellows and Gingrich were different kinds of men. Bellows gave you your head, but there was almost never any communication. Like a lot of editors, he was somewhat inarticulate. I worked for several editors who were inarticulate. They would tell you to do something and didn't know what to say. Gingrich wasn't like that. He was the most civilized, worldly, articulate man—one of the greatest people I've ever met. And there was one summer when we were off on strike with the *Herald Tribune,* and I took that summer to begin to plan a city magazine. And I planned it with Jerry Weidman, Wyn Maxwell (Jane Maxwell's husband), who had been Treasurer of the *Herald Tribune.* The next summer, we were off on strike, and I began revising the budget again, and doing a great deal of research with advertising, circulation people, trying to figure out how to raise the money, and I had to pick up odd jobs during the strike, and so while I was management and still on the payroll, we didn't know if the paper was going to fold or not. I would pick up odd jobs here and there, free-lance editing jobs. I was making an enormous amount of money in those days. I made more money in those years . . . people seemed to want to pay a lot of money for consultants. But I was not happy being a consultant. When you realize that in order to take that job as the Editor of the *Herald Tribune* magazine, I must have given up thirty or forty thousand dollars' income. I was much happier, and it was the right thing to do. It was a great newspaper and I was working with first-class people, and I wasn't just plugging in here and there. I hate the idea of having to sell my ideas.

It's demeaning to be a hustler. That's why Dan got so upset when he sold that paper. He no longer felt in control of it.

I came into the paper and I don't know Dan very well. I had almost no contact with him except on a very formal basis and it was strained out of necessity—it was correct in the sense that we never yelled at each other. But my feeling is that once he sold the paper his considerable intelligence and energy then went into holding on to control rather than the creative process.

The Voice *has been changing for quite a long time, but if I had to pinpoint a time it would be when Dan sold the paper and when he no longer felt in control. It was a key to Dan. He created it from nothing, after all.*

It's a key to anyone, but particularly somebody who goes through the kind of gut-tearing anxiety of nursing a publication to financial health when you're also attempting to make an editorial statement. I think I've always known this lesson of whoever owns it controls it. When I started the *New York* magazine, it was a key principle, and it was very current because most of my problems were that I didn't have any money. I took my severance pay from the *World Tribune* and bought the name of *New York* magazine. But I didn't have any money, and this was an expensive product, so I had to give away a great deal of the equity, and the financial backers insisted that I give away the business control, which to me was a violation of what I started for. I've always felt very strongly that the only way to protect yourself thoroughly was to own it or have financial control. You don't have to have a hundred percent. I had less than ten percent, but I made myself a publisher in order to know how to run the business, to protect myself against another publisher. To me, publishers are the enemy. Not that they're pernicious people; it's just that their basic discipline is shortsighted, and not longsighted. It is based on—and since I'm torn apart by this and have the battle going on inside myself all the time—a publisher works on a calendar basis—a fiscal year—and he has to make the numbers come out every year. It's an artificial—

Do you see yourself as a publisher?

I'm attempting not to be. Well, I am a publisher and I'm proud of that. But I'm attempting not to have that overtake my life. I had to appoint a publisher here and I've had to take over as Publisher of the *Voice*. But I was the Publisher from the day we bought it. The revenues had started to dip, and they were starting to take a nose dive in the inflation in newspaper products.

I read all the things that appeared about why you bought the Voice *and quotes from you. Maybe you can just sum it up.*

I haven't talked very much about it, but I literally bought it because I thinks it's terrific. I examined it, and I knew what to do with it. . . .

Let me ask a question here about Bartle. What happened?

Bartle was one of the owners of the paper whose only training was at the *Voice*. He was a lawyer. His only publishing experience was at the *Voice*. The basic style of the *Voice* was that they never had any budget. If you didn't spend any money, you could never get in trouble, and the idea was to never pay anything more than what you had because— Once they started making money, they set the price for seventy-five dollars an article, and they knew that they couldn't get into any trouble if they didn't pay more than seventy-five dollars for an article.

Don't you think it's genius on the part of them to pay so little and get some of the best people? I mean, financially it was shrewd. I don't think it was calculated.

I can tell you what we have found out. We found out something this week that was one of the biggest aspects of calculation. They kept taking away— The ad salesman would come in, and they'd go out and break an account and they'd get a commission, and they'd take it away and give it to the Ad Director in order not to pay the commission. They paid Sandy [Alexandra Fendrick, Director of Display Advertising] a lot of money, but even so, that was less than the commissions that they would have to pay for continuously running business.

Where did that money go?

Into their pockets. It was calculated. That's what I'm saying. The union organizers would say you've had this thing a year and you haven't done—But there was so much to do to put it on a professional basis. And we will undoubtedly continue finding some things like that. We found out that we were losing thousands of ads over the period of a year because . . . well, the prime example is Rosetta [Reitz, Director of Classified Advertising]. She was such a hardened feminist, and if she heard someone call her sweetie or honey, she wouldn't take the ad. But she would fire the ad taker who inadvertently used one of those words. They set up barriers to getting ads. We're trying to just take the barriers down.

Was the bookkeeping system up-to-date and systematic?

Ely was a professional, but he wasn't full-time. He was really a business architect, I would say. Ely was not a publisher. He was a very sophisticated man, but we use aggressive publishing techniques, which is: we say we want to expand our advertising, circulation . . . then you go out and spend money in order to make money. That was not the *Voice*'s style. That is where Bartle and I couldn't accommodate each other totally. Bartle and I are friends. There is not a personal break with us. The problem is that I have a particular management style which is not his. And neither he nor I wanted to get into a fight with each other, and he accommodated himself to me enormously, but he is not a publisher in the way that I am. What I want of management today is to be aggressive. We did not find that Bartle was taking enough initiative in the generation of new business.

And Carter?

Carter is basically an investor. He's an intelligent investor. He's made money, but he's got his own career and he does what any man like that does. He picks a manager, and the manager keeps him informed of the financial progress. But he doesn't interfere in the running.

You said you had different management ideas . . .

Bartle grew up in this technique of not spending any money. Now, if we tell—you know, backed by my company—and the other executives that if we are going to save the *Voice* financially we have to be very aggressive. We're willing to make a big investment, but that investment had to be able to pay off. This is what we proceeded to do. But we needed someone with my basic philosophy down there and . . .

What about Ross?

Ross is very intelligent, and I tried to put him in an execu-

tive position . . . but I've taken those responsibilities away from
him. And he's now more effective.

What is George Hirsch's relation to New York *now that he
is Publisher of* New Times?

Just as a stockholder. He has no connection now. We threw
him out of here, but George didn't get hurt by the experience. Sure,
it hurt his ego, but he made a lot of money and he learned about
publishing. He was in the Publisher's office of the *Life International,* but there again it was so segmented that he only saw a
tiny part of it.

To get back to the Voice. *I've interviewed a lot of people,
and there are very few—Jack Newfield seems one of the exceptions—
who don't have the feeling that Dan was a saint and you're the devil
or sort of the reverse.*

Jack and I worked together for a number of years. He saw
something that most people don't ever seem to focus on, which is
that although we insisted on a certain level of professionalism we
were very tough editorialwise. We would stand up against anything.
We ran Jack's "Ten Worst Judges" in *New York* magazine. There
wasn't any hood on the cover, and we ran it. And he saw the
process—how we went about it, the researching and the insisting
on being accurate. So he knew that I wasn't attempting to enforce
my political views on him. He automatically turned to me and said
he wanted to write a city politics, and I said, "Go!" Jack also moves
with the times and—

*You know his real break, however, seems to have come when
he asked Dan for more money and Dan said, "You weren't known
when you came here. We made you someone, and if you don't like
it—"*

I don't share that philosophy. I believe that if you pay somebody what they're worth—

*How do you decide that, though? Because there do seem to
be inequities. Cockburn's the only one, I'm told by Ross, who had
a special salary arrangement: he's paid both a salary and a fee for
each article.*

We're changing all of this right now.

*What about the rumor that Pete Hamill's getting sixty thou-
sand dollars a year?*

I wouldn't do it. *I wouldn't do it.* That's why Hamill writes
for us from time to time. I wouldn't agree to those things. Ross was

dealing—this was one of the problems—Ross couldn't make these deals. He couldn't make them stick. I said to Ross, "Here's what it is, here's the deal," and he just couldn't. He couldn't do it. We could never come to an agreement with Hamill. So we didn't. I was not going to do for Hamill what I wouldn't do for somebody else. When I first came in here I thought that I had to have a parity position. I said to everybody (and I was out front, and people found out that what I did was exactly what I said). So I said, I don't care who's been quoted as attacking me. I came out in the paper saying that everybody is going to get the same amount of money for the first year or so and then we'll be able to deal at the end of the year, and those that have produced, fine, and those that haven't . . . I'm not a writer myself, and as a result, I admire —writers a great deal.

How do you feel about the charges that have been made that you don't understand the process of writing the way Dan did, who was not a writer either?

Of course, I understand the process of writing. My problem is that in order to deal properly with a writer you have to spend a lot of time with them to understand their point of view, what they're interested in. As an editor, you have to interview the writer . . . What are you about? Now because of the complexity of this organization, I don't have the time. This is one of my problems at the *Voice*. It is that I'm not there to give them a personal direction as much as I would like.

But you've been there increasingly.

But I don't know how long I can keep that up because I have a lot of things I want to do. But I'm committed . . .

To what extent?

I have committed my career to the *Voice*. I said, "I'm going to buy this thing, and here it is . . ." I made a commitment, which is that I must make it a success. And I always understood that I had to make it a success on the *Voice*'s own terms. It's not on my terms.

But suppose on whatever the terms are, it isn't a success?

I know that I can make a success of it if I want to become the day-to-day editor . . . However, I don't think I can do that. Maybe I can. Dan was there all the time.

Would you like to?

I would love to. But I also have this problem. I created this thing in my image, and it's terribly responsive to me. And the audience responds to my own interests and passions and lacks thereof . . . This is a terribly personal vehicle. Because it's personal, there is a great deal of personal reward. I have to choose between being the Editor in the long run. Also, there is the dynamic of American corporations, that they must grow, and that means that I, despite the fact that what those stories say the *Voice* acquisition has been primarily digested now over the past few weeks, I would say, although it doesn't look like that to people on the surface, but I know that the major, pretty much all of the major, restructuring in setting a new direction has taken place now. A lot of it, of course, took place in the publishing area, which is not at all visible to the rest of the world.

What about the stories about Dan and Ed being fired? You said that that was distorted by the press. Why don't you tell me what happened?

Well, you see Dan felt that there wasn't any reason why they should have any confidence in me. Also, the economy was turning bad. They wanted to sell out. Also, any lawyer can tell you that a minority interest— It's very weak. The majority can totally screw the minority if it wants to. They didn't have anything to do with the negotiations. But when they found out about it at the first meeting, I told them, "I want to buy you out." The price was to be negotiated. A part of the negotiations was to throw a suit at us, saying that they, we, and Carter had violated their right of first refusal, which we had gone into great length about during the negotiations, and every lawyer we talked to—we got three different opinions—said that so-called first-refusal right was not applicable.

Why not?

It was so technical that I can't go into it. What it was was to attempt to put a pressure on us to get the highest figure possible. That's all it was. When we always in our own minds didn't want that twenty-percent interest. We were always having to think about them in terms of expansion. For example, if we wanted to start another *Voice* in Los Angeles, or start a national *Voice,* and we were going to finance the thing one hundred percent, they would get twenty percent of it. We bought the thing to expand it. We were going to put up all the money, take all the risk, and they were going to get twenty percent. We wanted to buy them out. But they were asking a skyrocketing price. So it was a matter of a negotiation.

But they filed a suit.

They filed a suit and put the pressure on us. But we assumed they would do this before we bought the thing, and so that's why we had these three different opinions, to find out if there was any merit in their case. We were convinced that there was no merit in the case. Not only were we convinced that there was no merit, but we made Carter and Bartle totally liable if there were. We never stood to lose anything. They had to pay the legal fees for the suit. We understood that this was going to happen . . . because we had a price in mind that we thought it was worth and they had a price which was so far apart . . .

I know, three million and finally settled for a half million, or something like that.

They wanted a million and a half, essentially. We said, "All right, sue us." Then this economy took this nose dive. We said, "Wait a minute. We're not going to do anything until we see what's going to happen to the economy, because conditions have changed. We'd better hang onto our money . . ."

Why didn't you correct the story if it was distorted?

I don't believe in battling things out in public. That is not my philosophy. I really strongly believe that it's the product that counts. I learned this the hard way when I had that fight with [Jimmy] Breslin; he was really tough. The *Voice* situation is nothing in comparison. But I never changed a word of what they've written.

What about the story of [Judy] Coburn about the baby lift?

Coburn wanted to write something that I didn't think—that she'd never written. She had been to Cambodia for six months. Everybody was saying the same thing about Cambodia, which was, "Look at the United States, ruining this marvelous little country." That's what she was going to say. My view about any publication is you got to jump over that, and I just didn't want to say the same thing that every other publication was having on page one. It wasn't a matter of saying, "You've written something and I'm going to cut this." It wasn't that it was too radical; it was a pure matter of news judgment.

We were talking about the business of Dan and buying them out.

So we then went through. Once they understood that we weren't paying for it—they—but we went through this. We said,

"We will buy you out, but it's gotta be at a reasonable price. Not the price you're asking."

Did you have any dealings with Mailer at the time?

I personally never had any dealings with him—I ran into him at a party. He assured me that there was nothing personal. Anyway, he felt that he had to go along with— I felt that he was pushing them. We were not that close—it was a professional friendship. Norman and I have talked—have had at least one long talk, maybe two, since the *Voice* and—Ed went through a long examination before trial. The examination went on for several days, at least two days. I think (this is just a conjecture on my part) that the lawyers said to them that they don't have a case and that they'd better sell. Then they began to give us signals that they were willing to negotiate. Because we wouldn't give them an offer under those conditions. So we made them an offer and they accepted it. And that was that. And then they dropped the suit. We said that this was a straight commercial negotiation and there wasn't any principle involved.

What about that business that they were supposed to be kept on until the end of the year and they were offed before that?

That was just our way of putting pressure on them. Once they hit us with a suit we said, "You're not behaving properly as officers, so we're going to cut you off." Incidentally, we paid them fully for their salary. We always knew we would. We accrued it in our books and we just kept paying them. It was a game, you know. You put pressure on us and we put pressure on you.

Was Dan getting seventy-two thousand at the end?

I can't remember, but I think he was. It was a combination of salary and bonus. I think he was getting sixty thousand in salary and twelve thousand in bonuses.

What about your own salary? It was reported you raised your salary from eighty thousand to a hundred and twenty.

They're accurate figures. That's my salary. Listen, this is a public company. Everything is out in the open. But I didn't give myself a raise. But that would be impossible. But I would love to give myself a raise because I don't think I'm making enough money, along with everybody else in the world, but I had to negotiate with the committee and the Board of Directors. It's a negotiation; I have to retain a lawyer. It's complicated and painful, but I sure as hell can't give myself a raise.

Now that business with Maurice.
I never really did understand that.
What happened?
As far as we have been able—I think you should talk to David Shanks about that—I got a letter one day: "What about Maurice?" I gave this to Judy [Daniels] and said what's this about—
Have you ever met him?
Sure. I met him. I was very happy to have him walking around as a promotion for the *Voice.*
Dan gave him twenty or thirty free copies a week to sell, and the story that goes around is that you won't give him any.
Here's what happened, as far as I can gather. One of the things—we didn't have a circulation department at the *Voice.* One of the things is that they were dumping a lot of papers in their entrance and people were stealing them. Not Maurice, but anybody. Including people who would come in and take a bundle of fifty papers and put them on their newsstands. So we moved it back. This is just one of the things we instituted. Because of the casualness, there was a lot of loss of papers, and we were losing eleven hundred a week to one dealer who was ripping us off. And they were losing them up at the plant. We installed all these things as a measure to tighten rather than just losing them. But we told Maurice to come in and we gave him up to a hundred and fifty copies a week, but he had to go to the back to pick them up. Well, it was a change in routine. He did that. Once he came in and asked us, and we happened to have a sellout. We didn't have any copies. He was a cranky old man, but we were also delivering them down to Bradley's because the bundles were getting heavier as we added editorial pages to it. So a bundle of fifty was too much for the old man, and we were taking them down to Bradley's. We were delivering them to him. For free. And we would give him up to three bundles free per week. We also gave him aprons, paperweights, calendars, and we said we'd give him a big commission on every subscription he sold. I was going bananas on this, frankly—it was the worst single thing. So when I got this letter from him, I said, "Judy, take care of this immediately." She did. She said there was nothing to it. It's just that we're delivering them to Bradley's now. And then this goddamned thing kept reappearing, and it sounds to me like somebody is pumping the story out—Howard Smith, or somebody—I don't know. I'm just giving you an example. Because Howard is a skilled kind of propagandist. So finally, because it appeared on page one

in the *Villager* here, I said, "Sue them for libel." And [*Voice* lawyer] Victor Kovner talked me out of it. I was so goddamned angry at this. Then we ran a letter saying, "Maurice come back."

He says it's filled with lies.

Where is he? Is he alive?

Yes. Is he alive? I bought my collection of Village Voices *from him.*

Well, why doesn't he come back?

Because he feels that the Voice *has thrown him out.*

We didn't throw him out. What the hell— I don't know what— I would like to talk to him personally because I am so goddamned irritated about this thing. I really would like to talk to him because this is the worst goddamned thing of all of the stuff. It really bugs me. I felt that I was being set up. I knew it wasn't anything that we had done. I have had the circulation people in here giving me a formal report on this goddamned thing at one point. I had talked to them before, but then I figured they just weren't paying enough attention, but finally I brought them up . . . And they said that they didn't know how to get in touch with him.

He's at the Lion's Head almost every night.

Where does he live?

Twenty-eighth, between Broadway and Sixth, in an old walk-up that used to be a brothel. It's in the artificial flower district.

What are you going to do about people who are accustomed to the old Voice *way?*

I really feel that in the long run they will have to adjust to our present method of operation. But, look, I'm hoping that some people will learn—some people have, most people have, in fact. I'm only talking about a handful of people who haven't—I don't tell them what to say. I'm really more concerned with length than I am with content at the *Voice.*

That's something that bothers people.

I understand that. But you go back and look at the old— *Voice,* you'll see that some stories are very short when they didn't have big papers. I mean, I'm concerned with content here. This is me, but even here, I give the writers— The essential thing that I do is to come to an agreement with the writer as to the point of view, but after that I don't interfere with what they have to say. I don't believe in that. And I think that you kill a writer's creativity by doing that.

The Voice *was a forum for differing opinions.*

I haven't done anything to stop that . . . It doesn't bother me very much. I think it adds a kind of interesting note to the paper. And I've expanded the letter space, which is very much used for that. In order to foster that.

Well, the question to ask now is: What do you see as the future direction—

The future direction is one in which we are going to have to continue to discover new writers. We have to be—we have to continue to be aggressive about the discovery of new writers because these new writers will then carry us into whatever the new direction is. As an editor, I feed my own kind of passions into *New York* magazine.

The Voice *is one of the few places I know of where a manuscript could be submitted and if it was any good it would get published. Who now deals with unsolicited manuscripts?*

A number of people do. Whether it's Karen [Durbin] or Judy [Daniels] or Richard [Goldstein].

So you're still accepting unsolicited manuscripts. Yet I have the impression that it is much more assignments now.

Well, it is a lot more assignments, because if you are going to raise the quality of the publication you've got to generate new ideas.

Who do you see as your readership?

It's younger—we know it's younger—

Right—you said an average reader is twenty-four years. You were quoted in SoHo News *as wanting to make it a national magazine—*

But I'm not sure that I can. I had a lot of ideas— Well, that interview was done last summer [1974]. But they got ahold of it and printed it in February. That was shortly after we acquired the *Voice.*

Have your ideas changed? It's been about a year.

Yes, very much. I've had to learn about the *Voice* and . . .

Have you sensed a receptive atmosphere?

Yes. Let me put it this way. The staff itself that I work with down there is extremely responsive to me. In fact, in some ways, they are more responsive than this staff here. And I often find myself working with the *Voice* staff a lot. They are more responsive. There are all kind of reasons, but they are more strong-minded editorial people here because they are professionals who made their careers and they know what they think and they will battle with me far more than the *Voice* people. I think a lot of the writers we have here have wild egos, far bigger than the *Voice* writers and the editors themselves. I'm used to a lot of combat, but the thing is that the writers who don't want to cooperate with me just stay out of my way. So it's a kind of— That's why I've never met Ron Rosenbaum before—so that writers that don't want to deal with me just don't show up very often and don't come into contact with me. But, to me, that is how you put out publications. It doesn't mean that you are saying to people, "Do this, write this, write that." What you say is, "What do we have for next week? If we don't have much, what can we think up?"

Rolling Stone hit on one thing—music—as the prime definition of the paper and then from there it could go on. What do you see as the distinguishing thing to make the Voice different from— to make it distinctive?

Well, here's what I see us doing. One is to take it into a more cultural direction because it really is strongly cultural, so play on that strength. But the advantage of the *Voice* is that it can move quickly—quicker than *Rolling Stone* or *Psychology Today*. You can write something like what we've done on gays recently, which the standard media are afraid to touch until the *Voice* does it. This doesn't mean that we're going to turn it into a gay publication, because we're not, but we can hit that very hard and then get off and find something else. With language, and take some chances and people will come to the *Voice* realizing that we'll take some chances. There aren't the penalties as there are with *Time* or *The New York Times*. So I want to emphasize that. And, again, this is going to be something that I hope people will understand—the *Voice* is a collection of voices—that's why I want Blair [Sabol] back and Vivian [Gornick] back and Richie and Christgau. They speak for themselves. They don't speak for me. The *Voice* is only a collection of unique voices. It doesn't have a central core.

You said earlier the paper is a reflection of you, of a point of view.

Yes, but the point of view in this case is the point of view which adds up with these unique voices. What I'm saying—and this is going to cause problems—is the writers who aren't unique are going to fall by the wayside. In other words, just straight reporters are not what we're looking for . We're looking for writers who speak

for themselves. We are looking for strongly held opinion reporters. . . .

*There has been adverse criticism. I wanted to ask you how
you deal with this—*

I've got to believe in my own news judgment and my own
methods. Sure, it causes you to reexamine them each time, but you
make the decision that you are going to stick with it. If it doesn't
happen to be right, then you move off it.

*You sound as if you are more upset about the inaccuracies in
figures about circulation than Hentoff's critical piece.*

Because I didn't agree with him. But aside from that, it didn't
make any difference. He just made me look good. But he doesn't
really know what he's talking about. But that's all right.

What about Jill Johnston?

Jill Johnston. Well, you see my quarrel with Jill is not what
she says, but the technique, the fact that she doesn't use capital
letters, punctuation, paragraphing. I feel that that is selfish. It is
noncommunicative and it is contempt for the readers. It is elitist in
the extreme. And nobody reads it.

How do you know that nobody reads it?

I am positive that nobody reads it because I have constantly
gone around asking people. Even the people that defended her said
that they never read it.

The Voice *did surveys on who's popular and who's not—*

Those surveys didn't really—I don't go by surveys. I can't
even tell you where Jill came out on the survey. It's my own perception. I know as many lesbians as anybody. Maybe not as many
as Jill. But I know enough. Gloria saying, "Let Jill alone." She
writes me letters defending Jill. If it weren't for Gloria—I am really
outraged by this noncommunication because that's my thing. I want
to communicate with people. And I think she's a terrific writer, that
she's really got something to say. She's moving, and she's one of these
unique voices . . . but she will not communicate with the reader.
There's no feedback whatsoever . . . It's a game. It's a real confrontation with me. She has beaten me at every step of the way. She's
the toughest negotiator of all. But I'm beginning to lose my guilt
about that, and she's got to write in capital letters. We will run her
columns from time to time. But she's got to write in capital letters
with punctuation. I agree that what she has to say is important, that
she is original and a unique mind, an important contribution, but

it isn't a contribution if nobody can read it. I believe in the great Luce dictum. It isn't news until it gets off of the page and into the reader's mind. That is one of the keys to my journalistic technique.

Whom do you admire most of the current writers—other than those of the Voice *and* New York?

There are a lot of people I admire but I am an unabashed admirer of Tom [Wolfe]. I admire Breslin a great deal, and I admire Dick Reeves enormously. I could pick out others—people who are just sensational.

How important is a good writer to a paper? Do you think no one writer is indispensable?

I think that's true, but I don't think I act that way. That's one of the terrible things about institutions. They are usually bigger than any one individual. I haven't changed any policies at the *Voice*.

First of all, you gave writers more money.

But I didn't do it to buy them off. I really believe that people should get paid adequate money, and that's been our policy here at *New York* magazine. If we made money, we passed it on to our employees, and we created some options for *Voice* employees. You can only do it once a year. And we did, fifty thousand shares, and we're going to start passing that out. I believe in all of that. It is what I believe in. My fight is often with our own Board of Directors. It isn't really with the employees.

What about the union?

I think that—having been on a paper that was killed by the union—obviously, I don't believe in them. I also believe that people would prefer to have the benefits without the union.

What about your attempts to keep the Newspaper Guild out of the Voice?

I don't want a union at the *Voice*. I think the only way to keep a union out of a publication is to remove the causes of the grievances, and this is one of my problems with Bartle. Despite the fact that he was cooperating whenever I asked him to do something, there were an awful lot of things I didn't know about—with his old *Voice* philosophy, but without, without love and the chicken soup that was passed out. That went a long way. When this union situation developed, I had to get him out of there immediately because he didn't have the ability to relate directly to those people, for whatever reasons. I mean . . . And so the department heads can relate to people. They relate to people.

How long has Jane been there?
Oh, about a month or five or six weeks.
Any indications of how that's working?
Oh, she's accomplished enormous things. Also, everybody was
working so hard, I had told Bill Ryan when he came on board last
November that I wanted to get a medical plan installed, and he had
been so busy creating the first budget that he didn't—it couldn't get
done until February. It had kind of fallen behind, although he had
periodically worked on it until Jane jammed the thing through with
Bill's help about a week after she got there. He had almost com-
pleted it, and all it needed was just a final push, and there was a lot
of that kind of stuff that they were just so busy that—holding the
place together.
How does it feel at the end of a year?
We're making strong progress. I can see finally that the
Voice is beginning to get on the tracks financially. Naturally, that
won't show up in our figures for a long time. As a result of the
economy, we had to take some emergency measures, like raising the
price, and also, the inflation was eating away at the purchasing power
of the employee—we couldn't have held onto our staff under any
conditions. Also, you can't—as a manager, you can't really live with
yourself if you think your people are existing under hardship. A lot
of the writers have other means of income, but not the classified and
display people and that's three-quarters of the staff. Nobody on this
[*New York*] staff comes from independent wealth. Maybe somebody
does and I don't know it, but as far as I know, this staff lives on what
they earn. It's a professional group of people, and I am used to
dealing with people at that level. When you have people with independent wealth, they can take all kinds of stands that are totally
O.K. for them, but may not be good for the rest of the people on
the paper . . . or the paper itself. They can be quite self-centered.
I have another policy which is better for the individual except for
these elitists. These people who suddenly become concerned about
how much the messengers are paid, and these are the people who
didn't really care before. For twenty years, they didn't care what
the messengers were paid. What they are perceiving is a different
set of circumstances, where they feel that they are losing their control. They can walk into the office on Monday and say, "Here's what
I have." And that's the crux of it. It is a struggle for control. It is
not a struggle for money. The impetus of this union is not really

money. It is their "hang something on me," because when they said it out loud, they lost their support among the employees. Most of the employees are not that handful of editorial staff. Most of those employees are kids who have never had a job anyplace else before, who need the money to live on. They're knocking their brains out— the first, second- and third-floor people. And that's the bulk of the employees in this company. We have been working as hard as we can to improve— Starting next week, I think it is, we are totally inspecting the first three floors in order to make better working conditions. We couldn't do that until we got that Language Lab out of there, because there wasn't anyplace to expand to. We had a physical problem, and the Language Lab thing didn't end until the thirtieth of June. We had the architects in there, and Jane is supervising the construction. We also had that goddamned problem with the Text Masters. I didn't get us into it, we inherited it. A deal where you set up your own particular typesetting company. It took us a year to get out of that. We had to close that down. I had a lot of immediate problems that I had to deal with in a hurry. I have since gone around and addressed every single department personally and tried to explain. It was mostly questions and answers, and also to listen to what they wanted and what their grievances were. As long as Bartle was down there, I couldn't do that. Once this union situation— I needed somebody to be in direct communication. Bill Ryan worked here, Steve Blacker, and now— David Shanks is a marvelous young man, and Jane—Jane doesn't even have to ask me because she sat next to me for eight years; she knows exactly what I think, so she can make decisions on her own. If she can't get through to me, she just goes ahead and does it. She was getting bored with what she was doing, and she didn't have editorial training. She was trained as a publisher, and yet she didn't have a specialty in sales or circulation or financing. So this was the perfect job. Of all the things she knows about, she's accomplished a lot in a very short period of time.

What do you see as the maximum growth in terms of circulation?

Well, I don't really know. All this talk that I said a quarter of a million, maybe I said it, but I don't believe it anymore. I'm not sure that's the way to grow. We could sell more advertising, higher prices, maybe start in other cities, maybe start a national edition, though I think that's very far down the list because I think as I know about the *Voice* I really think it is a thing that deals with people's local interest. It isn't a national product. Right now, we have so much potential, right in New York City. And that's taking all of our energy . . .

In other words, you're going to concentrate on local— I know you made this point when you spoke last week. You also mentioned that suburban readership has gone up. What about the potential there?

We are concentrating on that, and by doing a bit more promotion.

I was thinking about that. Since most of the Voice's *listing are local New York, would you consider expanding that?*

No. I feel that people—listings are one thing, but listings are not the main contributions to the *Voice*. It's individual point of view. What Sarris and Haskell have to say about a movie you are going to see eventually. What has Hentoff to say about this week's civil rights crisis? What do Phil Tracy and Ken Auletta have to say about the city and Jack about the city politic. I mean, this is what people are going to be reading. It's an alternative to television and broadcasting in general, which is where people get most of their news broadcast. But what we have to do is to design a publication. I'm not sure that people need daily newspapers anymore—maybe all they need is once a week a paper that they can read under their own terms, which is—I've got fifteen minutes free here and there—I don't have to spend an hour every morning, which they may not have because they may be driving that hour. We give an alternative point of view. Broadcast journalism is locked into this fairness doctrine, which is so much bland bullshit, really, but they're locked into it. They can't go as far as anybody in print. We can go farther out than anybody. And as a result, we can give sharper interpretation, more extreme, more experimental, more probing, so then you take what you get in the *Voice* and you got that in mind when you see and hear headlines, and it enables you to put it together in your own way.

Inevitably, it seems that there is an overlap between New York *and the* Voice.

There has always been overlap. It's just not been focused on . . .

How would you distinguish between the two?

The *Voice* is more experimental, more on the probing edge,

and *New York* has this system of researchers. They nail it all down and run it through a research machine. We're also interested in a very different area. It's not as cultural, more national political than local, and the *Voice* is more local. And also *New York* magazine itself is a collection of individual voices. So they're different voices than the *Voice* voices—see what I mean? You've got to believe in this. That is what I find staggering when Nat accuses me of thinking that writers are interchangeable. On the contrary, what I am always looking for—will pay a lot for—is a unique expression of something. That was my problem with Judith Crist. She wasn't unique enough. I want somebody who doesn't sound like anyone else. That's why we picked Simon. I don't necessarily agree with him, but he's totally unique. Now, I'm not talking about some nut. I'm looking for someone unique. I haul in someone for each publication. Are they interchangeable? No, they're not interchangeable. What happens is that the book publisher comes along and offers you more money. Cowan was saying, "I'm getting more outside assignments these days," and I can't help that. I don't know if I've said this to him, but the reason he's getting more assignments is that we've given him better display and focused more attention on him. Nevertheless, he doesn't think like anybody else. So other editors—and they're beginning to read the *Voice* for the first time—

The Voice *has always been a showcase. Probably more writers got a start—*

No question about it. It was a real farm team for the publishing ventures of New York City. But Dan didn't care whether they went out the other end. I happen to care. I want them to stay. One thing is that I am trying to hold onto them by paying them more, so that they're not quite as tempted. Realizing that some of this is inevitable, we are focusing on new talent. And the demands are so great, even the new talent goes. David Tipmore, I understand, has a job offer at *Rolling Stone,* and he's one of the guys we were focusing on. He didn't even totally develop before he went away. He hasn't left yet, and I'm not actually certain it's going to happen.

What about Alan Weitz?

Alan was one of the sons that you talked about. There was no hostility between us; not only that, there was a warm relationship between us, and he was very torn. I begged him not to turn his back on the *Voice.* In fact, I just got a phone call out there that he's now working with ABC News. I'm glad to see it, but he knows he can come back to the *Voice* if he wants to. He kind of felt torn apart. I understand that, and I wasn't attempting to increase the pressure, but they felt that. I have to go now.

O.K. Let's end here.